TAXPAYERS IN REVOLT

Taxpayers in Revolt

Tax Resistance during the Great Depression

David T. Beito

The University of North Carolina Press

Chapel Hill and London

The paper in this book meets the guidelines for permanence and
durability of the Committee on Production Guidelines for
Book Longevity of the Council on Library Resources.

93 92 91 90 89   5 4 3 2 1

Library of Congress Cataloging-in-Publication Data

Beito, David T.
    Taxpayers in revolt: tax resistance during the Great
Depression / by David T. Beito.
        p. cm.
    Bibliography: p.
    Includes index.
    ISBN 0-8078-1836-4 (alk. paper)

    1. Tax collection—United States—History. 2. Taxpayer
compliance—United States—History. 3. Depressions—
1929—United States. I. Title. II. Title: Tax resistance
during the Great Depression.
HJ3252.B45 1989   88-26032
336.2'91—dc19   CIP

343559

To my parents, Rangvald and Doris Beito,
with admiration and affection

CONTENTS

ACKNOWLEDGMENTS

It is impossible to thank adequately all of the individuals who helped me in preparing this book. At the onset, I would like to express my debt to Allan G. Bogue. His insightful comments and suggestions have greatly enhanced this book on both a stylistic and a conceptual level. Stanley K. Schultz also deserves special praise. He never hesitated to take time out of his busy schedule to offer suggestions and encouragement. James L. Baughman brought home the necessity of putting this work into an historiographical context.

Had it not been for the help of Walter E. Grinder and Leonard P. Liggio, of the Institute for Humane Studies at George Mason University, Fairfax, Virginia, this book might not have been completed. Walter proved instrumental in introducing the manuscript to Paul Betz of the University of North Carolina Press. The Institute awarded me a postdoctoral fellowship to continue my research and rewrite my dissertation for publication. The enthusiastic support and comments offered by Ralph Raico and Lawrence H. White, also active with the Institute, helped get my work started on the right foot.

Through the recommendation of Lester Hunt, of the University of Wisconsin, I was awarded a fellowship at the Center for Study of Public Choice at George Mason University. While at the Center, I received much helpful advice from Charles Rowley, Robert Tollison, Jennifer Roback, and Viktor Vanberg.

The many other individuals who provided assistance include Tom G. Palmer, Tatia Payne, Ralph Kloske, Lee Cronk, Deborah K. Hunt, Anne M. Hudson, Thomas McCormick, Christine and John Blundell, Mary S. Lyman, W. Elliot Brownlee, Eric Lampard, Steven Vaughn, Beverly Morrison, Earl Mulderink, Emilio Pacheco, Sheldon L. Richman, R. Dale Grinder, David Boonin, Jeremy Shearmur,

Sharon Kern, Andrea Salsberg, Margo Reeves, Todd J. Olson, and Keith Shimko. Judy Cochran, in the Department of History of the University of Wisconsin, Madison, rendered invaluable and patient aid in arranging for my defense. Most of all, I want to thank my parents Rangvald and Doris Beito. Without their constant and heartening encouragement, this book would not have been possible.

INTRODUCTION

The United States owes its birth in part to a tax strike. Despite this fact, tax rebellion has not been a favorite topic of American historians. Remarkably few studies deal with the politics of taxation—much less tax revolt—after the Whiskey Rebellion of the 1790s. This neglect is lamentable not only because the taxpayers' protest merits consideration as a historical phenomenon in its own right but because it also it offers a suggestive approach to several vital questions. Chief among these is the relationship of taxation conflicts to the following issues: the perpetuation of legitimacy by the state, class theory, and the strengths, weaknesses, and persistence of anti-big-government thought during American economic crises.[1]

Two historians who stand out in this still-sparse field are James Ring Adams and Clifton Yearley. Adams pointed to the role of the radical Jacksonian Locofoco Democrats in promoting tax-resistance initiatives, such as voters' approval of bond issues and constitutional limitations on state debt. He expanded on work by historians, such as Lee Benson, who have highlighted the "extreme antistate doctrine" of the Locofocos. William Leggett, the chief intellectual spokesman of the Locofocos, advocated the strict laissez-faire doctrine that government "possesses no delegated right to tamper with individual industry a single hair's-breadth beyond what is essential to protect the rights of person and property."[2]

Unlike Adams, Yearley did not focus on taxpayers' revolts per se. Instead he explored at length the uneasy and complex relationship between big-city political machines and middle-class taxpayers during the Gilded Age. In most urban areas during the nineteenth century, real estate owners—usually a minority of the citizens—paid most local taxes. Many taxpayers resented having to pay for the spending programs voted in by the nontaxpaying majority. According to Yearley, political machines depended on nontaxpaying voters for their base of support. Nontaxpayers not only included the poor but also the wealthy owners of untaxed personal property. As Yearley put it, real estate owners had become convinced that "they were financing both the revels of the new wealth and the bread and circuses of the new democracy."[3]

On the whole, the period between 1900 and 1929 brought a lull in tax resistance. Taxation, though always an important issue, did not bite hard enough to provoke substantive rebellions of either a legal or an illegal nature. Tax strikes do not seem to have been contemplated, much less practiced, and legal limits on local property taxation—all the rage in the late nineteenth century—did not enjoy a renaissance.[4]

The Crash of 1929, and the economic collapse that followed in its wake, sparked a revival of taxpayers' revolts throughout the country. Between 1932 and 1934, seven states put into place overall limitations on the general property tax (meaning both real and personal property); six through popular initiative and one by a vote of the state legislature. Several dozen similar limitations won enactment at the local level. In addition, every state and hundreds of counties witnessed the formation of taxpayers' and economy leagues. Measured in numbers of organizations, the tax revolt of the 1970s and 1980s looks puny by comparison.

The tax strike was the most serious weapon of resistance. Although taken seriously, and threatened often, an organized tax strike rarely took hold. One place where it did was Chicago. From 1930 to 1933, Chicago was the scene of one of the largest illegal tax boycotts in American history. At its pinnacle, the organization that led the strike, the Association of Real Estate Taxpayers (ARET), had a paid membership of 30,000 and a budget of $600,000.

The tax rebels of the early 1930s, both in Chicago and elsewhere, wanted to put constraints on government via tax and spending reduction. They combined these ideas with a general (though usually inchoate) distrust of politicians, bureaucrats, and municipal bond holders. Many resisters advanced a kind of class theory under which receivers of government funds were characterized as a "tax spender" (or "tax eater") class. Support for economy in government and tax slashes did not go into hibernation after 1929; in fact, if the statements of prominent civic, political, and business leaders are taken at face value, these beliefs enjoyed a resurgence lasting well into 1933.[5]

In the last twenty years, historians have begun to take more seriously the existence of anti-big-government popular attitudes during the 1930s. In *Voices of Protest*, Alan Brinkley pictured the movements led by Huey Long and Father Coughlin as symptomatic of the "urge to defend the autonomy of the individual and the community against encroachments from the modern industrial state." Leo Ribuffo, in *The Old Christian Right*, also detected a nostalgia for small, decentralized government in these and other movements of the period. Although Brinkley and Ribuffo noted the pre–New Deal roots of the old Christian right, they focused, for the most part, on the period after 1933. Further, their almost exclusive concentration on national issues, while quite germane to the period they discuss, says little about economy-in-government agitation from 1929 to 1933, which was predominantly a local and state affair.[6]

The credentials of Long and Coughlin as opponents of big government have been rightly questioned by historians. Less open to dispute is the centrality of this sentiment to depression-era tax revolts. The dedication of the tax rebel to limited government was rarely consistent and well thought out. Those who resisted taxes were, for the most part, political amateurs. They railed sincerely against high taxes, political paternalism, and grafting bureaucrats, but often fell short when it came to formulating their own proposals for retrenchment in government. Frequently, the tax rebel did not have a systematic philosophy as such but rather a set of loosely connected and sometimes murky attitudes about the need to curb government's power. For reasons we shall see, this lack of a clear-cut agenda contributed to the ultimate undoing of the tax revolt of the 1930s.

The best of the few treatments of public attitudes at the state level before the time of the New Deal is James Patterson's *The New Deal and the States*. He noted that the voters continued to elect large numbers of economy-minded and veto-wielding governors and legislators during the most severe years of the depression. By and large, Patterson credited this phenomenon to voter apathy and low turnout at elections. But this explanation left much to be desired, especially in light of the considerable and persuasive evidence showing the significant *popular* base beneath economy-in-government sentiment.[7]

The state's claim to power over society would be a toothless pretension were it not backed up by a system capable of extracting money from the population. Max Weber, whose work inspired a whole debate over how governments achieve and maintain legitimacy, recognized this. Weber prefaced his analysis with the assumption that the distinctive attribute setting the state off from other institutions is its claim to a monopoly on the legitimate use of force. "Even a casual reader of Weber," Sheldon S. Wolin observed, "must be struck by the prominence of 'power-words' in his vocabulary; struggle, competition, violence, domination, *Machtstaat*, imperialism."[8]

Confronted by the greatest tax crisis of the twentieth century—perhaps since the American Revolution—opinion molders of the depression era could not afford to avoid the relationship between taxation and legitimacy. To scores of reformers, public finance economists, bankers, and businessmen, taxation had an intimate connection with the survival of government itself. In localities far and wide, they took the leadership in unprecedented "pay-your-taxes" campaigns, which were nothing less than undisguised advertisements, backed up by threats of force, to bolster state legitimacy.

Conflicts over taxation brought to light differing conceptions of the state's proper role in society. True to their roots in the Progressive Era, the civic reformers, academics, and officials of professional government associations who led the fight against tax resistance applauded the expansion of government. They conceived of government as the cooperative manifestation of society's will. Government, especially if efficiently administered, was a necessary, positive tool to fight poverty, ensure public health, provide sanitation, and promote economic planning. For them, expanded government and advancing civilization were inseparable.

The promoters of tax resistance were often less clear and resolute in their philosophy. In general, however, they upheld a more constrained or negative conception of the state. Most tax resisters looked with skepticism on government's expansion beyond providing courts, police, and national defense. They feared that, unless limited in its power to tax, government would become the protector of entrenched special interests, retard economic recovery, and sap individual autonomy. In contrast to their opponents, tax resisters argued that government could best fight the depression by deflating to the same level as the economy. Indeed, many resisters blamed excessive taxes and spending for causing the depression in the first place.

The taxpayers' revolt of the 1930s gives the historian a window into a whole set of larger questions. Do political and economic classes play any role in tax crises and, if so, how do these classes arise and how are they constituted? How do governments maintain authority and legitimacy when their source of money is challenged? Lastly, a study of depression-era tax resistance challenges prevalent historiographical interpretations of the vitality and continuity of popular wariness of big government during the worst years of economic decline in American history.

CHAPTER 1

Tax Resistance:
Origins and Development

Only in the past twenty years have historians, such as James Patterson, begun to cast more discerning eyes on taxation policy during the 1920s. Even now, the famed Coolidge tax cuts in the later part of the decade stand at center stage in the debate. The preoccupation with Coolidge's taxation reduction policy as the touchstone of the "new era" has unfortunately obscured the enormous tax increases that took place at the local level. Per capita tax collections for all levels of government rose from $68.28 in 1922 to $80.30 in 1929. Because economic growth kept pace with tax increases, the tax burden as a percentage of the national income remained fairly steady, falling slightly from 12.1 in 1920 to 11.6 in 1929.[1]

A closer examination reveals that federal and state/local taxing authorities embarked on markedly divergent paths during the 1920s. In 1920, local taxes accounted for 3.3 percent of the national income and state taxes for .83 percent. By 1929, these percentages stood at 5.4 and 1.9 respectively. Meanwhile, federal tax collections actually fell as a percentage of the national income, from 7.9 in 1920 to 4.2 in 1929. Looking back from the vantage point of the early depression years, several commentators in both academia and the media recognized what had happened. In a 1932 article for the *Forum*, Jay Franklin challenged the image of the 1920s as an era of relief for the taxpayer. "For every penny saved in taxes at Washington," he pointed out, "five cents were added to his [the taxpayer's] taxes at the City Hall and State House."[2]

Throughout the 1920s, the general property tax accounted for over 90 percent of taxes levied by all cities over 30,000 in population.

As the decade wound down, the real estate component of the tax yielded an ever-mounting percentage of total general property tax collections. By 1928, real estate owners picked up 83 percent of all property taxes. At the state level, the general property tax (of which real estate accounted for 77 percent of the total) made up an ever dwindling share of tax collections; down to 25 percent in 1928. Even so, the real estate tax remained the primary extractive revenue source for the states.[3]

On the face of it, the real estate tax seemed almost designed to incite rebellion. Only vaguely did it meet the definition of a tax based on ability to pay. In theory, it fell equally on all landowners in proportion to the assessed value (based, usually with greatly imperfect approximation, on market prices) of their real estate. This standard had diminishing applicability in a society where the ownership of real estate had become a notoriously poor barometer by which to measure the comparative wealth of individuals. For homeowners, the real estate tax had a particularly onerous side. Unlike owners of rental property, they could not resort to the option of shifting part or all of their tax burden onto third parties.[4]

If the real estate tax failed to meet even the rather dubious criteria of justice and equity as set down in the public finance tomes of the period, such as ability to pay, what accounts for its remarkable staying power as an extractive source? For one thing, it involved a low administrative overhead. Since real property could not be effectively hidden from their purview, the assessor and collector did not have to engage in costly and unpopular detective work. For all intents and purposes, taxpayers could not conceal their taxable real estate from the authorities. When real estate taxpayers, either by choice or necessity, lapsed into arrears, their delinquency became apparent for all to see.

The origins of the real estate tax predated the American Revolution, thus possessing a cardinal administrative virtue: "The old tax is the good tax." Taxpayers may have grumbled about the injustices of the burden but at least they knew what officials expected of them. Under any substitute form of taxation, the political authorities ran the risk of disrupting ingrained taxpaying habits. This administrative advantage, which the public finance texts and tax officials readily acknowledged, was a *necessary* but by no means *sufficient* condition to ensure continued reliance on the real estate tax. "Oldness" had not prevented the abandonment of the personal property tax (which in pure form applied to all movable property), even by those states whose constitutions required *all* property to be taxed at a uniform rate. Under the rural conditions of the eighteenth and nineteenth centuries, when most movable property took the uncomplicated form of household furniture and livestock, the assessment and enforcement of the personal property tax had been a relatively pro forma matter. Strict enforcement became impossible when, with urbanization and industrialization, personal property (literally defined) took on more dispersed forms, including factory machinery, stocks and bonds, art objects, and jewelry. When affixing value to real estate, the assessor had always been able to use market value as a guide. By the 1920s, this yardstick could not be approximated for many kinds of personal property, especially those with a rare or nonexistent market turnover. Since the assessors' subjective opinions about the market value of an item of personal property were arguably as good as any other, they could, and frequently did, arbitrarily raise or lower assessments to discriminate against or in favor of particular taxpayers.[5]

The system, with all its widely recognized examples of corruption, made evasion much more tempting for the taxpayer. This was particularly true with respect to the taxation of intangible personal property. Most states defined taxable intangibles as paper, such as stocks and bonds, *representing* ownership in a tangible asset. Occasionally, the taxing authorities also classified bank accounts as intangible property. "The final outcome of the enforcement of such laws," wrote one of many critics of the tax on intangibles, "is to create a situation in which a taxpayer must choose between being a fool or a liar." Not surprisingly, the average taxpayer preferred the latter option. First, it took no effort (unless the act of hiding a stock or bond in a desk drawer can be classified as effort) to conceal intangible personal property from the eyes of the assessor. Second, taxpayers could see no reason to pay a tax so universally regarded as manifestly burdensome and unjust. In effect, the taxpayer, if subject to the requirement, had to pay taxes twice on the *same* property: once, through the personal property tax on the intangible piece of paper (usually a stock or bond), and another time through the real estate tax on the tangible asset it represented.[6]

By the 1920s, the general property tax, while still a de jure uniform levy on all forms of property, was fast becoming a de facto real estate tax. Yet, as long as it did not too severely pinch taxpayers, whose incomes remained high, local governments found that the extractive productiveness of the real estate tax counterbalanced the various constitutional, moral, and practical objections. Tax rates gave but an imperfect measure of mounting reliance on real estate taxation by local governments because the relationship of assessed value to market price varied significantly depending on the taxing jurisdiction. Nevertheless, the upward trend was unmistakable. Between 1918 and 1928, the average tax rate per dollar of assessed valuation for all cities over 30,000 in population rose from 20.2 mills (a mill equals one thousandth of a dollar) to 27 mills. Added to this, in 1928, most property owners paid state taxes, averaging 2 mills, and county taxes, averaging 5.9 mills.[7]

Even amidst the relative prosperity of the 1920s, taxpayers showed telltale signs of cracking under the mounting pressure of the tax burden. In a study of Detroit's tax delinquency, published in 1932, Virginia L. Eyre, an economist for the U.S. Department of the Treasury, came across a puzzling trend: in spite of a booming local automobile industry and the supposed municipal prosperity it should bring, real estate tax delinquency (the percentage of taxes levied but not collected) had gradually climbed from 4.5 in 1921 to 6.2 in 1926, and reached an all time high for the decade of 12 percent in 1929. This paradoxical divergence between economic expansion and waning tax collection moved Eyre to speculate that "even if business activity had actually continued to increase after 1929, Detroit could have anticipated an increased tax delinquency in 1930." While nobody ever tallied comprehensive national statistics, available local studies of cities like Cleveland; Columbus, Ohio; Fall River, Massachusetts; and Jackson, Michigan; and states such as Michigan, Missouri, Virginia, Minnesota, and Ohio tell a recurrent story of slow but steadily increasing percentages of real estate tax delinquency. According to the final report of the President's Conference on Home Building in 1932, "The growth of delinquency is apparently not due to the present business depression but has been going on since 1920 at the latest; it applies to city lots and the wealthier counties as well as to wild or cut-over lands." The report concluded that the delinquency problem was "apparently due to the increase of the property tax more than any other one cause."[8]

Tax increases put an added strain on the real estate industry, which had already begun to sag by 1926. According to estimates of the National Bureau of Economic Research, the value (in millions of dollars) of all contracts for residential building in the forty-eight states dipped from 4,754 in 1925 to 3,813 in 1928. Unfortunately, we have no detailed breakdowns of these statistics. If measured by the less precise standard of numbers of nonfarm dwelling units built, regional variations can be discerned. The number (in thousands) of new dwelling units built each year nationwide declined from 938 in 1925 to 753 in 1928, a decrease of 20 percent. Of the nine regions in the country, the West North Central, at 40 percent, and the South Atlantic, at 31.4 percent, registered the sharpest declines. The West South Central states, with a six percent climb in the rate of increase in the number of new dwelling units built annually between 1925 and 1928, stood out as the only exception to this overall record of decline.[9]

On top of this, municipal governments discovered and utilized a multitude of devices to hurdle or evade debt limits and thus spend in excess of their tax take. In their most common form, debt limits, mostly dating to the late nineteenth century, put a legal cap on the ratio of bonded debt to assessed valuation. Local governments outdid each other in coming up with ingenious methods to escape debt limits. These included the creation of new taxing and assessment districts (outside of the recognized municipal borders), the levy of special assessments, and the juggling of the value of the assessments themselves. Again, local/state and federal debt policy worked to cancel each other out. Per capita federal debt fell from $209.01 in 1922 to $139.32 in 1929 while localities and states ran up their per capita debt from $90.04 in 1922 to $137.91 in 1929, an increase of 53.2 percent. Although total debt per capita for all levels of government actually declined during this period from $299.05 to $277.23, this was scant compensation for owners of real estate. They took over the lion's share of responsibility for ultimate repayment of the new state and local debt.[10]

By the end of the 1920s, local governments hit on the "tax-anticipation warrant" (a bond payable in future taxes) to evade the debt limit. For many vote-conscious politicians in the 1920s, the tax-anticipation warrant proved an irresistible temptation. Since it did not meet the legal definition of a municipal bond, it fell outside the restrictions of most debt limits. More importantly, politicians had every reason to gamble that continued prosperity would ensure the safe retirement of the warrants or at least put off the final day of reckoning. In short, the tax-anticipation warrant seemed a foolproof method of financing the expansion of local government and at the same time circumventing tax resistance.

The 1929 crash introduced many Americans—who had hitherto taken matters of public finance for granted—to the painful realities of an unprecedented tax burden. Per capita tax collections actually fell from an all-time high of $83.40 in 1930 to a low of $59.64 at the trough of the depression in 1933. As a percentage of the national income, perhaps the most pertinent measure of the burden's impact, taxes nearly doubled from 11.6 percent in 1929 to 21.1 in 1932. In just three years, the tax load on the American people increased more than it had in the 1920s. Not even during World War I had taxes ever taken such a large percentage of the national income. Taxes at the local level more than doubled, rising from 5.4 percent of the national income in 1929 to an unheard of 11.7 percent in 1932. Surging even faster, state taxes went from 1.9 percent in 1929 to 4.6 in 1932. At the same time, federal tax collections stayed relatively constant, inching up from 4.2 percent in 1929 to 4.7 in 1932.[11]

Motivated by some combination of willful rebellion and economic impoverishment, tax delinquency ballooned steadily after 1930. In a study for Dun and Bradstreet, economist Frederick Bird estimated that the median tax delinquency for all cities over 50,000 in population had climbed from 10.1 percent in 1930 to a record 26.3 percent in 1933 (figure 1-1). The severity of the delinquency rate varied greatly from a high of 68.6 percent in Shreveport, Louisiana, to a low of 2 percent in Providence, Rhode Island. No region of the country escaped increases over the 1930 level. While their condition had grown more acute, delinquents could take some solace from the fact that they no longer stood alone. Richard Olney, a former Democratic congressman from Massachusetts, confessed at the 1934 convention of the National Tax Association, "I am one of the great army, not of the unemployed, but, of tax delinquents." Had he made this confession in 1924, he would, instead of finding a receptive audience, have been dismissed as a pariah.[12]

Plummeting land values put a double squeeze on the already strained resources of real estate owners. The value of new residential

Figure 1-1

Median Year-End Tax Delinquency for All Cities
over 50,000 Population, 1930–1936 (percent of collections)

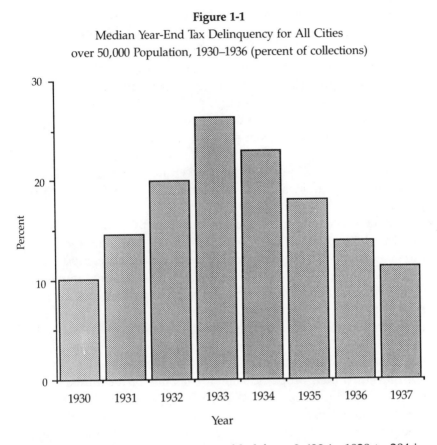

building (in millions of dollars) tumbled from 2,623 in 1929 to 204 in 1933 (a decline of 92 percent), making the real estate sag of 1925–28, when values fell 20 percent, look trivial by comparison. During the same period, the number (in thousands) of nonfarm dwelling units constructed annually fell 89.4 percent. The decline spread to every part of the country and ranged from an astounding 97.3 percent in the East North Central Region, on one extreme, to 81.6 percent in the South Atlantic Region, on the other.[13]

The impossibility of secret evasion of real estate taxes and the consequent visibility of delinquency, quite convenient to the tax assessor and collector in the 1920s, now became an embarrassment. Heretofore, local and state governments had relied on the tax sale to coerce recalcitrants. In most states, a tax sale would be declared when a certain period of time had elapsed after the property had gone into delinquency. At the sale, the tax title, in the form of a tax certificate, would be awarded to that bidder willing to pay all the accrued delinquent taxes and penalties. The owner of the tax certificate did not immediately obtain ownership of the property itself. He merely gained the right to collect future penalties from the delinquent property holder. Redemption periods (the time in which the delinquent owner could clear title by paying off the back taxes and accrued penalties) varied from state to state but usually ran an average of two years. If, in that period, the original owner could not meet these payments, the owner of the tax certificate would be issued a tax deed which could be used as a basis to sue for full title to the property.[14]

This tax-sale machinery had operated effectively in the years before the depression; in fact, there had been a thriving and highly profitable market in tax titles. Traditionally, private corporations who specialized in tax titles had dominated the market. They purchased the tax title not to gain ownership of the property itself but to collect penalty payments from the delinquent owner. In normal times, since the penalty payments required of the delinquent owner were higher than the going interest rate, tax titles netted a better than average profit when compared to other investments. Owners in arrears usually redeemed their property while the tax title buyer turned a comfortable profit in the process. With the collapse of real estate values and subsequent glut of tax titles on the market, buyers could nowhere be found. Those investors unlucky enough to hold tax titles purchased before the crash found themselves burdened with full ownership to real estate forfeited by owners who had defaulted on penalty payments. Wade Smith, a contributing editor of the *National Municipal Review*, exaggerated only slightly when he blamed these conditions for "wiping out the tax title buyer."[15]

By 1931, the political side to the tax system's collapse made its presence felt. For the first time in decades, local and state officials had to confront organized and far-ranging tax revolts. In 1932, journalist Anne O'Hare McCormick observed:

> Wherever you go you run into mass meetings called to protest against taxes. That is nothing new, of course, but opposition has seldom been so spontaneous, so universal, so determined. The nearest thing to a political revolution in the country is the tax revolt. For the first time in a generation taxpayers are wrought up to the

point of willingness to give up public services. "We'll do without county agents," they say, "We'll give up the public health service. We can no longer pay the cost of government."

Speaking from a viewpoint critical of revolt, Harold S. Buttenheim, the editor of the *American City*, advanced a particularly concise description of how matters had changed since the quiescent 1920s. "It has become fashionable to decry government and taxes," he observed. "Demands for indiscriminate budget-slashing are the order of the day. So-called economy leagues are springing up all over the country. Embattled taxpayers are organizing strikes. Fluent orators are taking to the air to attack government and the costs of government." The forms of tax revolt—as Buttenheim's comments showed —ran a wide gamut. The tax-limitation movement and its more radical cousin the tax strike sparked the most controversy.[16]

The Rural Dimension

For the farm sector, the rising tax load exacerbated an already desperate situation. In its gloomy report for 1932, the Department of Agriculture estimated that the "real weight [of the farmers' tax burden] has been doubled by falling prices since 1929." Furthermore, it concluded that it "takes more than four times as many units of farm produce to pay the farm tax bill now as it took in 1914." In Iowa, a startling 48 percent of all farm properties came up delinquent in 1932. During the same year, Mississippi's tax-title auctioneers turned in a pathetic performance. As Robert P. Swierenga explained, tax titles for "one-fourth of the entire land area [of the state], including 20 percent of all farms and 12–15 percent of all town property" went up for sale in the space of one day. Because of a lack of bidders, virtually all of the titles "reverted" to the state government.[17]

Some of the strategies employed by farmers to fight high taxes and tax-law enforcement long ago entered the realm of popular legend. In January 1933, a crowd of farmers in Doylestown, Pennsylvania, overran a tax sale, purchased the title for $1.18, and then returned it to the owner. All across the country, farmers emulated this "dollar sale" strategy not only to resist taxes but also to prevent mortgage foreclosures. "Farmers," a 16 November 1932 editorial in the *New Republic* observed, "are in fact revolting against this burden

in many parts of the country. They are doing so by direct action—
they are not paying their taxes. The authorities are, in many of these
cases, not trying to collect. That is why armed resistance has not
followed."[18]

In late 1931, a mass meeting of tax protesters in Freeborn
County, Minnesota, demanded the abolition of the county agent,
county nurse, weed inspector, and home demonstration agents, in
addition to a 20 percent salary reduction for all government employees. In neighboring Faribault County, a protest gathering of 2,000
taxpayers, which voiced almost identical demands, prompted this
sarcastic salvo from Merle Thorpe, the editor and publisher of Nation's Business, who had long been a critic of such programs: "But
what's this? We thought it had been proved by agricultural departments, federal, state, and county all over the United States, that
what the farmer really wanted was demonstration agents, weed in-
spectors, etc., that Government only went into such work in answer
to an insistent demand for these services from the people among the
grass roots."[19]

The rural tax protest had a distinctly spontaneous air. Taxpayers'
organizations would appear, disappear, reappear, and then disappear again into oblivion at dizzying rates. On occasion, a group
achieved dramatic victories, but over the long haul, permanent and
effective organization proved elusive. Farmers may have been in a
rebellious mood but this did not portend—as many critics of capitalism hoped at the time—that they had embraced socialism. To journalist Mauritz A. Hallgren, it meant just the opposite. Hallgren, in
his book Seeds of Revolt, published in 1933, rejected as absurd the
suggestion, propagated by his fellow leftists, that because farmers,
"our most ardent champions of the rights of private property," had
"in hundreds of communities resorted to direct-action methods" that
"they were as a class becoming radical or revolutionary." On the
contrary, because farmers had used these methods only to protect
their private property, they had, according to Hallgren, "become increasingly reactionary."[20]

Hallgren's conclusions were only partly right. The farmer's stand
against the tax collector may not have been a Marxian attack on private property, but it nonetheless qualified as a genuinely radical and
revolutionary act. In fact, from the perspective of local and state governments, the rural tax protest may have merited greater animus

because, unlike a challenge to capitalism, it posed a direct danger to the state apparatus.[21]

By any standard, J. M. Setten, an unschooled farmer and tax-protest activist from Bloomington, Illinois, penned a radical and revolutionary indictment of political authority in a letter to Governor Henry Horner on 10 January 1933. "A tax strike is brewing," proclaimed Setten, who had just returned from the state convention of a tax league. "In some states at tax sales the people bought their property for 50 cents with shot guns," he warned the governor. "Politicians only understand the language of bombs and bullets." Although in timeworn populist rhetoric Setten denounced the "chain stores and the trusts," he directed most of his complaints against "racketts" like public health, welfare, and conservation, which "should be abolished." He predicted that the state tax league, then contemplating a tax strike, "will become the most powerful organization in the U.S.A. as WE taxpayers have all the money to back us. The goose that lays the golden eggs is dead and turnips are not giving blood any more. . . . The schools are just a graft and rackett for jobs, keeping lobbyists at Wash. and Springfield at 10,000.00 a year to have unjust laws passed against us."[22]

Although most farmers did not go this far, Setten's views reflected a continuing rural animus toward big government. The Ohio State Grange, a member of a coalition that brought a tax-limitation law to Ohio, spoke for granges across the country when it inveighed against paternalistic statism. "We are building up by legislation and poor relief," resolved its state convention, "a class which will more and more take away from those who are industrious, thrifty, self-dependent." Writing in 1934 for *Social Forces*, James Babcock highlighted the anti-big-government overtones of the farm revolt. Babcock noted that in the 1920s, " 'education for cooperation' was looked upon as a solution for economic ills. Today the farmers are saying: 'Schools cost too much.' 'Teachers are paid too much money.' 'We are going broke supporting our schools.' 'I say abolish the county agent.' 'He was wished on us by the state college.' "[23]

The Urban Dimension

Like their rural compatriots, urban tax resisters lacked an overall national movement to tie their efforts together. The closest facsimile was the National Association of Real Estate Boards (NAREB). It managed to foster a limited measure of interstate cooperation and communication. The founding of its Property Owners' Division, which organized autonomous chapters in localities throughout the country, brought a modicum of vigor and determination to the NAREB's fight against high taxes. Limited in membership to nonrealtors and intended as a populist vanguard for tax reduction, the Property Owners' Division movement enjoyed a notable record of success. After one year of operation, the total membership of all the divisions topped 8,000. Less than a year later, the Chicago division alone could boast 7,000 members.[24]

The property owners' divisions did not sit by at the beck and call of either the NAREB or the individual local boards. To be sure, most of the divisions started out as mere appendages to the local boards, but as time went by, they embarked on separate and occasionally conflicting courses. Tax reduction being their raison d'être, they usually lodged much more strident critiques of high taxes than the parent boards. In contrast to their real estate operator patrons, division members did not have the luxury of shifting any of their taxes onto tenants or homeowners. This predisposed them to consider desperate and sometimes illegal measures, like the tax strike, that local boards could not countenance.

Without exception, the local boards and divisions stressed rollbacks in government spending as a necessary prerequisite for real estate tax reduction. In certain cases, they coupled this demand with proposals to broaden the tax base. The preference for a particular method of replacement taxation depended on the board in question. The Colorado Real Estate Board, for example, called for an income tax while the Iowa board, on the other hand, suggested a gasoline tax as a means to relieve real estate owners from paying all road costs. The Chicago board added still more variety to the brew by supporting renewed collection of the then moribund, but still legally sanctioned, personal property tax. Proponents of base broadening repeatedly emphasized how unjust it was for real estate owners to bear 80 percent of the local tax load and in turn receive what they estimated as 20 percent of the services of government paid for via these taxes. Local boards always took pains to stress the purely replacement function of any new tax. They insisted that new taxes could not be enacted unless completely offset by a reduction in real estate taxes. "We favor broadening of the tax base," read a resolution adopted by the Indianapolis Real Estate Board in October 1932, "but in no event and under no circumstances to raise more funds merely to support governmental extravagance."[25]

For this reason, the NAREB's leadership urged that real estate tax limits and reductions should always precede any consideration of replacement taxes. In defense of this stand, a study of tax limitation by the NAREB observed that in "scores of instances promises that the real estate taxes would be lowered when new revenue measures had been enacted have not been kept." Consequently, partisans of base broadening, within the Board's ranks, usually framed their arguments in purely theoretical terms. When it came to proposing legislation, such as the tax limit, local and state boards rarely made provision for replacement taxes of any kind. This policy not only avoided the pitfall of *replacement* taxes becoming *added* taxes but also won the support of those owners of real estate, and other segments of the public, who favored tax reductions but opposed base broadening. It also deserves emphasis that even the most fervent defenders of base broadening promoted an *aggregate* reduction in the tax load. When the Massachusetts Association of Real Estate Boards called for tax and spending cuts "comparable to the reduction and economies of private life," real estate operators throughout the country agreed.[26]

The Ohio tax-limitation campaign of 1933, headed by Adam Schantz III, typified the board's approach (or more precisely nonapproach) to base broadening. Schantz attributed the success of this campaign, which brought about by popular initiative a 1 percent limit to all property taxes, to "an unusual and widespread public support by 'butchers, bakers and candlestick makers.'" He suggested that this unanimity had been achieved because of the Ohio board's strategy of not "even peeping the words 'Sales Tax,' 'Income Tax' and 'Other Taxes.'" Schantz warned the NAREB's members that any talk of base broadening would be poison to a tax-limitation campaign. "Had we," Schantz pointed out, "begun to suggest . . . some other form of tax, we would immediately have incurred the enmity of groups and individuals specifically touched by such new taxes advocated."[27]

Schantz's efforts in Ohio so impressed the NAREB's leadership that, in 1934, they asked him to head their new Committee on Taxation. Under Schantz's leadership, the committee steered clear of divisive replacement taxes and instead set its sights on two narrow objectives at the state level: a constitutional real estate tax limitation, and a homestead exemption of up to $5,000. The adoption of this strategy by Schantz (who, although an unpaid volunteer of the NAREB, was not a real estate operator) went far beyond a pragmatic desire to relieve owners of real estate. He unashamedly embraced the anti-big-government implications of real estate tax limitation and argued in terms remarkably similar to modern public choice theory. Schantz's defense of tax limitation as a check on encroaching "tax spenders" closely resembled economist Giovanni Montemartini's discussion of the "political entrepreneur." "It is normal and human," said Schantz, "that they [the tax spenders] should want to advance and expand their activities just as people in private enterprise like to advance and expand their enterprises. The only difference is that private enterprise expands and grows according to economic circumstances while tax spenders' organizations want to expand, and do expand, their enterprises much faster than private enterprise can pay for." Lawrence G. Holmes, the secretary of the Committee on Taxation, shared Schantz's distrust of bureaucracy and politicians. He saw the "fact that the multitudinous tax-spenders' organizations are concentrating efforts to defeat limitation [as] one of the arguments in its favor."[28]

The NAREB's coordinating role, while significant, is easy to overstate. Its decentralized framework of organization ensured a weak national office. Also, while the NAREB's members agreed on the necessity of real estate tax reduction, local boards exercised complete autonomy. Lastly, although the NAREB and its affiliates at the state and national level enthusiastically backed real estate tax limitation, they not infrequently played a subordinate, and sometimes nonexistent, role when it came to originating and waging local campaigns. In Michigan, for instance, the editors of the *Michigan Farmer* framed and (along with the Grange and a group called the Home Patriots) did most of the campaigning for that state's successful constitutional initiative limiting general property taxes to 15 mills. When voters approved the limitation by a vote of 671,124 to 641,962 in November 1932, the *Michigan Farmer*, rather than the Michigan Real Estate Board, could justly claim most of the credit. The amendment piled up its largest majorities in rural areas where the board had no real presence, while in Detroit—the center of the board's strength—it actually lost by a narrow margin.[29]

The Taxpayers' League

More than the NAREB and its affiliates, the individual taxpayers' league, usually organized on a county or municipal basis, acted as the main conduit for resistance. Harold Groves, a member and later chairman of the Wisconsin State Tax Commission, wrote in 1932 that taxpayers' leagues had "entered their golden age during this depression." In the same year, a writer in the American Library Association *Bulletin* observed that the "taxpayer is indeed in revolt. Local and state taxpayers' leagues multiply." Thomas Reed, a leading political scientist and municipal reformer, lamented that taxpayers' groups "spring up like mushrooms; every time you go out in the morning, you find more of them." Although estimates varied as to the number of local taxpayers' organizations, everyone agreed that the movement was growing. Edward M. Barrows, a frequent writer on the subject for the *National Municipal Review*, calculated that "there are not less than three thousand and probably not more than four thousand such local groups now in action, and that their number is rapidly increasing." Nineteen thirty-three turned out to be the banner year for taxpayers' leagues, with several hundred formed in the spring alone, according to an estimate by Howard P. Jones of the Committee on County Government of the National Municipal League. The contrast with the 1920s could hardly be more manifest. One 1927 study placed the *total* number of state and local taxpayers' organizations at only forty-three.[30]

Daniel Hoan, the Socialist mayor of Milwaukee, looked on the spread of the taxpayers' league with particular alarm; so much, in fact, that he took time off from his mayoral duties to write several articles for leading municipal-reform publications and a booklet on the subject, *Taxes and Tax Dodgers,* for the Socialist Party of America. Hoan equated taxpayers' organizations with tax dodgers' leagues and years later recalled that they sprang up "like weeds" during the depression. He charged that taxpayers' groups "who are always damning their government because they have to pay taxes are doing more to undermine faith in government than all the communists in the world." Hoan decried taxpayers' organizations as mere fronts for the real estate swindler and other greedy capitalists and traced their origin to a "conspiracy [that] was hatched in New York power and banking offices." Nonetheless, he conceded that they had a broad base of support. "Thousands of workers who own their own homes," Hoan wrote, "are attracted by the cry against taxes and assist these selfish groups masquerading as leagues of *small* taxpayers."[31]

Other leading figures in civic-reform circles, to which Hoan belonged, recognized the popular nature of taxpayers' organizations. For Barrows, taxpayers' leagues personified "the popular thought of thousands of communities crystallizing into national sentiment." Barrows advised a halt to the search for a conspiratorial master plan. Instead, he implored fellow critics to come to terms with the indigenous nature of the taxpayers' league. Howard P. Jones concurred with Barrows. He noted as evidence for the spontaneity of taxpayers' leagues that there "were few paid organizers, traveling the highways and byways to weld such groups together."[32]

An inside account of a taxpayers' league is hard to find. Probably the most detailed and dispassionate came from the pen of journalist Hal Steed. In 1933, he wrote "Adventures of a Tax Leaguer," a two-part article for the *Saturday Evening Post*. Basically, Steed recounted the experiences of an official of the Taxpayers' League in an unnamed city of 400,000 people from 1932 to 1933. "For convenience of narrative," he wrote in the first person. He also changed the names of the leading personages in the league. Fortunately, in a later work on a different subject, Steed revealed Atlanta as the unnamed city. (I have placed quotation marks around the invented names in Steed's account.)[33]

Like most taxpayers, Steed, owner of an apartment building, had paid his ever-mounting tax bills during the 1920s without objection. Only when his taxes came up delinquent for 1930 and 1931 because of bankrupt tenants, did political action cross his mind. "Taxes, for the first time in my life," Steed recalled, "became a problem. . . . No meeting of our real-estate board was complete without a denunciation of high taxes and dishonest or incompetent politicians." In response to these worsening conditions, Steed and other local businessmen founded the Taxpayers' League (in actuality the Taxpayers' League of Atlanta and Fulton County). From the beginning the league targeted the "outrageously high" salaries of public employees. It also deplored the influence of tax-spending "organized minorities."[34]

After one week, the fledgling organization could boast 1,000 members, most recruited from the ranks of the homeowners. From the outset, the membership squared off into two camps. One group opted for a confrontational stance toward the city government. Although not active with the league, Julia O'Keefe Nelson, a member of the Atlanta school board and a supporter of tax slashes, exemplified this strand of resistance. She called a county tax boost highway robbery. Nelson implored voters to show politicians that "every one of us will go to jail before we will pay it." The other wing, to which Steed belonged, wanted to "conciliate, not fight" the authorities. Fluctuating between these extremes, the league chalked up a mixed record in its dealings with the city. City expenses, although trimmed slightly as a result of the league's pressure and negotiation campaign, did not fall nearly as fast as had the economy. Still, according to the *Atlanta Constitution*, membership passed the 3,000 mark in April.[35]

In spite of assurances they had given to Steed, local politicians raised tax rates. This action emboldened the militant wing of the league. "Horace Doughty," one of the directors, took Steed aside in November 1932 and warned him that, unless it could be headed off, there would be a rebellion of taxpayers. Steed reacted with disbelief. He found it difficult to imagine the prospect of "our staunch leading citizens, taking part in any sort of strike. Why, the thing was simply not done!" The prostrike faction, led by "Timmons Thorndike"—another one of the directors—pointed to newspaper accounts of tax-striking farmers in the west as a source for inspiration. In the end, "Doughty" and Steed managed to derail the strike proposal. Steed credited their victory to a last minute appeal by "Doughty," who had counseled the membership, 5,000 strong, that the "remedy is not in striking, but in orderly cure at the polls."[36]

Proponents of tax reduction frequently linked their efforts to a general hostility toward governmental paternalism. The president of the Wisconsin Taxpayers' Alliance lamented, "Instead of simply protecting the citizen in the enjoyment of the natural right to live and to follow his vocation unhindered, government is now telling him how he must live, and is, regardless of his wishes, charting the path which he must follow."[37]

Leading eighteenth- and nineteenth-century American political thinkers and economists, including Thomas Paine, Jefferson, John Taylor of Caroline, and William Leggett, had argued that increases in government spending translated into a net loss for society. Many Americans still shared this view of government. As Ashton C. Shallenberger put it in the American Taxpayers' League's *Handbook on Taxation*, published in 1932, "No nation ever can or did make itself prosperous by taxation. Taxes prey upon national wealth and industry. Governments do not produce wealth. They consume it." The *North Dakota Taxpayer* reasoned that "until our public officials realize that they have not been elected to imitate Captain Kid[d] the Taxpayers of North Dakota or any other state in the Union will never enjoy Tax Relief." Speaking for a constituency threatened by tax-revolt sentiment, William G. Carr, the director for research of the National Education Association, pointed to what he regarded as a common economic fallacy that "money put into governmental enterprises is in some mysterious way swallowed up and lost to humanity forever." The *Illinois Teacher* charged that "demagogues, tax dodgers and scheming politicians" had exploited the widespread suspicion of the taxation system as "a rapacious monster ravening over the state seeking whom it may devour."[38]

Tax resisters wondered aloud why government expenditures had not declined commensurate with the economy. A pamphlet of the West Virginia Taxpayers' Association proclaimed, "Taxes should not continue to go up when the ability of the taxpayer to pay has been so greatly curtailed. . . . The price of government should undergo the same measure of deflation as every other branch of human activity." William B. Munro, a former president of the American Political Science Association and the author of several widely read books on local government, framed the issue in even more succinct terms. "The loudest protests today," he suggested, "are not being directed . . . against the proposal to tax this or that, but against the idea of levying any new taxes at all. 'I buy less food, less tobacco, less recreation,' says the man who still holds his job, 'and I would like to buy less government.' "[39]

Taxpayers versus Tax Spenders

The wages of government employees, which had not fallen at the same rate as those who worked in the private sector, provided an especially inviting target for tax resisters. According to the National Industrial Conference Board, the cost of living had declined by 28.5 percent between 1929 and 1933 while (according to a study by *Public Management*) the wages of government employees for 210 selected cities had fallen only 17 percent. Thus, in contrast to wages in the private sector, the real wages of government workers had increased significantly.[40]

Distrust and suspicion of bureaucrats resurfaced during the depression. The *Iowa Taxpayer*, for example, feared that "our local, state, and national government is passing from the stage of being an agency to serve the people, to a huge bureaucracy whose chief aim is to enlarge itself." Over and over again, municipal employees and civic reformers portrayed themselves as under siege by a hostile population. A few examples will suffice. In 1933, the American Municipal Association and the Federation of State Leagues of Municipalities published a joint report in which they deplored the "present popular tendency to assign to public employees the role of villain in the tragedy of present economic conditions." The report continued, "It is generally accepted as an established fact that all public employees are extravagant bureaucrats, time-serving payrollers and nonproductive parasites whose mere existence is an unwarranted imposition on all long suffering taxpayers. It appears that all public officials therefore have forfeited their right to be considered as human beings. They should be driven from the public trough and their salaries slashed ruthlessly." Clarence A. Dykstra, the president of the International City Managers' Association, bemoaned, "There seem to be no game laws of any kind to protect public officers and the establishment we call government. Taxes have been assailed as economic waste and those who spend tax money have been pictured as wastrels."[41]

Municipal reformers had labored for over a generation to restructure and professionalize government and thereby improve the tarnished prereform image of the government employee; now they feared that all this effort had been for naught. Many predicted that if these attacks on government continued, the reform edifice that they had constructed would be irreparably damaged. University of Chicago professor Charles Merriam, America's most prominent political scientist, warned that these recurrent criticisms of government employees threatened to poison permanently "the springs of governmental interest, enthusiasm and service." Glenn Frank, the president of the University of Wisconsin, went further. In an article for the *National Municipal Review*, the leading municipal-reform publication, he entertained the prospect that spreading antigovernment ideology would "divert men of capacity and self-respect from the public service for a generation to come."[42]

On occasion, the tax resisters' indictment of government, and of those who benefited from it, approached a high level of sophistication. They advanced a theory of class, with taxpayers on one side and the tax spenders, (or tax eaters), who exploit them, on the other. The *Washington Taxpayer*, which spoke for defenders of that state's real estate tax-limitation statute, predicted that unless taxpayers took action, "some group of tax spenders, better organized and more versed in political pressure, will get the ears of the candidates and formulate their program which will always be for more money and more government." The *Wisconsin Taxpayer* took Nicholas Murray Butler, the president of Columbia University, to task for some comments he had delivered in a speech on taxation. Butler had proposed that the tax burden should be more evenly spread to instill "tax consciousness" (i.e., an awareness of the need to stop "the mounting costs of government") among the American people. The *Wisconsin Taxpayer* responded: "It might be suggested to Dr. Butler that the masses of the people are now bearing the tax burden and that they are now tax-conscious, but that in their every effort to affect a reduction, they meet with stubborn opposition from those selfish individuals and organized groups who prey upon the government."[43]

Professor Harley Lutz, of Princeton University, author of several widely read public finance texts, seemed taken aback by the degree to which resisters played up the class theme. He particularly singled out their "trick of speaking and perhaps thinking, of the taxpayers as one group, and of those responsible for public policy as another quite different group." Lutz disparaged the resisters' unflattering portrayal of the tax-spending class. "Municipal bondholders," he observed, "are visualized as a group of wealthy investors who loaned their money when prices are high and are now demanding their pound of flesh when prices and incomes are low. Public employees are visualized as living in luxury." Lutz rejected the class model as an invalid description of the political system. Instead, he pictured government as a kind of giant cooperative purchasing agency in which all citizens participated as equal shareholders.[44]

Wherever proposed, tax-reduction and tax-limitation initiatives ran into opposition from state employees, municipal reformers, and others who depended directly or indirectly on tax money. In Michigan, for example, the Michigan Education Association and the Michigan Municipal League led the fight against the 15 mill tax-limitation initiative. State education and teachers' associations, with the help of the National Education Association, formed the core of unsuccessful campaigns against limitation proposals in Ohio, Indiana, and Washington. In addition, national municipal-reform and rationalization organizations, like the American Municipal Association, the National Municipal League, and the Municipal Finance Officers' Association, gave ideological and logistical succor to these campaigns.

These groups discovered unfamiliar but greatly helpful allies in the municipal bond and investment banking trades. In its report for 1934, the Municipal Securities Committee of the Investment Bankers' Association of America exuded a hostility to tax limitation matching a typical article on the subject in the *National Municipal Review*. It labeled tax limit laws as the most damaging of all forms of legislation to municipal credit. The report made a special point to laud "every Municipal Securities Committee of the Association [that] had struggled with some local [tax-limitation] movement for it." Often with notable success, local bond committees instigated or financed litigation to repeal or loosen tax limits. Unlike many other groups on both sides of the taxation issue, municipal-bond dealers and investment bankers made no secret of their pecuniary stake in the defeat of tax-limitation legislation. The *Bond Buyer* summed it up with refreshing candor: "The municipal bond buyer is not interested in a bond supported by limited taxing power."[45]

The local taxpayers' league became a common fixture throughout the country. No state, and few localities, escaped protests of one kind or another. Because it touched the lives of so many powerful constituencies, the urban tax revolt generated most of the publicity. Civic reformers, real estate business groups, municipal bond holders, and organized government professionals drew their sustenance from America's larger cities. In the following pages of this chapter, I focus on Milwaukee, Detroit, and New York City. Many other cities could have been selected as case studies, but these three received especially close attention from leading journalists, politicians, civic reformers, real estate interests, and municipal bond investors.

Milwaukee

Daniel Hoan, the Socialist mayor of Milwaukee, made a special point, when speaking before municipal-reform audiences, to denounce "tax dodger leagues." In the course of his speeches, Hoan often recounted his own struggles with one of these leagues in Milwaukee, the Taxpayers' Advisory Council (TAC). From its formation in April 1932, with the support of the Real Estate Board, the Association of Commerce, and the Building and Loan Association, the TAC proved a constant headache to Milwaukee's Socialist administration. Initially, the TAC adopted a two-pronged strategy of court suits and intensive lobbying to lower assessments and thus achieve its overarching goal of a 25 percent reduction in municipal spending. Thwarted in these efforts, leading members of the TAC strongly intimated that they were considering a tax strike. This talk sparked an angry reply from the *Milwaukee Leader*, the city's Socialist daily and a backer of Hoan. "If the taxpayer should go on strike," the *Leader* predicted, "all services would have to stop. . . . Epidemics of disease would sweep the city. Burglars would ply their trade unhindered. Fires would rage unabated, burning up the homes of the taxpayers."[46]

Threats of a strike abated after the TAC garnered enough signatures to place a tax-reduction initiative on the ballot for November 1932. It proposed drastic restrictions on the city's tax levy and limited annual spending to a maximum of $17 million until 1937. The local Socialist party organization targeted defeat of the initiative as a key priority and the *Milwaukee Leader* ran a string of front page editorials critical of the TAC. Not unexpectedly, Hoan campaigned hard against the proposal. He accused the TAC of "hysteria, falsehoods, and bulldozing" and portrayed the initiative as a smoke screen to "save money for those who are already much too wealthy." He alleged that, if passed, it would give the city a black eye in credit markets and place its services on "a level with small villages." Despite a strong showing by candidates running on the Socialist ticket, the voters turned a deaf ear to Hoan's pleas and approved the tax-reduction initiative by a vote of 91,752 to 81,507.[47]

Undaunted, critics of the initiative secured enough signatures to put a measure on the ballot in April 1933 to repeal the results of the November vote. As the 4 April election date drew nearer, the rancor reached a high pitch as each side charged the other with ulterior motives. The Milwaukee Contractors' Association, which had gathered most of the signatures to place the repeal measure on the ballot, proved a costly ally for the Socialists. In an open letter to the press, Henry H. Otjen, the president of the TAC, suggested that the contractors wanted repeal because it would open up the prospect of tax-funded city contracts. Edward Buer, the head of the Milwaukee Contractors' Association, played into Otjen's hands by, in effect, admitting the truth of his accusation. As Buer put it in his reply to Otjen, the contractors "admit . . . that they are an organization of men engaged in public works whose capital is invested therein and whose loyal employees . . . look appealingly to their bosses for work which cannot be given them because of your charter ordinance."[48]

Not without some justification, Buer and the Socialists tried to tar Otjen and other of the TAC's leaders with the tax-delinquent brush. Buer's claim that they accounted for 50 percent of the city's tax delinquency may have been wide of the mark but several TAC members did owe substantial sums. Otjen, for example, had run up a delinquency bill of $3,162 for his 1932 taxes while Leonard Grass, president of the Real Estate Board, was in arrears to the tune of $39,195. By early 1933, however, with over 40 percent of Milwaukee's taxes uncollected, this charge had lost a great deal of its potency. For every delinquent Grass and Otjen, there were thousands of voters in the same boat. Hoan and his allies were routed in the April election as the repeal measure went down to defeat by a vote of 63,000 to 49,000. The Socialists forced themselves to swallow substantial retrenchments in the city budget, including reductions in museum, library, and park services.[49]

In their response to the tax revolt, Milwaukee's Socialists argued in terms befitting the most conservative defender of governmental authority. This really should not give much cause for surprise. In Milwaukee, the Socialist party and the political establishment were one and the same. Beyond this, the Socialists, as proponents of expanded government power, were the natural enemies of tax revolts. They needed an efficient and unrestrained government to carry out their societal vision. Historian Kenneth Fox noted that moderate socialists, like Daniel Hoan, and municipal reformers had often gotten along well with each other. Socialists and good-government reformers shared a dislike for the leading anti-big-government figures of the period. Merle Thorpe alienated socialist and civic reformer alike with his use of laissez-faire credos. Hoan, on the other hand, won many plaudits from the National Municipal League for his efficient style of government.[50]

Detroit

Throughout the early years of the depression, Detroit also had an active tax-resistance movement. Unlike Milwaukee, however, fragmented organization and disagreement over strategy greatly limited effective action by taxpayers. The story of Detroit's tax revolt began in 1932 when Mayor Frank Murphy announced plans to stage a tax title sale for 90,000 parcels of delinquent property, which had a total value of $500 million. This proposal met determined opposition from Frederick A. Wayne, the head of the Taxpayers' Protective Association, who called Murphy's plan communistic and vowed to work for the recall of any councilman who voted to hold the sale. Although the sale went ahead, it was a grand flop, because of a paucity of bidders. Returning to the trenches in March 1932, Wayne demanded a 25 percent reduction in taxes for 1932–33 at a hearing of the city council where, according to newspaper accounts, he was wildly cheered by a large audience.[51]

After mid-1932, another group stole the tax-resistance limelight, the Associations for Tax Reduction (ATR). The ATR had close ties with the Detroit Real Estate Board—so close, in fact, it was considered by many a mere stalking horse for the board. In the past, the ATR's president had been president of the board while its manager had served the board as both secretary and president. Nevertheless, the ATR had a base of support extending well beyond real estate interests. Over forty civic, business, and neighborhood organizations made up its membership. The ATR staked all its hopes on a petition drive to force a special election on a far-reaching proposal for a tax-limitation charter. If passed, the proposal, dubbed a limited tax strike by its sponsors, would have legally limited property taxes to $61 million for the 1932–33 budget and reduced collections thereafter by $1 million a year until 1937–38, when there would be a permanent cap of $56 million. After it collected the required number of signatures, the ATR staged a large parade through downtown Detroit to celebrate. A truck pulled by horses, which contained all the petitions, led the procession. Finally, "amidst a storm of denunciation" from the Real Estate Board the city council agreed to hold a special election on the proposal.[52]

In many ways, the charter election campaign in Detroit closely paralleled that of Milwaukee during the same year. Like Hoan, Murphy alleged that the tax-reduction campaign had been instigated by a small group of wealthy real estate operators who wanted to get out from under their back taxes. Also, as in the case of Milwaukee, these charges had some validity. The president of the ATR, for example, was delinquent in his taxes by $150,000. Murphy overreached himself when he tried to blame Detroit's *overall* tax delinquency on speculators who owned vacant property. On the surface, these accusations were credible, because vacant lots accounted for a hefty 48 percent of the total delinquent *parcels* of property, a fact emphasized repeatedly by Murphy. But, in reality, the 48 percent figure becomes meaningless when it is taken into account that vacant lots made up a minuscule 6 percent of the city's total tax collections. In fact, as Sidney Tickton discovered in a 1932 study for the Detroit Bureau of Governmental Research, "there is no one group more than any other responsible for the delinquency. All groups are represented on the delinquent tax roll in about the same proportion as on the general tax roll."[53]

In addition to zeroing in on allegations of tax dodging, Murphy charged that the backers of the proposal, having been unable to defeat him for reelection in 1931, were now intent on "wrecking our government." Following a similar tack, other critics hammered relentlessly on the theme that if the ATR had its way there would be chaos and disaster for Detroit. The ATR's manager suggested in response that the "only 'chaos and disaster' that will result will be the 'chaos and disaster' that befalls a few non-essential and over-paid hangers on who should have been eliminated long ago." The statistician of the ATR tried to seize the offensive by playing up the class dimension. The campaign, he declared, "was a struggle between the taxpayer and the tax spender." An ATR broadside pointed out that U.S. Senator James Couzens, a vocal opponent of the limitation, owned more municipal bonds of the city government than any other individual. It went on to warn that "immediate reduction of taxes is the only means by which a tax strike can be averted."[54]

Backers of the limitation saw their campaign as part of an assault on big government. One supporter of ATR framed it in these terms: "Our government officials say, that the government must have an increasing amount in order to operate efficiently. . . . I believe that two-thirds of our governmental activities could be dispensed with, and the great mass of the people would get along quite as well."[55]

Despite the ATR's aggressive strategy, it became more isolated as time went on. Detroit's two leading good-government organizations, the Citizens' League and the Bureau of Governmental Research, pulled out all the stops to defeat the charter amendment. They called the tax-limitation proposal a straightjacket and claimed that its provisions would impinge on governmental flexibility, experimentation, and rationalization. Since civic reformers predicated their ideology on these attributes of government, this opposition could be expected. Not so easy to explain was the stand taken against the amendment by people who would seem to have been a natural constituency for such a law. Groups and individuals in this category included the Board of Commerce, the head of the Property Owners' Division of the Detroit Real Estate Board, the Ford Motor Company, Chrysler, and the Committee on City Finances.[56]

The opposition of the Committee on City Finances wrought particular damage to the amendment's chances. An understanding of the committee's role is essential for two reasons: the committee gave an added respectability to the forces against the amendment, and (more crucially) the study of its activities reveals much about how Detroit's leading financial institutions fit into the city's fiscal crisis. The committee had been formed in 1929 at the behest of the common council to advise the city on its finances. It was popularly known as the Stone Committee, after its head, Ralph Stone, chairman of the board of the Detroit Security and Trust Company. Stone's colleagues on the committee included representatives of the Michigan Manufacturers' Association, the Real Estate Board, the Board of Commerce, the Citizens' League, and the Bureau of Governmental Research.[57]

Because its members controlled a major portion of Detroit's lendable capital, the committee enjoyed automatic entrée into policy formulation at city hall. Thus, as the percentage of Detroit's tax levy devoted to debt payments grew, so too did the committee's power to extract concessions from the city government. Even by standards of the depression era, the increase in Detroit's municipal debt had been higher than average. In part, the stage had been set by Detroit's territorial annexations in the 1920s. The annexed areas had a weak tax base and proved a net drain on already overextended city finances. Debt service as a percentage of the tax levy climbed from an already staggering 21.6 percent in the 1929–30 fiscal year to a crippling 42.5 percent in 1932–33.[58]

During this period, the Stone Committee pulled the city out of more than one financial crisis. In 1932, for example, Stone and Henry Hart, the vice-president of the First Detroit Company, persuaded the New York banks to advance over $40 million in short term loans. As a quid pro quo for this subsidy, the common council adopted the "Stone recommendations," a rigid economy program that included reductions in welfare and other city services. The Stone Committee knew full well, however, that it could not push local politicos too far. Interdependence between local bankers and politicians followed in the wake of extended credit lines. Members of the Stone Committee had become nearly as dependent on the maintenance of tax collections as their enemies the tax spenders. Furthermore, Murphy let it be known that, under certain circumstances, he considered repudiation of the city's debt a live option. "I am not for repudiation," Murphy remarked in a thinly veiled threat. "I am simply not for permitting the City and the government to be wrecked and ruined, if we can stop it."[59]

The forebodings of the bankers and other bearers of Detroit's debt that repudiation would come about as a result of the amendment's enactment were well founded. Assuming a tax-delinquency rate of 25 percent, local government, under the terms of the tax limitation, would be assured of only $45 million in tax collections. Of this amount, $31 million would be needed to pay off the fixed annual debt charge, leaving only $14 million for the rest of the city government. To receive education subsidies from the state government, the city would have to spend $10 million of the $14 million on schools and public libraries. As Sidney Fine, Frank Murphy's biographer, explains, "This left a grand total of $3,668,610 to operate the rest of the government which was only 13 percent of the amount for the same purposes provided by the revised Murphy budget." In all likelihood, Murphy and the city council would have reacted to this prospect by imposing either a total repudiation or a radical debt rescheduling (in effect, a de facto repudiation). The results, in any event, could be none too reassuring for those who held Detroit's municipal debt.[60]

The amendment seemed clearly headed for trouble as the 9 August election date approached. Murphy, with his impassioned and well-polished speaking style, found a receptive audience in the voters. His predictions that chaos would befall the city after the amendment's enactment must have swayed many voters, especially those dependent on tax-funded relief programs. Murphy even indulged in a bit of red baiting. He claimed that local members of the Communist party supported the amendment. "The Communists," he charged, "have recognized their opportunity in this election. They are out for revolution. . . . They look for anything that will produce chaos and confusion."[61]

Murphy skillfully exploited the prerogatives of his office. About a month before the election, he called in all the city department heads and ordered them to "furnish leadership for the people in this fight." The ATR termed these tactics the "City Hall lash." Fine described some of the methods used by the city's political leaders to carry out these orders: "The Department of Recreation posted literature at all playgrounds and community centers explaining the implications of the tax plan, employees sent out personal letters about the proposal to friends of the department, and the department hired a sound truck to urge votes against the plan at baseball games and other recreational events on the Sunday before the election."[62]

Commissioner L. G. Lenhardt denied that these actions constituted a political stand by the Murphy administration. He depicted the city government's campaign against the amendment as not a question of politics but a question of "whether the government is going to keep going or whether it is not." On election day, the amendment lost in a landslide of 126,578 to 40,050. By any standard, Murphy and his allies had scored a decisive victory. They had carried all but one of the city's 895 precincts.[63]

New York City

Throughout most of 1932, Mayor "Beau" James Walker, the reigning head of New York City's Tammany political machine, was being investigated by the state legislature for corruption. At the same time, the mayor had become embroiled in a bitter political feud with Charles W. Berry, the city comptroller. Amidst this background of political corruption and factionalism, New York's real estate and tax-payers' groups debated the merits of nonpayment. The West Side Taxpayers' Association (WSTA) led off the militant forces with a resolution in March 1932 encouraging taxpayers to withhold their 1932 taxes. As a corollary, it called for reductions in municipal salaries, the lowering of assessments to reflect market value more nearly, and a boost in fares to make the subways self-supporting.[64]

That same month, Frank Demuth, president of the WSTA, carried forward the prostrike cause to the Greater Brooklyn Property Owners' Association (GBPOA). "A tax strike soon would demonstrate that the Mayor is killing the goose which is laying Tammany's golden eggs," Demuth told a March meeting of the GBPOA. He implored the 400 assembled members to realize that "you all have the weapon in your own hands. Without us the city government cannot continue and it is high time that they recognize that fact." As evidence that taxpayers could no longer depend on the city government to give them relief, Demuth recalled a meeting he had attended with Walker where the mayor had said, "I'm going to give the city decent homes to live in." Pointing to Walker's comments, Demuth posed a rhetorical question to the audience: "But if our throats are cut by taxation—who's going to foot the bill?" After applauding Demuth's speech enthusiastically, those present at the meeting appointed a committee to press the GBPOA's demands in person to Walker. These demands included, in addition to the retrenchment program previously adopted by the WSTA, a call for the mayor to reopen the current city budget. If Walker proved intransigent, the members agreed to meet on 18 April to plan a strike for 1 May, when tax collections began.[65]

Right from the start, the association's tax-strike campaign ran into stiff opposition from the more conservative and cautious New York Real Estate Board (NYREB). On 24 March 1932, Anton L. Trunk, the president of the board, told the New York Times that the fledgling strike movement was playing with dynamite and touted cooperation with city officials as the best method to bring down tax rates. Nonetheless, he joined his pleas to the strike enthusiasts with some friendly advice to the city government. "Of course we [the Real Estate Board] realize the growing resentment of taxpayers, and that unless something is done for their relief they will take things into their own hands." Even more ominously for city authorities, Trunk warned that if the situation got out of hand, the NYREB might be reluctantly forced to take leadership of the tax-strike movement.[66]

Trunk's forebodings about the unwanted disorderly implications of a tax strike prompted one supporter of nonpayment to suggest in jest that "for those conservative taxpayers who shudder at the term 'tax strike,' the term 'tax pass' might be used." Under any name, the board would not brook nonpayment proposals and managed to quash the sentiment, at least temporarily. On 25 March 1932, the Brooklyn Real Estate Board, with help from the boards of both New York City and the state, persuaded a conference of thirty civic and business groups to adopt its resolution condemning a tax strike. Even so, the prostrike forces mustered a sizable minority, which included the United Real Estate Owners' Association, the West Side Chamber of Commerce, the Broadway Association, and the Twenty-Third Street Association, against the resolution. The board's herculean efforts won them an editorial pat on the back from the *New York Times*: "The Real Estate Board is well advised in cautioning its members against joining any tax strike. The time has come for action, but not for resort to that doubtful weapon."[67]

Serious talk of a tax strike continued to be heard throughout April. While Trunk's fence-mending campaign with the city government won praise from the press, Walker did not reciprocate. He spurned offers of a private conference with the board and the thirty other organizations which had attended the 25 March meeting. Instead, when the board and its allies called on him at city hall on 28 March, he demanded that they tell him the names of all the groups and individuals who had endorsed a tax strike. "If there is going to be a strike," the mayor warned, "I want to know who is causing it. Then we will deal with them in the manner prescribed by law and we'll find out if treason is still a crime in this state." At a stormy meeting of the Board of Estimate in April, the audience greeted Walker with hisses when he ruled out a general salary reduction for city employees and refused to consider proposals to increase subway fares.[68]

Trunk grew impatient with Walker's unwillingness to conciliate the board. On 6 May he wrote, and later released to the press, a bluntly worded letter to the mayor. In the letter, which the *New York Herald Tribune* dubbed an ultimatum, Trunk castigated Walker for his persistent refusal to meet with the board and other groups of taxpayers. He belittled the mayor's oft-expressed "pride . . . that two-thirds of one per cent may be saved from this year's budget," and predicted that "unless you put into immediate effect definite and substantial economies, the budget for 1933 will be so large that even you will be fearful of the effect when it is announced what will have to be collected in taxes from property owners."[69]

Seemingly in response to Trunk's accusations, Walker shifted gears toward a more conciliatory policy. On 12 May, he held a meeting at city hall with Trunk and other representatives of the Real Estate Board. According to M. V. Casey, the real estate editor of the *New York Herald Tribune*, "The Mayor was told in ungarnished terms what the situation was and what the result would be unless drastic economies were affected in the city government." Apparently, Trunk's warning letter had been sufficient to change Walker's approach. Instead of daring the board's members to strike, as he had done in the past, Walker tried to win them over. He promised to propose a budget at, or lower than, the last year's level and vowed to fire any of his department heads who failed to reduce their spending. In the space of an afternoon, Walker had been able to dispel months of acrimony and, according to Casey, lift "high . . . the hopes of real estate owners." In addition, Trunk and the rest of the board pledged their full support to Walker's economy efforts. With much justification, Casey concluded that as a result of the parley "possibilities of a tax strike in the city [had] faded."[70]

While Walker's turnabout can, in great part, be explained by the board's pressure campaign, it should not be forgotten that by May 1932 he was badly in need of political support. Only eight days before the meeting on 12 May, Berry had delivered some damaging testimony to the Hofstader Committee about the mayor's political manipulation of bus franchises. On 26 May, the last day of his questioning before the committee, Walker devoted the final portion of his testimony to a long plea for taxpayers' relief. In particular, he blasted the "unworkable Charter that makes the cost of the municipal government far beyond that which it should be, and which as a result becomes a burden on the taxpayers in this city that is almost unbearable."[71]

By the second half of 1932, the tax-strike musings of the previous months had subsided. The Real Estate Board had played a key role in the restoration of taxpayers' quiescence, but other factors as well made a well-organized tax-withholding campaign unfeasible. For one thing, the would-be strikers did not have many cards to play. Although the city's tax-delinquency rate reached even higher levels—from 14.6 percent in 1930 to 26.4 percent in 1933—it never really attained crisis proportions. These percentages may seem high, but they were no worse than the national average of 26.3 for all cities over 50,000 in population. Had the rate of nonpayment been a bit higher, New York's tax strikers could have thumbed their noses at the tax authorities with little fear of effective retaliation. As it was, the city's threat to prosecute leaders of any tax strike—backed up by a pledge of leading bankers to use their ownership of mortgages to force owners of real estate to pay their delinquent taxes—had a chilling measure of credibility.[72]

Beyond this, tax-resisters lacked unity. The plethora of real estate and taxpayers' groups in the city led to a situation where taxpayers fought each other more than they fought taxes. No one organization—not even the Real Estate Board—spoke for enough taxpayers. Be that as it may, both the board and New York's political leaders never hid their concern about the strike threat, with the result that Trunk and the Real Estate Board won enough concessions from Walker to prevent demands for tax relief from taking too extreme a turn. At the same time, Comptroller Berry offered attractive monetary inducements to taxpayers. During an especially tense chapter in the history of city/taxpayer relations, on 18 March 1932, Berry endorsed legislation to give 6 percent rebates to taxpayers who tendered early payments on the second installment of their taxes due 1 November.[73]

Parallels between all these cases abound. In every city, taxpayers made opposition to high real estate taxes the centerpiece of their activism. Although frequently serving to unify taxpayers, the National Association of Real Estate Boards, its local chapters, and affiliated organizations pursued variegated and occasionally conflicting strategies. In New York City and Atlanta, local boards worked closely with the authorities and sought to restrain strike-prone elements while in Milwaukee and Detroit they chose to confront, through the initiative process, rather than conciliate.

Taxpayers had three available roads to relief: replacement taxes, economy in government, or a combination of both. Replacement taxes alienated potential supporters and gained few allies, a fact widely recognized by tax resisters. Many, though by no means all, resisters saw the issue of replacement taxes as a snare that would only divert attention from the first priority of taxpayers' organizations: tax reduction. Frank G. Arnold, the president of the Nebraska Federation of County Taxpayers' Leagues, spoke for taxpayers' associations around the country when he warned that "practically every state that has been inveigled into these new forms of [replacement] taxation pays far more taxes eventually, and we know from experience that public expenditures cannot be curbed by furnishing more money for the tax spenders to waste." Of the tax limits enacted by seven states in the 1932–33 period, only one, West Virginia's, made any provision for replacement taxes. Even the West Virginia law did not establish a new tax; it only gave the legislature the power to enact an income tax if it so chose. Beyond this, those real estate and taxpayers' organizations that pressed for the income, sales, or personal property taxes to "relieve real estate" carefully warned that they sought replacement taxes, not added taxes.[74]

What motivated these long-quiescent taxpayers to rebel? Or still more specifically, were those who chose the route of resistance ideologically motivated or merely hard-pressed Americans who sought economic relief via tax relief? Obviously, economic motivations played a central role in bringing taxpayers to the point of rebellion, but it would be both facile and misleading to conclude that tax resistance was automatically caused by economic self-interest. A more rewarding line of analysis would treat the onset of economic decline as a *catalyst* to action by taxpayers. It was not so much that taxpayers like Hal Steed cynically adopted an anti-big-government pose when the depression cut into their incomes. Rather, as Steed himself put it, the depression forced taxpayers to *think* for the first time about the burden and perforce the purposes of high taxes. To use a popular term of the period, the depression motivated taxpayers to become "tax conscious," to look more critically at how a bureaucracy they could once afford to ignore spent their tax dollar.

Though the specter of the tax strike was common, strikes rarely materialized. Nonetheless, those dependent on tax money took this threat seriously and acted on it. David Wood, the leading municipal bond lawyer in the United States, saw organized tax evasion as the most important danger to municipal credit. "This taxpayers' strike," he charged, "is a result of the campaign which has been waged for the reduction in municipal budgets. Many cases have come to my attention where real estate organizations and similar civic bodies have urged taxpayers not to pay their taxes." Melvin Traylor, the president of the First National Bank of Chicago, went still further. He characterized the tax striker as "the greatest menace to American governments today." When speaking these words, Traylor may well have had in mind events that took place in his home city of Chicago. For in Chicago, more than any other place, these often expressed fears became reality.[75]

CHAPTER 2

Chicago: Portrait of a "Tax Racket"

In Chicago's tax strike from 1930 to 1933, the tax revolt of the 1930s found its most dramatic expression. If degree of tax controversy is a criterion, Chicago provides a poor choice for a typical case study. Chicago's importance to the historian lies in the explosive example it served as for the rest of the country. Its plight stood out as a reminder to other localities of just how bad the tax revolt could potentially get. When compared to other American cities, Chicago's fiscal situation was a portrait of extremes. The corruption of the local taxation and assessment process had long been pervasive. When taxpayers struck back against this system, they did it in a big way. Chicago's organized tax-resistance movement was unrivaled for its time in both breadth of support and extremity of tactics.

In the kinds of tax problems it faced, however, Chicago was quite typical. By the early depression years, tax corruption, heavy reliance on the real estate tax, tax delinquency, and the resistance had moved to center stage in many large and small American cities. These tax afflictions, although especially acute in Chicago, were not specific to it. For these reasons, uncovering the story of its tax strike can also yield profitable insights into the general character and potential of tax resistance during the depression.

Taxation had always been a hot potato in Chicago's local politics. By the late 1920s, the intractability of Cook County's corrupt assessment system had become an embarrassing mark of local distinction. Herbert D. Simpson, professor of economics at Northwestern University, wrote *Tax Racket and Tax Reform in Chicago*, a highly readable and perceptive chronicle of Chicago's tax troubles in the 1920s. Writing in 1930, at the height of the Capone era, Simpson used Chicago's notoriety for organized crime as his point of departure. He complained about a glaring omission in a recent article describing the activities of locally based gangster rackets. According to Simpson, the article left out "what is probably the greatest of them all—the Tax Racket."[1]

To get a better picture of what Simpson meant by the term "tax racket," some background is necessary. Political scientists of that era scarcely could have asked for a better example of extreme government fragmentation than Chicago and its environs. More than one public administration text of the period cited the eye-catching statistic that Cook County contained within its borders 446 separate units of government, each possessing autonomous power to levy taxes. These figures did not even include a like number of governmental units without taxing authority but with budgetary demands.[2]

In comparison, the county's assessment system seemed an exemplar of centralization. A five-member elected Board of Assessors supervised the assessment of all personal property and real estate in the county. The law required the board to make a countywide assessment at least once every four years. Taxpayers could appeal their assessments to a three-member Board of Review, also elected on the county level. Outside of the city limits of Chicago, Cook County voters elected their own township assessors. These township assessors worked under the supervision of the Board of Assessors and the Board of Review.[3]

Tax assessment, like much else in Chicago politics, defied the comfortable simplicity of official appearances. An extralegal system of assessment, under the control of the dominant political machine, worked in tandem with these government bodies. As Herbert Simpson put it, "The tax system has become the mere adjunct of whatever political organization is in power." "Tax fixing" (the basis of the tax racket) provided the motive force for this ex officio assessment setup. Basically, tax fixing involved the juggling of assessments to reward those who cooperated with the local political machine and punish those who did not. By the 1920s, Chicago's rival Republican and Democratic machines had farmed out most of the tax-fixing authority to precinct captains. Simpson recalled that "one could sit in the Board of Review and Board of Assessors' offices and see these men [precinct captains and other party officials] come in with their pockets bulging with the crumpled tax bills of constituents to be 'fixed.' " The upshot was that assessments fluctuated wildly, both within and between precincts.[4]

Busting the Tax Racket

Although the assessment status quo was remarkably durable, it had, by the 1920s, been under fire for quite some time. The teachers, who wanted more tax money to fund salary increases and other school expenses, formed the vanguard of the reform movement. Since the turn of the century, the Chicago Teachers' Federation (CTF), under the leadership of its business manager, the indefatigable Margaret Haley, had initiated a long series of court suits to force the property of public utilities onto the tax assessment rolls. The CTF had also spearheaded successful efforts in 1907 to exempt the schools from the Juul Law, which limited property tax rates to five percent. From 1915 to 1925, real estate and personal property taxes paid for about 90 percent of all school costs. Unfortunately for the CTF, its setbacks often negated its victories. Although overall salaries of teachers more than doubled between 1913 and 1925, much of the increase went to high school teachers instead of to the elementary teachers who belonged to the CTF. In addition, the CTF had to fight off rival interests for school money such as janitors and building contractors. Elements from both of these groups benefited from close ties with local politicos.[5]

After a long lull in tax agitation, Haley decided to take the offensive once more. As historian Marjorie Murphy put it, "Her timing proved disastrous." Haley's last tax crusade initiated a long chain of events that threw Chicago's schools into the worst fiscal crisis of their history. In 1926, the CTF and the Board of Education persuaded the City Council to make a selective survey of the tax assessment rolls. The findings showed that properties in the Loop (Chicago's central business district) had been assessed substantially under appraised value. Superficially, these results appeared to confirm Haley's long-time depiction of the Loop as a haven for rich tax dodgers.[6]

Throughout 1926, the CTF suffered one defeat after another. The Board of Assessors, the Board of Review, and ultimately the State Supreme Court stymied Haley's push to require a full-value assessment. Then, the CTF's fortunes took a dramatic turn for the better. It obtained the help of a powerful ally, the Joint Commission on Real Estate Valuation (JCREV). The JCREV had been created in late 1926 at the behest of the Cook County Board of Commissioners and over the protests of Mayor William Dever. Although offered membership, the members of the Board of Assessors and the Board of Review refused to participate in commission activities. As a result, business elements and civic reformers took effective charge. George O. Fair-weather, business manager of the University of Chicago, became the chairman of the commission. The university owned a great deal of property in the Loop. John O. Rees, who had been active in the assessment rationalization campaign of the Cleveland Bureau of Municipal Research, took over as director of the JCREV. The campaign also received full backing from the Building Managers' Association which represented many of the larger commercial properties in the Loop.[7]

Fairweather and the leadership of the Building Managers' Association knew what few others, including the CTF, even suspected. Relative to other classes of property in the city, Loop property had been overassessed by the Board of Assessors. At first, the JCREV campaign for assessment reform duplicated the failures of the teachers. The Board of Assessors, Board of Review, and the new Republican administration of Mayor William Hale "Big Bill" Thompson spurned the commission's requests for access to the records of the just-completed 1927 assessment.

Finally in October 1927, the CTF, with JCREV support, filed a petition for a hearing before the Illinois Tax Commission on "the appalling conditions of assessment in Chicago." The CTF and the JCREV complained that the local authorities were in violation of a long-ignored 1898 law requiring the publication of all assessments. The Tax Commission seemed impressed with the CTF's case. In January 1928, it ordered the Board of Assessors to obey the law and publish all tax assessments. After months of legal and bureaucratic wrangling, the local authorities backed down and grudgingly published the assessment lists in July.[8]

The published results shocked even the most cynical observers. "It was plain as noon," wrote Chicago journalist Milton Mayer, "that hundreds of politicians were growing rich and that tax-fixing had become a major industry." Properties in Cook County showed an average assessment of only 35.9 percent of sales value. This average, however, should not be taken too seriously, as a majority of properties had assessments either well above or below 35.9 percent. Assessments ran the gamut from 1 percent to over 100 percent of sales value. Properties in the county showed an average deviation from uniformity (uniformity defined in this case as 35.9 percent) of 36.5 percent.[9]

As the JCREV had surmised, the Loop suffered from overassessment relative to other classes of property. The average assessment in the Loop, 74.1 percent of sales value, was more than double the countywide average. Simpson and other contemporary analysts of the assessment tried their best to reconcile this apparent anomaly. First, they pointed out that the variation and complexity of Loop property made an accurate assessment much more difficult. A second, and more plausible, explanation was that the members of Chicago's money-hungry political machine believed that the financial rewards of Loop overassessment outweighed the political risks.[10]

In more ways than one, the political situation in Chicago recalls the experience of other machines in the late nineteenth century. As historian Clifton K. Yearley has argued, the political boss in large urban areas depended on the support and mobilization of poor to lower middle-class voters. Since heavy Loop assessments did not alienate (and indeed may have bolstered) this constituency, local politicians saw no reason to change their ways. Moreover, as Simpson noted, the lower echelon of Chicago's party functionaries came from economically modest backgrounds. This may have predisposed them to accept the common perception that the Loop "can afford to pay more." In a statement that doubtless won the empathy of Loop businessmen, Simpson judged that the assessment status quo, "provides assessing officials with as arbitrary power over the property and fortunes of wealthy citizens as any Central American dictator could desire."[11]

One should not conclude from these observations that Chicago had somehow stumbled on a unique form of progressivity in property taxation. Other aspects of the 1926 assessment contradicted any such pat explanation. Owners of expensive residential property received a notably lower tax assessment than other homeowners. The disparity in assessments is more profitably viewed from a political rather than an economic perspective. The newspapers had a field day publicizing the way that politics distorted the assessment rolls. The *Chicago Tribune* printed a picture of two similar adjacent houses. One of them, owned by Chief of Police Detectives Michael Grady, had an assessed value of $500 while his neighbor's house showed an assessed value of $2,450. To confound further any simple "soak the rich" explanation of the assessment, the Board of Assessors assessed vacant lots at only 35.2 percent of value, slightly under uniformity.[12]

The "Reform" Reassessment

On 19 July 1928, the Tax Commission, well assured of significant support from taxpayers, issued a second order for a reassessment in Cook County. This time it prevailed. After a few last-ditch attempts to thwart the order, the Board of Assessors buckled down to work on the reassessment in October. Justifiably suspicious of its vanquished foe, the Tax Commission limited the board's discretion by requiring it to follow what was known as Rule Fourteen. Among its stipulations, Rule Fourteen required the board to follow standard "unit-foot values" when making assessments. The board put Harry Cutmore, formerly of the Manufacturers' Appraisal Company, in charge of reassessment—a choice well suited to the wishes of the JCREV.[13]

A split quickly developed among the interests responsible for the reassessment order. The teachers kept up their campaign to transform the reassessment into a tax boost. The downtown property owners, including the JCREV, staunchly opposed a tax increase. Many of them even turned the revaluation effort into a platform for tax reduction. The teachers really had little hope for victory in this confrontation. Their original case had been based on the premise that the Loop was underassessed. This assumption had been completely undermined by publication of the 1927 assessment. Revelations of tax corruption led to a realization of the teachers' worst nightmare: a taxpaying alliance between homeowners and Loop business interests. Much to the chagrin of the CTF, its erstwhile comrades-in-arms from the business community easily derailed any prospect for tax increases. They ensured that the reassessment would be, in the terminology of a later era, revenue neutral.[14]

Pressures for an outright reduction, however, overwhelmed the standard of neutrality when the depression forced the board to consider the decline in real estate values. When its work was finally completed in 1930, the board had reduced the average assessment from 35.9 to 27 percent. In substance, the board chose to redress inequalities of the past almost exclusively through reductions on property previously overassessed. It slashed Loop assessments from 74 percent to 41.3 percent and brought down single family residential assessments from 32.6 percent to 28.2 percent. In addition, it lowered the average deviation from uniformity, which had been 37 percent in 1927, to 20 percent. When all was said and done, the reassessment hardly proved worth all the trouble, not only for the CTF but for the other original sponsors. The actual work dragged on interminably. The Thompson machine and the bureaucracy of the board did their best to obstruct and underfund Cutmore and his associates. Finally, on 23 April 1930, with the April primaries safely behind them, the Board of Review put its final stamp of approval on the new assessment.[15]

The Taxpayers Have a Holiday

In the meantime, Chicago's taxpayers went on a two-year tax holiday. From May 1928 until July 1930, no general property taxes were levied. To meet annual expenses, Chicago, and other political subdivisions in Cook County, issued tax-anticipation warrants redeemable from the tax levies of the following year. Even before the tax holiday, the city's dependence on tax-anticipation warrants presaged a major problem. In 1928, when the city government levied taxes on the 1927 assessment, it financed that year's budget on warrants payable in 1929 taxes. When these anticipated taxes failed to materialize, the government merely pyramided new warrants on top of the old.[16]

Naturally the banks looked askance at these sleight-of-hand borrowing practices. Where New York and Detroit, hardly paragons of fiscal responsibility, could borrow at an interest rate of 3.5 percent, Chicago's city government had to settle for rates of 6 percent and above. By the time the stock market crash hit in October 1929, the city's borrowing power had nearly dried up. Long before the practice spread to other municipalities, local government employees went on "payless paydays." In December 1929, the city government suspended salaries for police, teachers, and other key employees. Mayor Thompson seemed a man with his head in the clouds. He appeared either unwilling or unable to win the confidence of major creditors through a serious program of retrenchment.[17]

In late 1929, contrary to Thompson's wishes, the Finance Committee of the City Council put the onus on the JCREV to provide a solution for the city's fiscal problems. Eager to lend a hand, the JCREV formed a citizens' committee of leading civic and business leaders in January 1930. The chairman of the committee, Silas Strawn, boasted corporate and banking connections almost without rival in

Chicago's business community. At the time of his appointment, Strawn was vice-president of the U.S. Chamber of Commerce, chairman of the board of Montgomery Ward, and a director of the First National Bank of Chicago. Coincidentally or not, the First National Bank owned several million dollars' worth of tax-anticipation warrants.[18]

The Civic Federation, the city's oldest and most powerful reform organization, cooperated closely with the Citizens' Committee. In fact, the committee did its day-to-day work in the offices of the federation. Five members of the Civic Federation, including financier Rufus Dawes, brother of Charles G. Dawes (of "Dawes Plan" reparations fame), sat on the executive committee of the Citizens' Committee. The Civic Federation's importance in Chicago's fiscal situation is revealed by the composition of its leadership. Only one of the twenty-one officers and executive committee members of the federation failed to win inclusion in the 1931 edition of *Who's Who in Chicago*. Ten of the twenty-one also appeared in the *Social Register* of the same year. Many of the twenty-one listed multiple corporate directorships in their biographies, most commonly in regionally or nationally based banks and utilities. These banks and utilities owned a large block of Chicago's outstanding warrants and municipal bonds.[19]

With the help of the Civic Federation, the Citizens' Committee formulated a rescue program that had two key features. One mandated the creation of a subcommittee under Phillip R. Clarke, president of the Central Trust Company of Illinois, and charged it with raising sufficient funds to tide the city over. To facilitate this campaign, the subcommittee created the "Cook County Warrant Trust." As funds came in, the subcommittee deposited them into the trust. The subscribers, in turn, received certificates bearing 6 percent interest with 1928, 1929, and 1930 tax-anticipation warrants serving as security. Clarke, who had headed Liberty Bond drives in World War I, brought all of his talents to bear to put the campaign over the top. By early March, the Clarke subcommittee had met its goal of raising $74 million. The largest subscribers to the rescue fund included a number of regional and national corporations such as Standard Oil of Indiana, Sears Roebuck, the Pennsylvania Railroad, and Armour and Company. The leading Chicago banks, no doubt relieved to shift some of the city government's debt to nonfinancial corporations, acted as intermediaries for the subscription sales.[20]

The Citizens' Committee tried to keep a tight rein on the allocation of subscription proceeds. Strawn, for example, vowed that money would go only to the necessities of government. Predictably, Thompson and other members of the Republican machine resented these restrictions. They charged that a banker-controlled dictatorship was usurping the functions of city government. In an attempt to get around the restrictions, Thompson sent his ally on the city council, Oscar Nelson, to New York City to arrange a subscription sale of warrants. Given Thompson's dismal fiscal record and his lack of Strawn's and Clarke's connections, it surprised no one when the sale flopped.[21]

The second part of Strawn's program set the Citizens' Committee on a collision course with taxpayers. To get stalled tax collections back on schedule, the committee instituted the so-called "Strawn Plan." The Strawn Plan stipulated that 1928 taxes would become due in July 1930, 1929 taxes in February 1931, and 1930 taxes in November 1931. In effect, the plan left taxpayers with only sixteen months to pay three years' worth of tax bills. Moreover, each tax bill in this sequence would be higher than the previous one. The 1930 tax collections of $284,221,000, for example, would be a hefty 23.6 percent higher than the 1928 total of $219,815,000.[22]

The Onset of the Revolt

This increase threatened to put an unbearable strain on payers of real estate taxes. Even under normal circumstances, real estate owners paid more than 80 percent of the local tax bill. As elsewhere in the country, land values had fallen sharply. Between 1927, the tail end of the real estate boom, and 1931, the heaviest year of the Strawn tax increases, the value of new building construction fell 86 percent. During the same period, the value of real estate declined by a less spectacular, but still severe, 38 percent.[23]

Owners of real estate faced special difficulties when they tried to liquidate their assets on the market. Many of them had overmortgaged during the boom years. Between 1927 and 1931, for example, the number of foreclosures had rocketed upwards by 457 percent. Hence, real estate, in contrast to most other, more liquid, commodities, was so encumbered with debt that buyers frequently could not be found at any price. The number of real estate transfers in Cook

County declined by 42 percent between 1927 and 1931. Still, owners of rental property could probably have weathered the storm had not the decline of income relative to fixed costs been so marked. According to one survey, operating expenses of a typical office building increased by 2 percent between 1927 and 1932. At the same time, net income declined 70 percent. This narrowing of profit margins only fixed attention on that portion of operating expenses devoted to taxes. The results of a study of steam-heated apartments in Chicago in 1933 found that taxes made up the single largest portion of all operating expenses, including heat, repairs, water, light, and management.[24]

Disheartened by the Strawn tax increases, a small group of wealthy real estate operators decided to take action in early 1930. Prime instigators of the initial agitation included Henry E. Hedberg and James E. Bistor (partners in the firm Hedberg and Bistor) along with fellow real estate operator Benjamin Lindheimer. All of them had extensive holdings in the Loop. After several meetings, they formed the Association of Real Estate Taxpayers of Illinois (ARET) on 9 May 1930. They did not lack for money. Bistor, Hedberg, and Lindheimer recruited thirty other real estate investors who donated approximately $30,000 in seed money. The original statement of purpose seemed innocuous enough. It described ARET as "an organization with which all Illinois real estate tax payers may become affiliated to permit united protection for themselves in matters of taxation and legislation, and to prevent an inequitable distribution of tax burdens on real estate and all incidentals thereto pertaining."[25]

Bistor remained a central figure in the association throughout its history. His background could have provided grist for a Horatio Alger novel. He was born in Macomb, Illinois, in 1890. Bistor's parents died during his childhood, so at age 12, he supported six brothers, the surviving members of the family, by lighting streetlamps in Macomb. Two years later, Bistor sought better job opportunities in Chicago. He started as a bicycling rent collector for the prestigious firm of Chandler, Hildreth, and Company, which specialized in loans and real estate.[26]

Along with Henry E. Hedberg, he organized the firm of Hedberg and Bistor in 1917. The two were a good business team. Hedberg, the older, had excellent business connections that complemented the qualities of the hard-driving Bistor. Edwin J. Kuester, a

Association of Real Estate Taxpayers officials and attorneys pose in 1932 with books listing the 26,000 colitigants in *Reinecke* v. *McDonough*. *Left to right:* James E. Bistor, president of ARET; Perry Ten Hoor, ARET attorney; George W. Reinecke, member of ARET's board of directors; and Ferre C. Watkins, ARET attorney. (International News Photos)

former employee of the association, remembers Bistor as "a strong powerhouse of a guy. He wouldn't stop for a brick wall. You could just back him into a corner and he'd fight his way out of it." One of their other associates in ARET jokingly ascribed the secret of the firm's success to the theory "that Hedberg would bring in all of these prosperous Swedes and Jim would hit them on the head." The two enjoyed a booming business during the 1920s and acquired some prime property, including a fifteen-story skyscraper in the Loop and a massive apartment complex located on Lake Shore Drive (Chicago's so-called gold coast). They financed much of this expansion through two devices, the sale of real estate bonds and the use of land mortgages. Unfortunately, for Hedberg and Bistor, these debt obligations made it quite hard to adapt when real estate values tumbled in the late 1920s and early 1930s.[27]

While Bistor described himself as a Republican, he had taken little interest in politics until the formation of ARET. Like other ARET leaders, he used the association as the launching pad for a long career of involvement in political causes. Bistor's political outlook must be viewed as inseparable from the depression-era context from which it arose.

Despite ARET's claim to represent the taxpayers of Illinois, all of the original eleven officers and members of the executive committee made their homes in Cook County. Eight of the eleven appeared in the 1931 edition of *Who's Who in Chicago*, and two others made later editions. Biographies of nine of the ten (in *Who's Who in Chicago* for 1931 and subsequent years) showed real estate to be their primary business interest. The one exception, Barnet Hodes, worked in a law firm that specialized in real estate matters. Of those whose partisan affiliations can be identified, eight listed themselves as Republicans and two as Democrats. Ethnicity and religion were the most significant divisions. Four of the eleven can be identified as Jews, two as Catholics, and three as Protestants. In contrast to their opponents in the Civic Federation, none merited a listing in the 1931 edition of the Chicago *Social Register*. This probably reflected the comparatively nouveau riche and Jewish cast of ARET's membership. Though they were wealthy, the business prestige of most of these men paled beside the high-powered corporate and banking connections of the Civic Federation's leadership. Biographies of these ARET leaders in *Who's Who in Chicago*, for example, contained little evidence of multiple business directorships or chairmanships.[28]

All of the eleven—save lawyer Barnet Hodes—belonged to the dominant trade association for real estate operators, the Chicago Real Estate Board (CREB). During this formative period, ARET and the CREB shared much more than a similar membership roll. Newton C. Farr, the president of the CREB, described the relationship between the CREB and the ARET as that of an interlocking directorate. Lindheimer, in addition to his duties at ARET, headed the CREB's new property owners' division. Also, every member of the CREB's executive committee sat on ARET's executive committee. If viewed in this light, Lindheimer's declaration that the "two organizations will act in harmony" qualifies as a major understatement.[29]

Facts like these only beg the question: why did the real estate operators who dominated both groups bother to form a new and separate organization? In part, the division of labor had a strategic basis. Lindheimer explained it in the cryptic words "the Association of Real Estate Taxpayers . . . will be able to do some things that would not be considered with as good grace from the property owners' division of the Board." He undoubtedly meant that ARET would be able to take controversial stands that the more cautious CREB and property owners' division could not. Perhaps, too, Lindheimer believed that an organization of *taxpayers* would have more credibility with those who were not real estate operators.[30]

Despite Lindheimer's rosy portrayal of the CREB and ARET as members of a united front, personalities definitely entered the picture. The formation of the ARET predated the CREB's property owners' division by about three months. During that short period, ARET's organizers had already amassed a war chest of $30,000. Given this power base, it is reasonable to assume that strong-minded men like Bistor would resist any attempt to subsume their organization under the CREB's rubric.[31]

In August 1930, ARET hired newspaper executive John M. Pratt to take over as paid executive director. For nearly three years, Pratt, along with Bistor, dominated the affairs of ARET. Pratt's wealthy background more than compensated for Bistor's humble origins. Pratt was born in Sharpesville, Indiana, in 1886. His family owned some of the largest tracts of farmland in the county. In the 1890s, his grandfather, Thomas G. Pratt, and father, Bennett R. Pratt, branched out and started a tomato cannery. Between 1899 and 1905, Pratt attended Marion College in Illinois, where he studied to be a teacher. Sometime during this period, the family lost most of its money because the cannery business failed. Pratt permanently shelved plans for a teaching career and, along with his parents, pulled up stakes and moved to Canada to homestead farmland in northern Saskatchewan. Eventually John, through purchase, expanded his homestead to make it the largest farm in the immediate area.[32]

In 1913, Pratt began a long career in politics. The councillors of

Lost River, a new rural municipality, selected him, at age 21, as their secretary-treasurer. A secretary-treasurer is comparable to an American town clerk. His duties in this job included the supervision of local tax collection. The irony was not lost on Pratt, who often joked about it during his stint as a tax rebel in Chicago. Even during this early period, one of the locals noted his "talent for elocution." The life of a tax collector, however, did not suit Pratt, who moved to Winnipeg in 1917 to become the municipal editor of the *Grain Growers' Guide*. By this time, the *Guide*—which spoke for the nascent cooperative movement in Canada—enjoyed the largest circulation of any Canadian farm publication.[33]

Pratt's interest in taxation reform was already apparent. Under his tutelage, the *Guide's* column on municipal affairs devoted more space to taxation than any other single subject. Pratt's work for the *Guide* also underscored the beginnings of a lifetime attraction to the tax theories of Henry George. Like George, he supported the abolition of the predominant local tax on acreage and its replacement by a "system of taxing the unimproved values of land." These years were marked by the formation of the famous Canadian Wheat Pool with the *Guide's* support. Western grain farmers, who owned and operated the Wheat Pool, employed it as a private cooperative device to bypass the marketing network of the large corporations. At about the same time, Pratt participated in the formation of the National Progressive Party, a rural-based third party in western Canada.[34]

In 1921, Pratt returned to the United States, where he stayed for the rest of his life. He accepted a job with the Universal Feature and Speciality Company, a newspaper syndicate with headquarters in Chicago. In 1926, he became the advertising manager for the *Chicago Herald and Examiner*, one of the two Hearst papers in Chicago. There, in addition to his other duties, Pratt organized public relations for the tour Hearst sponsored for Queen Marie of Romania. He left the *Herald Examiner* in 1930 and shortly thereafter took over the reins at ARET. Pratt's reasons for accepting this job remain unclear to this day. That it complemented his longtime interest in taxation and paid a substantial salary of $20,000 were undoubtedly important factors in his decision.[35]

Some who knew Pratt remember him as a promoter and an opportunist; others believed him highly principled. Pratt's employment record lent superficial credence to his characterization as an opportunist. His employers since 1917 had been a diverse lot, ranging all the way from the *Grain Growers' Guide,* on the one hand, to the Hearst press on the other. Without question, these occupations engendered in him the ability to promote a company line. While Kuester stressed Pratt's honesty and integrity, he also recalled him to be "a public relations man and a salaried fellow who made the most of a situation. Nothing crooked about him; people were doing it all the time."[36]

Other evidence, however, reveals a more complex figure. Because of ideological scruples, he turned down a lucrative job offer from an executive at Seagram's. Though no teetotaler himself, childhood memories of his grandmother's temperance admonitions had left their mark. After the demise of ARET, Pratt quit a job with newspaper publisher Frank Gannett's anti-Roosevelt Committee for Constitutional Government. Although Pratt agreed with the Committee's stand against Roosevelt's "court-packing" plan, he resigned because he feared that Gannett would turn the organization into a springboard for a presidential bid.[37]

Pratt, who described himself as a "Jeffersonian Democrat," saw no contradiction. To him, participation in the *Guide,* ARET, and eventually anti–New Deal causes bespoke a deep distrust of centralized political bureaucracies and paternalism. Each cause, in its own way, hearkened to the *Guide*'s Jacksonian front page slogan: "Equal rights for all; special privileges for none." Pratt's reading of George no doubt reinforced these beliefs at an early age.[38]

Few questioned Pratt's organizational acumen and none his exceptional ability as a speaker. According to all accounts, he had that most enviable knack for making a successful pitch to potential contributors. Pratt added to all these talents a thorough knowledge of Chicago's real estate situation. These attributes complemented his long track record of experience with general questions related to taxation. Pratt did not come to this new job from the perspective of a real estate investor. This fact alone must have colored his outlook. True, he owned a house in Park Ridge, a suburb of Chicago. This small holding, however, in no way compared with the vast personal stake that men like Bistor invested in ARET's success or failure. Pratt, if he so chose, could find a well-paying job elsewhere; most of the others could not. As we shall see, this situation had its advantages. Pratt's lack of real estate assets left him much less vulnerable to outside pressure.[39]

The Program of Revolt

From its inception, ARET put priority on one goal above all others: bringing personal property onto the tax rolls to lower real-estate taxes. Theoretically, personal property included everything from automobiles to intangibles such as stocks and bonds. The bare bones of the original and, with some small changes, later program of ARET called for municipal economy and cancellation of Strawn's 1929 and 1930 tax increases, with the resulting deficit to be made up by "funding." Basically, "funding" entailed selling of low interest bonds with repayment spread over twenty years. Projected collections of personal property taxes served as collateral to induce buyers to purchase these bonds.[40]

ARET's leaders recognized the personal property tax as their legal ace in the hole. They only had to quote the so-called uniformity amendment of the 1870 Illinois Constitution to underscore a seemingly airtight case. The amendment provided that "every person and corporation shall pay a tax in proportion to the value of his, her, or its property." Like the proverbial Johnny-one-note, ARET constantly reiterated that the amendment had long ago become a dead letter for Illinois and its localities. In 1920, personal property constituted 24.2 percent of tax collections in Cook County. After that, the percentage fell until, in 1930, it reached 13.5 percent. The part of the general property tax paid by real estate owners, on the other hand, rose from 70.2 percent to 84 percent during the same period.[41]

Nevertheless, relative to real estate, the amount and dollar value of personal property skyrocketed during the 1920s. Reliable estimates placed the approximate taxable value of personal property in Cook County for 1929 at $30 billion. By contrast, real estate had an estimated taxable value of $10 billion during the same year. To say the least, these figures did not square with the official assessment records. According to the assessor, personal property showed more taxable value in 1920 than it did in 1930. ARET estimated that, under a uniform assessment, real estate would provide only about 30 percent of Cook County's general property tax while personalty would pay the rest.[42]

Like their counterparts in the rest of the country, office holders in Cook County had plenty of practical reasons for lax enforcement of the antiquated personal property tax requirements. Strict enforcement would have brought such invasions of personal privacy and other political abuses of power that a tax rebellion of untold proportions might have been set off. "The absence of any standards of appraisal and assessment," observed the Joint Commission on Real Estate Valuation in 1930, "leaves the person declaring his personal property at the mercy of the assessors." For assessor, the term "tax fixer" seems just as appropriate. During the "reform" assessment of 1930, one precinct captain instructed the deputy assessor in his area to classify potential payers of personal property taxes into two groups. First, those who were not to receive schedules and, secondly, those who were to be "hit extra hard."[43]

Since the general property tax rate for Cook County hovered around a high 5 percent, the personal property tax had confiscatory implications for owners of intangible assets. Herbert D. Simpson estimated that in "the case of a 5% bond, this [literal enforcement of the law] would take nearly a third of the income, leaving the investor a net return of 3.5%, out of which to pay income taxes and investment expenses." Faced with these consequences, the vast majority of taxpayers ignored the law and followed their common sense. They chose either not to file a schedule or to grossly understate their personal property holdings. As Simpson aptly put it, "All the law breakers under prohibition would scarcely make a frog-pool in Lake Michigan compared to the number of law breakers developed under the present personal property tax in Illinois." Even among those who bothered to file schedules, personal property tax delinquency reached a staggering 45.9 percent in 1930.[44]

Obey or Revise

If ARET's members wished to move personal property onto the tax rolls, they had two options: to press for literal enforcement of the 1870 Constitution or to support a revision. At first, they chose the second option. ARET's members, however, always protected themselves with an alternative. Failing revision, they demanded strict enforcement of the existing law. This message rang clear in ARET's rallying cry, "Obey or Revise."[45]

To force revision, ARET marshaled its forces against the planned Strawn tax increases. It staked hopes on a proposed revenue article that appeared on the November statewide ballot. The amendment permitted the state legislature to classify personal property for taxation. Under classification, state and local governments had discretion to tax specific forms of personal property, such as stocks and bonds, at lower rates than real estate. The article also permitted the legislature to adopt an income tax. This portion of the amendment did not interest ARET's leaders. Barnet Hodes, then chairman of the group's legislative committee, ridiculed suggestions that an income tax would naturally follow if voters approved the article. Hodes did concede it worthwhile to be on guard that any proposed income tax be used solely to reduce real estate taxes. "It is very questionable," Hodes feared, "whether *if* an income tax law is passed that it will result in removing the burden from real estate or relieving those oppressed by real estate taxes."[46]

ARET put the main emphasis on the provision in the amendment that allowed classification of personal property for taxation purposes. Hodes, for example, argued that the lower rates allowed under classification would induce taxpayers to declare their personal property assets more readily. He condemned the "unjust" standard of uniformity for real property and personal property tax rates. "Owners of real estate are in agreement," declared Bistor in support of classification, "that this [taxation at the standard rate] would work an undue hardship on the owners of intangible securities."[47]

ARET's leaders resorted to something resembling a benefit theory of government as their theoretical starting point. The benefit theory, in contrast to the ability-to-pay theory, held that taxes should be levied in proportion to the services that an individual received from government. Bistor questioned why real estate owners should be required to pay 80 percent or more of the general property tax. "Not more than 10 per cent of the benefits of government," he charged, "accrue to real estate owners. The organized groups get the advantages while the poor property owner pays the bill." In the same vein, Cornelius Teninga, ARET's first president, pleaded for the "equitable principle that those who derive the benefit should pay for that benefit."[48]

Bistor and other key ARET figures predicted that if taxes reflected the benefits people received from government services, spending reductions would quickly follow. ARET published a booklet, *Taxes, Unemployment, and Business Recovery*, that maintained that voters would be less likely to approve bond issues if everyone had to pay the bill. It estimated that the "real estate of Cook County is held by less than 22% of the voting population. The 78% vote the issues but pay no taxes." Teninga warned that real estate owners "cannot afford to leave recommendations of purposes for which money should be raised to those who have an interest only in spending those funds." The new executive director rapidly took up this line of argument. Pratt blamed the "wanton wasting of public funds" on the fact that real estate owners had to pick up most of the burden.[49]

ARET's members mounted a major push for the amendment. They erected billboards at prominent locations in the city and ran ads in the major newspapers. The publicity gave a special place to the slogan—and implied warning—"Obey or Revise." One booklet, produced by ARET, showed a picture of a house sold for back taxes. The evicted owner stood out in the street shaking his fist.[50]

All of this activity was only a prelude for yet another in ARET's unbroken string of defeats. Voters, both in Chicago and downstate, rejected the amendment by clear-cut majorities. Somewhat surprisingly, it garnered the lowest vote in less well-to-do areas. The Chicago Federation of Labor ran several negative editorials in its publication, *Federation News*. These editorials reflected widespread fears that the amendment, contrary to the claims of supporters, would result in added taxes rather than replacement taxes. One of these editorials read in part: "The tax eaters are always hungry. . . . What Illinois needs is honesty and economy in its governing bodies, not new devices for extracting money from the pockets of the taxpayer. . . . Those who are ready to give unlimited power to the tax eaters to prey upon the public at their will should vote 'yes' on the amendment. All others should vote 'no.' " Some, no doubt, voted down the amendment out of sheer confusion over its complicated phrasing and implications. The defeat was hardly surprising. From the beginning, the amendment bore the marks of a doomed measure. Even key ARET leaders, who campaigned for its passage, could not hide their lukewarm attitude toward the income tax provision.[51]

"Obey" Becomes "Revise": Challenging the Assessment

ARET spent no time mourning the defeat. Frustrated by the electoral process, it went after the jugular of the Strawn program: the recently completed 1930 assessment. ARET's leaders reasoned that without a legal assessment the planned 1929 and 1930 tax increases would never come off. They did not base their complaint, as had the opponents of the 1927 assessment, on an allegation of discrimination between different classes of real estate. Instead, ARET challenged the assessment because it failed to correct the imbalance between the assessments for real and personal property. Ironically, the underassessment of personal property had been an issue of little consequence during the earlier imbroglio over tax corruption.

On 5 November 1930, ARET mailed out 5,000 copies of its first systematic attack on the assessment, *Taxes, Unemployment and Business Recovery.* The bulk of the mailing went to the leading businessmen of Cook County. Using a myriad of statistics, the booklet painted a dire picture of the plight of property owners since the onset of the depression. It described how the decline of income for real estate owners had been much greater than the reduction in the assessment. To illustrate the tax burden on real estate owners, the booklet drew an analogy between the Strawn tax increases and a recent German moratorium on reparations: "The total amount involved in payments to allied governments is $427,000,000.00. Cook County's two tax bills for 1931 total $548,648,000.00 or $121,000,000.00 more than the amount that is to start a distressed and faltering world back on the way to economic recovery." Another section predicted that these tax increases would only perpetuate Cook County's long-time notoriety "for an unequaled, wanton extravagance in the expenditure of public funds."[52]

The booklet explained ARET's two-part plan for cancellation of the 1931 tax increases and "funding." It abandoned the previous flirtation with classification and an income tax. Its pages do not reflect much concern for legislative solutions of any kind. The overriding goal now focused squarely on "forcing recognition of the illegality—the unconstitutionality of the tax assessment." Put simply, ARET had moved from a strategy of "revise" to one of "obey." For the first time, ARET leaders seemed concerned enough to entertain desperate and perhaps illegal alternatives. There was a glimmer that a tax strike might be a possibility. After describing how business conditions had led to "depreciation in values that rob them [real estate owners] of their entire interest in properties," the booklet asked the provocative question: "Under such circumstances, why should they pay?"[53]

Despite hints of subversive coming attractions, *Taxes, Unemployment and Business Recovery* won general applause from the press. An editorial writer in the *Economist and Magazine of La Salle Street*, the voice of the downtown business upper crust, concluded that the only thing unfortunate about the booklet "is that its circulation in Illinois could not be at least a million." The *Chicago Daily News* also ran a favorable editorial. The *Chicago Tribune*, on the other hand, was more circumspect. Its editorial writer believed that the reparations analogy overstated the burden of the 1931 tax increases, observing that "though the two payments will come in the same calendar year, they will be separated by ten months." The editorial distanced itself from ARET's call to void the 1930 assessment, on the grounds that it would cut off revenues for needed government services. Somewhat paradoxically the *Tribune* then took the association to task for inadequately stressing the need for economy in government spending. These criticisms aside, the editorial echoed the substance of ARET's critique of the "unjust and inequitable" tax system in Cook County.[54]

On 12 December 1930, Pratt and Teninga filed a demand before the Illinois Tax Commission. The demand (actually a petition) proposed that the 1930 assessment be scuttled because it unconstitutionally underassessed personal property. Pratt and Teninga alleged, in their letter to the commission, that the "practice of placing practically the entire burden of the costs of government on one form of the community's wealth, representing less than 20% of the population" had led to "reckless squandering of public funds to a point where government costs are becoming ruinous."[55]

Intrigued with ARET's case, William Malone, the chairman of the commission, quickly scheduled a hearing for 17 December. During his testimony, Pratt displayed a list of general classes of non-assessed or underassessed personal property culled from census and income tax records. These included over $4 billion in trust departments of local banks, $550 million of inventories in retail and wholesale establishments, and $400 million in automobiles. If one took the word of the assessor at face value, much of this personal property did not even exist.

In place of ARET's old program, Pratt now proposed a blanket tax rate limit of 1 percent for both real and personal property. A rate this low, Pratt suggested, would relieve real estate owners and, at the same time, induce taxpayers to declare their personal property. The implications of this stand come into clearer focus when we remember that local tax rates ran at about five percent. Even with renewed personal property assessment, massive municipal budget cuts and perhaps repudiation of outstanding warrants would be necessary to make up for the shortfall in spending created by enactment of such a proposal. By calling for a 1 percent limit, ARET signaled the doom of any real prospect for compromise with their tax-starved foes in the banks and local government.[56]

At first, Malone seemed destined to stage a replay of his 1928 invalidation of the 1927 assessment. He excoriated the administration of the personal property tax as a criminal farce. He had little praise for the politicians in Cook County who, he said, had been on a spending orgy for years. A new source of pressure, however, complicated Malone's decision. The Citizens' Committee and the Civic Federation, whose members had been slow to act, now mustered their forces in defense of the 1931 assessment. These organizations prevailed on Malone to hold a rehearing on 26 December.[57]

Silas H. Strawn predicted at the hearing that a new reassessment would delay tax collections for so long that the credit of Chicago would be absolutely destroyed. At yet a third hearing before Malone on 29 December, he reminded the Tax Commission of the banks' position. According to Strawn, those "who loaned money to the city on tax anticipation warrants want to know that the taxes, with which to pay them, will be collected, and collected at the prescribed time." Strawn did not attempt to defend the justice of the 1931 assessment. He granted the overall validity of ARET's complaint. Rather he focused on how a new reassessment would harm Chicago's credit and lead to chaos and anarchy in the local body politic. [58]

Like the Citizens' Committee, the Civic Federation had a large stake in Malone's decision. Its leading lights came from the summit of Chicago banking power. Among them were Sewell Avery, a director of Continental Illinois, and Melvin Traylor, the president of the First National Bank of Chicago. An adverse decision from Malone promised to endanger their large investments in tax-anticipation warrants. Also, no doubt, they looked suspiciously on ARET's proposal to tax intangible personal property like deposits and securities.[59]

Lastly, the Civic Federation's reputation rested on its track record as a sober and responsible advocate of municipal rationalization. A new reassessment could have thrown the governments of Cook

County into an irreversible tailspin. To support another reassessment would have run completely counter to the cautious mind-set of the Civic Federation's leadership. The Civic Federation had, to be sure, supported—indeed helped to usher through—the voiding of the 1927 assessment. Conditions had changed radically in the interim. Not only did the city now face a depression, but its credit had almost dried up. In 1927, the leaders of the Civic Federation had believed— naively, as time proved—that the reassessment would take only a few months. They had not imagined in their wildest dreams that it would drag on for two years. They were not in a mood to endure that headache again.

The testimony of Douglas Sutherland, the secretary of the Civic Federation, before the Tax Commission hearings in late 1930 provided a clear barometer of this change in attitude. In terminology befitting a conservative champion of the status quo rather than a crusading enemy of the machine, he summarized the case against a new reassessment. Like Strawn, Sutherland assured the commission that he had no quarrel with ARET's allegations about the underassessment of personal property. Instead, he rejected ARET's demand on the grounds that it showed "a lack of practical consideration of vital factors involved." He guessed that a new reassessment would take months at the minimum and thus unravel the "close-knit schedule" of tax increases for 1931, which had been worked out by the Citizens' Committee. Sutherland repeated Strawn's prediction that invalidation of the assessment would hopelessly demoralize Cook County's creditors. Even under the present situation, he pointed out, "Chicago's corporate borrowing power is practically exhausted."[60]

Sutherland left unaddressed ARET's contention that placing personal property on the tax rolls would double Cook County's bonding capacity. He deemed it unlikely, however, that personal property could ever be assessed, much less taxed, to the extent that ARET claimed. Sutherland agreed, at least in theory, that real estate owners should be ultimately relieved from part of their tax burden. Ever the hardheaded defender of bureaucratic efficiency, he realized that real estate had well-tested superiority over personal property as an extractive source for government. "Real property," Sutherland declared, "cannot hide or escape. . . . Personal property, whether it be the kitchen table, a share of stock or a bond or note, is here today and gone tomorrow."[61]

Sutherland did not speak to ARET's claim that a maximum 1

percent rate would encourage owners of personal property to declare their assets to the tax collector. Nonetheless, he could hardly have been unaware of the experience of several states that had actually tried to lower personal property tax rates, usually via classification. In one respect, the record bore out ARET's case. Low rates did lead to higher assessments. On the other hand, they did not bring in higher tax collections. Enlarged assessments simply could not compensate for the tax reductions brought about by lower rates. Reduction of the general property tax rate may have promised relief for property owners but it was a poor bet for those dependent on local government.[62]

Faced with opposition like this, Malone backed away from any previous inclinations to overturn the assessment. On 5 January 1931 he officially turned down ARET's demand for a reassessment. Three days later he resigned as chairman of the commission. Shortly thereafter, a majority of the other commission members also resigned. Governor Louis L. Emmerson went on vacation rather than accede to demands that he appoint a new commission.[63]

ARET's leaders shrugged off their defeat on the reassessment as a temporary setback. As before, defeat only induced a shift in strategy and tactics. In every obvious sense, the association withdrew from the political process. Instead, it sought relief in the courts. In February 1931, the executive committee entered into a two-year contract with the eminent law firm of Watkins, Ten Hoor, and Gilbert. Under the terms of the contract, ARET acquired the full-time services of two attorneys and, in turn, paid them a salary of $1,500 a month.[64]

In a brilliant strategic move, the executive committee hit on the idea of building a mass base to help fund the litigation. It set membership fees at an affordable rate for small taxpayers. New members paid 1 percent of their tax bills, with a minimum fee of two dollars. No one tried to conceal the fact that ARET was now primarily a de facto legal defense service. Each membership form required a separate legal fee of ten dollars (five dollars for taxes under $200) for each parcel of property owned by the taxpayer. It also stipulated that a new member must sign this agreement: "I hereby make application for membership in your Association and authorize you to represent me through your attorneys, WATKINS, TEN HOOR AND GILBERT, in all court actions they deem necessary to protect my properties from tax sale or forfeiture, pending the decision of the courts on the validity of the 1929 [1930] assessment."[65]

The first litigation began when the Board of Review shut its door to further assessment appeals from taxpayers. The board had been swamped with complaints; over 40,000 cases still had not been heard when it cut short the appeals process in early 1931. On 3 February, fifty members of ARET, led by Pratt and attorney Ferre C. Watkins, marched on the offices of the board and, with a petition in hand, demanded that hearings be reopened on the 1930 assessment.[66]

Undeniably, ARET had the better case. The law explicitly required a board hearing for all pending appeals from taxpayers. In no mood to listen, the board's members ignored ARET's petition and delivered the assessment rolls to the county clerk. ARET was not caught off guard. It promptly retaliated with a suit asking that the Superior Court of Cook County force the board to reopen the assessment books and hear the remaining appeals. If the court upheld ARET's suit, it would also suspend the upcoming 1929 tax levies pending completion of the appeals process. "The action of the board in refusing to hear the objections," declared Pratt, "is unconstitutional and illegal, and amounts to confiscation of Property without due process of law."[67]

ARET put an added twist on its membership drive and court litigation. It recommended that members withhold their taxes until a final ruling by the courts. As we shall see, the decision to pursue a strike was not unpremeditated. It embodied the culmination of long and repeated frustrations with the political process. By early 1931, the association had shifted 180 degrees from its rather conventional and bland position in May 1930. This turnaround guaranteed that ARET would have to face political pressures and social ostracism quite unfamiliar to most of the solid citizens who comprised its membership.[68]

CHAPTER 3

Taxpayers on Strike in Chicago

During an age of tax revolt, Chicago easily qualified as a potential trouble spot. In most of the rest of the country, the effects of the depression fueled the onset of taxpayer unrest. In Chicago, economic decline only fired the embers of a revolt well under way before the 1929 crash. These conclusions are fairly clear. The problem starts when we begin to wrestle with the tricky questions of how and why the legal forms of revolt evolved into an outright strike.

The breakdown of the tax-appeals system provided the immediate spark. A flurry of protest overwhelmed the traditional outlet for complaints, the Board of Review. In one day alone, 29 November 1930, 4,000 taxpayers jammed into the board's offices to file protests. When the board's members turned a deaf ear to the mountain of pending appeals, aggrieved taxpayers resorted to the only avenues of protest left open to them. In Chicago, this meant court litigation and/or nonpayment of taxes.[1]

The long-term causes were more complex, but no less crucial. By the late 1920s, Chicagoans had earned a well-deserved reputation as hard-boiled cynics about politics and politicians. On this score, Herbert D. Simpson asked, "Isn't it pretty bad when people go on the assumption that all government is crooked—and think nothing of it?"[2]

Simpson's opinion did not lack for corroboration. In 1929, political scientist Leonard D. White, a member of the Chicago Civil Service Commission, decided to test "the feeling widely held by [Chicago's] city employees that their occupation was held in contempt by their fellow-citizens at large." He surveyed a sample of 4,680 Chicago residents. White expressed dismay at the results. He discovered that residents from all walks of life regarded public employees and politicians with disdain. White lamented that " 'politics,' in other communities a word of honor" had in Chicago become "one of reproach."[3]

Before 1927, those taxpayers who resented the tolls that politics exacted on their pocketbooks could seek relief through the tax fixer. To describe how tax fixing worked in practice, however, the phrase "fiscal illusion" would be more fitting than "relief." Economist James M. Buchanan could have been referring to Chicago when he paraphrased another writer's description of fiscal illusion: "The ruling group attempts, to the extent that is possible, to create fiscal illusions, and these have the effect of making taxpayers think that the taxes to which they are subjected are less burdensome than they actually are." One could come across taxpayers during the old tax-fixing regime who counted themselves lucky to be assessed at only 60 percent of market value. "It is said in Chicago," wrote William G. Shepard for *Colliers* in 1930, "that ninety per cent of its taxpayers thought they were getting the best of other taxpayers. However that may be, at least half of them were wrong." The publication of the assessment lists in 1928, showing the average assessment to be 35.9 percent of market value, knocked a central prop out from under the tax-fixing system. It stripped away the veil of secrecy and thus undermined tax fixing's political value as a safety valve for keeping discontented taxpayers under control. Owners of real estate that had been taxed higher than 35.9 percent of market value could now see that, contrary to the tax fixer's promises, they were not getting relief.[4]

No ranking of long-term causes would be complete that did not include the two-year lull in tax collections. Many defenders of renewed collections feared permanent damage to the psychology of orderly taxpaying. Silas Strawn commented, "The fact is that some of our property owners, not having paid taxes for two years, have got out of the habit." In 1929, the *Chicagoan* published a play, *The Municipal Follies*, that satirized the weakening of the tax habit. One of the characters, Mrs. People, complained to a bribe-taking Chicago policeman: "But what is my shame to the needs of our wretched family? Their father is a tax addict. . . . Every cent he could lay his hands on he spent for his vile taxes. Taxes are an obsession with him. He can't pass a tax window. . . . Oh, Oh, Oh! (Weeps.) Save him from himself!"[5]

If habit and legal circumstance made nonpayment more attractive, the changing character of real estate ownership enhanced the potential of a tax strike to win a mass base. Since the turn of the century, the prospect of home ownership had opened up to a wide spectrum of Chicago's residents. In 1930, 42 percent of immigrant and 28 percent of second-generation families owned homes. This was a dramatic turnabout from 1908 when the same figures had been 15 and 20 percent respectively. Moreover, according to the 1930 census, half of all the owner-occupied homes in the city showed a value of less than $8,250.[6]

Genesis of the Strike

All these potentialities for conflict would have counted for little without the Association of Real Estate Taxpayers to bring it all to fruition. The decision to resort to a strike did not come overnight. Some members of ARET evidently toyed with the idea as early as November 1930. In a speech at the Realty Club of Chicago, John M. Pratt employed the term "taxpayers' strike" to characterize mounting tax delinquency. He quickly ruled out ARET's participation in such a campaign.[7]

These statements, however, were straws in the wind. ARET did not commit to a strike in any visible way until after the State Tax Commission refused to invalidate the assessment. Days after that decision, ARET sent an ultimatum to Strawn. Turning Strawn's own words against him, the letter warned that any attempt to put 1929 taxes into collection would result in "calamity, chaos, or anarchy."[8]

Predictably, ARET's intensified rhetoric alarmed Strawn and his allies in the Civic Federation. It cast a pall over their recent victory in defense of the 1930 assessment. ARET, the very same group that they had so recently routed, now returned with a new but no less potent challenge to the Strawn tax increases. The Civic Federation devoted its *Bulletin* of February 1931 to the topic, "Dangerous Not To Pay Tax Bills," striving to nip the strike movement in the bud. It took this action "in the hope of saving many property owners from suffering heavy expenses, or perhaps even losing their properties, through heeding the dangerous advice of inexperienced persons as to non-payment of tax bills and the so-called 'funding of 1929 taxes.' " The terminology employed by the *Bulletin* foreshadowed future critiques of ARET. A tax strike, it predicted with some alarm, would be "disastrous to the general welfare of the community" and lead to the suspension of essential government services.[9]

The Civic Federation had ample cause to believe in the potentiality for a general tax strike. Throughout the early months of 1931, ARET mounted a remarkably widespread membership drive. By signing up, taxpayers of modest means could secure professional legal service for a grand total of fifteen dollars in fees. The attorney general of Illinois estimated that ARET's nine suits, if paid for by one person, would cost a total of $200,000! By offering this legal service, ARET put within reach of the ordinary taxpayer an avenue of protest otherwise prohibitive to all but the wealthiest. Most of these new recruits came aboard as a result of the weekly radio talks over WIBO that Pratt began in January 1931.[10]

At this point, the Chicago Real Estate Board started to put some distance between itself and ARET. In mid-1930, the CREB's property owners' division and ARET's executive committee had been of a piece. By March 1931, the boards shared only two members. During the same month, H. H. Haylett, the business manager of the CREB, disavowed any connection with ARET. "We understand," said Haylett, "that the 1929 tax money already has been spent and we are not in sympathy with any kind of a taxpayers' strike." Yet, as shall soon become clear, the CREB's stand on this issue was a good deal more complex than meets the eye.[11]

Exemplifying the trend toward a more extreme strategy, Barnet Hodes and Benjamin Lindheimer repudiated ARET and the tax strike. Both responded to the call of political opportunity. Hodes won election as an alderman and Lindheimer secured appointment to the Board of Improvements. Lindheimer owed his appointment to Anton Cermak, recently victorious over Thompson in the mayoral election. Chicago's political, reform, and business elites had come to look on Thompson as a supreme embarrassment. Lindheimer and Hodes alike played major roles in Cermak's campaign.[12]

Many others in the real estate industry shared this confidence in the new mayor. Cermak, who had been a realtor himself, won plaudits during the campaign for his attacks on Thompson's free-spending ways. No doubt they also felt like cheering when Cermak's inaugural address condemned recent (and by inference upcoming) tax hikes as "glaring instances of excessive taxation amounting practically to confiscation."[13]

ARET Takes to the Courts

ARET's litigation drive and support for nonpayment doomed any possibility for a lengthy honeymoon. Less than two weeks before Cermak took office, ARET won its first victory when a lower court judge ordered the Board of Review to hear more than 30,000 pending appeals from taxpayers. The board promptly retaliated by appealing to the Illinois Supreme Court. In the meantime, the county collector mailed out the 1929 tax bills.[14]

ARET had taken precautions against just such an occurrence. It distributed en masse membership blanks carrying this recommendation: "No taxpayer should pay one dollar of the 1929 tax until the Supreme Court rules on its validity." Interestingly, these words left open the question of *which* Supreme Court: that of Illinois or of the United States. To obtain a distribution network for membership blanks and other literature, ARET's leaders needed only to call on their colleagues in the real estate industry. A mailing directed toward real estate operators in April 1931 ended with a promise to send literature in mass quantities on the "understanding that you mail them to your clients with your recommendation."[15]

Ironically, a quirk in the law helped push many taxpayers toward nonpayment. Payment of *any* part of the real estate tax still left the unpaid portion subject to sale and forfeiture, victory or loss in the courts notwithstanding. ARET's literature repeatedly underscored this fact. Especially for those taxpayers in imminent peril of losing their property, nonpayment must have seemed the best means of warding off the tax sale. The same quirk in the law also aided ARET's litigation recruitment drive. Defaulting taxpayers who left their properties unshielded by court actions risked greater chance of sale and forfeiture than their organized counterparts who signed up with ARET. These circumstances fused litigation *and* total nonpayment into one highly attractive package for the taxpayer.[16]

During the rest of 1931, ARET's litigation machine rolled forward at full throttle. Two of its most notable suits were the James Bistor equity action and the George F. Koester mandamus action. For the Bistor case, ARET signed up 2,500 new members as plaintiffs. The combined legal fees of these new plaintiffs financed necessary legal costs. These two cases, and subsequent ARET court suits, emphasized the same general premise: the 1930 assessment should be voided because it ignored vast amounts of personal property. In bringing these suits, ARET's leaders had two major goals: a massive real estate tax reduction (in excess of 50 percent) and a delay in tax sales until economic recovery restored the ability to pay.[17]

This Way Ruin Lies

The ink barely dry on his inauguration speech, Cermak locked horns with ARET. He aimed his first volleys at John Pratt. Of Pratt's highly successful weekly radio broadcasts, Cermak alleged, "Hurling advice over the radio every night against paying taxes is just a scheme to get the taxpayers' money." In contrast to the emphasis on tax-reduction in his campaign, the mayor blamed the city's financial plight on an overemphasis relief for taxpayers.[18]

Cermak secured backing from a broad spectrum of the press. All five of Chicago's daily newspapers closed ranks against the strike. An editorial in the *Chicago Evening Post* opined, "Not to pay tax [sic] in the hope that the court will give a reduction is to shirk the responsibilities and duties of citizenship." Surprisingly, though noted for passionate critiques of high taxes, the *Chicago Tribune* led the charge against the strike. In a seemingly unending series of editorials, the *Tribune* warned Chicagoans to ignore the counsel of don't-pay-your-taxers. One editorial asked ARET's leaders to explain "why they are not to be considered undesirable citizens, racketeers or worse."[19]

Throughout the 1930s, the *Tribune*'s publisher, the redoubtable conservative Robert McCormick (later an unbending critic of the New Deal) dominated editorial policy. His opposition to the strike was explainable on several levels. McCormick—and hence the *Tribune*—fervently backed Cermak, ARET's new nemesis. McCormick also disliked ARET's support of personal property taxation. He argued that broadening the tax base, through personal property taxation only detracted from the goal of overall tax reduction. Most importantly, McCormick espoused Conservatism with a capital C. The genuinely Jeffersonian aspects of McCormick's philosophy often clashed with his defense of law and order and established government institutions. The part of a radical agitator subverting the state simply did not suit him. A strike, McCormick feared, would open up a Pandora's box of radicalism: "This [nonpayment of taxes] is not the proper method to pursue. This way ruin lies—the very ruin that the

Reds seek to bring about. Unorganized lawless resistance to taxation must give way to organized lawful organization of tax levies."[20]

Broadsides from the press and politicians notwithstanding, ARET grew stronger each passing day. The city government's downward slide, on the other hand, continued unabated. Even a Madison Avenue public relations expert would have been hard pressed to put a good face on the situation. In May 1931, Joseph McDonough, the city treasurer, disclosed that only 55 percent of total tax levies, an all-time low, had been collected prior to 15 May, the penalty date. When, after months of delays, the city held tax sales in September, the results proved humiliating. The *Chicago Daily News* observed that professional tax buyers, the backbone of the tax sale process, "were conspicuous by their absence."[21]

The Kelly Plan

Unlike his predecessor, Cermak stayed on close terms with the city government's leading creditors. Even so, the bankers were losing patience. They gave an ultimatum to Cermak. Without fundamental reforms of the assessment machinery, the confidence of tax-warrant investors would be lost. Leading bankers and reformers supported one reform in particular: abolition of the elected Board of Assessors and Board of Review. In its place, they wanted to substitute a single appointed assessor. The idea took shape in the later months of 1931. It became embodied in a bill written by D. F. Kelly, the president of the Fair. Kelly also had impeccable banking credentials. He was a director of the Continental Illinois Bank and Trust Company and two other Chicago banks.[22]

The bill placed all power for assessments in the hands of a county assessor to be appointed jointly by the County Board and the governor. It also replaced the elected Board of Review with an appointed Tax Board of Appeals of two members. Cermak worked hard for the Kelly plan. He persuaded the city council to pass a resolution endorsing the bill. In addition, he went in person to the newspaper publishers and lined up their support (only one of the Hearst papers, the *Chicago Evening American*, dissented). The bankers, who scarcely needed to be asked, put their resources at the mayor's disposal.[23]

In his speeches for the bill, Melvin Traylor of the First National Bank of Chicago never concealed his special scorn for ARET. Traylor branded the strike "a discredit to any man who carries the badge of citizenship" and accused ARET of "devoting its energy to murdering the credit of Cook County and indirectly of the Commonwealth of Illinois." "If it is the fault of the taxing body," he contended in a follow-up speech, "that the taxpayers are refusing to pay. . . . We should remove those taxing bodies and leave no further defense to the objecting taxpayers."[24]

All of the leading teachers' unions, including the CTF, the Men Teachers' Union, the Federation of Women High School Teachers, and the Illinois State Teachers' Association, campaigned for the bill. This must have been a bitter pill for Margaret Haley to swallow. Her reputation had been built on crusades against the "tax dodging" banks. On this critical question, the common interest that Haley's CTF and the bankers shared overrode past differences.[25]

The Chicago Federation of Labor and the Illinois State Federation of Labor (ISFL) parted ways with the teachers' unions over the bill. The ISFL charged that an appointed assessor "violated the principle of popular government." Charles S. Richards, a real estate operator and chairman of one of ARET's branch offices concurred. His language bespoke a Jacksonian suspicion of elites in government. He assailed the Kelly plan as a usurpation of the right of the "plain people" to elect their representatives.[26]

Richards addressed the argument that appointment would take politics out of the assessment process. On the contrary, he maintained, an appointive system would only entrench political control because the politicians did the appointing. According to Richards, "There is no particular merit to a man because he is appointed. The political bosses control in either case."[27]

Nathan MacChesney, the new chairman of the CREB's property owners' division, may have been cool to the strike but he agreed with ARET on the Kelly plan. He faulted supporters of the appointive system for placing inordinate faith in the allegedly apolitical expert. To bolster his case, MacChesney quoted Harold Laski's famous article, "The Limitations of the Expert." According to Laski, the expert "confuses learning with wisdom, and tends to make his speciality the measure of life."[28]

Michael Igoe, an old rival of Cermak in the Democratic party, led the legislative fight against the Kelly plan. Not without good cause, ARET's leaders distrusted the motives of their new ally. Igoe's faction of the party controlled approximately 45 of the 592 patronage jobs on the assessor's payrolls, jobs that the Kelly plan would take from its grasp. Whatever his motivations, Igoe put the debate within the standard class framework of tax resisters. He characterized the Kelly plan as another chapter in an unending struggle between "the tax spenders on the one side and the taxpayers on the other."[29]

For both sides, defeat or victory of the Kelly plan became a question of major importance. ARET and other taxpaying groups organized a car caravan to Springfield and held a rally on the capitol lawn. John Pratt addressed the assemblage as the "cream of the tax strikers," and won applause with his vow that "1930 taxes cannot and will not be paid!" Every time Pratt mentioned Melvin Traylor's name, the audience booed. The teachers answered with a mass meeting of their own at the Chicago Stadium on 4 January. The *Chicago Daily News*, an avid enemy of the strike, paid for the rental of the stadium.[30]

For a while, the opponents of the Kelly plan seemed about to prevail. The legislature adjourned without taking action and Cermak proclaimed in desperation that "the ship is sunk." The reluctance of the bankers to promise that credit would be extended if the bill passed was the sticking point. Traylor told Igoe at a legislative hearing, "You can pass this legislative program in toto, or any other, but until the people of Chicago go to paying taxes you will have no credit." He could offer no other encouragement than to praise the bill as a useful first step toward restoring the confidence of creditors.[31]

On the issue of nonpayment of taxes, it appeared that there might be a consolation prize for Cermak. Concurrent with the legislative adjournment, the Illinois Supreme Court upheld a lower court rejection of the Bistor case. The court held that ARET had failed "to allege facts from which it might be determined whether the omitted property was liable to assessment."[32]

Even Otto Kerner, Jr., who later played an instrumental role in the prosecution of the strikers, agreed that the court had demanded an insurmountable task of ARET. "The impossibility," wrote Kerner, "of carrying out these requirements of listing and identifying all omitted personal property was not considered by the court, but as a practical problem this would in effect be delegating the duties of the assessors to an individual taxpayer." Whatever its legal merit, the foes of the strike hailed the ruling. The *Chicago Daily News* proclaimed the decision "a death blow to Cook County's tax strikers."[33]

Not for the first or last time, ARET's critics spoke too soon. Less than two weeks after the Bistor decision, County Judge Edmund Jarecki made banner headlines by voiding real estate assessments on the 1928 and 1929 taxes. The case had been brought by Lillian Cesar, the wife of a draftsman, and 2,000 others. "Can it be maintained," Jarecki asked, "that an assessment so flagrant, so reeking with fraud can be held to be a good roll?" Ironically, though a great boon to its fortunes, ARET had not even brought the case. Nevertheless, ARET's leadership maintained close ties with the litigants. Cesar's lawyers, Roy Keehn and Morris Schaeffer, had been partners of Barnet Hodes. The basis of the case, the underassessment of personal property, was cut from the same cloth as ARET's litigation.[34]

Jarecki's literal application of the uniformity clause of the Illinois constitution completely undermined the well-planned tax timetable of city officials. It reversed judgment on tax sales and put off future sales indefinitely. The only ray of hope available for foes of the strike turned on Jarecki's recommendation (although not requirement) that taxpayers pay the portion of their taxes that they deemed fair. The city government was not about to gamble all its prospects for more tax money on proselytizing the taxpayers. It promptly appealed the case to the Illinois Supreme Court. If the court sustained Jarecki's ruling, the likely result would be a new reassessment. Keehn predicted that in that eventuality, real estate taxes would be reduced by more than 60 percent. Pending a ruling, however, local taxes became, legally speaking, purely voluntary. The town of Winnetka in Cook County made it official. It printed up a "Voluntary School Tax Bill."[35]

The Cesar case brought the Kelly bill back to life. At this juncture, the city was desperate to do just about anything to reassure the hard-pressed banks. Both the *Chicago Evening Post* and the *Chicago Daily News* ran rare front page editorials urging passage of the bill. The *Chicago Daily News* foresaw a disintegration of city government unless the legislature took quick action. "The danger of violence, fire and disease," it declaimed, "is so imminent as to warrant immediate preparation of possible invocation of martial law, under which civil rights in a normal community are automatically suspended." An editorial writer for the *Chicago Evening Post* wondered whether ARET might be liable to a legal charge of sedition adding that "refusal to pay taxes strikes at the very root of government as effectively as an armed revolt."[36]

In the end, the ardent and powerful backers of the Kelly bill

were too much for the taxpaying coalition. The bill won overwhelm-
ing passage in both houses of the legislature and became law in late
January 1932. The members of the Board of Assessors and the Board
of Review were now out of a job. The final law did not give the
proponents everything they had wanted, but it came close. In their
one setback, the supporters of the bill conceded a provision to re-
store election for these offices after December 1934.[37]

Not only the Jarecki decision but also the appalling economic
situation in Chicago spurred politicians to support the Kelly bill.
When the *Literary Digest* asked, "Can America's Second City Survive?" it voiced a common fear. The depression hit Chicago especially hard. Unemployment passed 40 percent in 1932. That same
year the relief rolls listed over 100,000 families, up from 16,000 in
November 1930.[38]

Building a Mass Movement

Kelly plan or not, ARET had never been in a stronger position.
The Cesar case enhanced the drawing power of nonpayment. It rewarded taxpayers who had joined ARET's litigation and tax-withholding campaign. At the same time, it invited demoralization of
those taxpayers who had heretofore refused to take part in the strike.
They had paid their taxes but now were left without a legal course to
obtain a refund.[39]

ARET issued a stream of pamphlets urging taxpayers not to pay
their upcoming 1930 taxes. Although the Jarecki decision only cov-
ered taxes for 1928 and 1929, it clouded the legality of all other taxes
levied on the 1930 assessment. These included the 1930 taxes just
coming into collection. ARET rejected Jarecki's appeal for partial payment for the same reason it had turned down a similar proposal a
year earlier. One pamphlet closed with the question: "Shall I pay a
tax which by general admission is unfair and illegal and which by
court order is fraudulent and void and which is more than double
the amount that would result from a fair, reasonable, legal assessment of the taxable wealth of Cook County?" By October 1931, membership had grown to 8,000 (it had been approximately 35 before
February!). In June 1932, it passed 20,000.[40]

The same economic conditions that prodded the legislature into
passing the Kelly bill also worked in ARET's favor. Real estate values

continued their precipitous slide, reflecting a mounting inability to repay mortgages and taxes. Fred Sargent, no friend of the tax strike, observed, "Why, these [taxpayers] asked themselves, pay taxes on something that belongs solely to the mortgage holders?"[41]

Taxpayers who wanted to sign up for the tax strike did not have too far to look. By August 1931, ARET listed 161 branch offices in the city (76 in the north and 85 in the south) where new members could join. Most of these branch offices doubled as real estate or other business firms. Pratt's radio broadcasts greatly amplified the ability of these branch offices to attract members. Though his audience was limited to Chicago, Pratt should be classed, along with Father Coughlin and Franklin Roosevelt, as a pioneer in the use of radio to promote a political cause. By all accounts, he possessed a laid-back, conversational, and highly persuasive style, ideally suited to winning an audience in the radio age. Pratt knew how to infuriate Cermak by publicizing newspaper accounts of local political corruption.[42]

From the beginning, ARET's leaders recognized the importance of radio as a vehicle to win new members. In the first year of broadcasts, they allotted $11,000 of their $20,000 advertising budget to the radio campaign. By 1932, two stations carried Pratt's broadcasts, now tri-weekly. The attorney general of Illinois made the most of this when he brought suit against ARET in 1933: "[When] the sensational radio speeches made three times each week by the Executive Director of the respondent [ARET] over Chicago radio stations are considered, we have not far to look for the cause of this general failure and refusal of taxpayers to pay taxes. The wonder is that anybody at all paid taxes during the period between February, 1931, and the filing of the Information herein."[43]

"Shame" and "Pay Your Taxes!"

In the meantime, it became common knowledge that the city government stood helpless in the face of the strike. Alfred G. Erickson, a judge of the Municipal Court of Chicago, complained that when he paid taxes in 1931 his neighbors jeered and laughed, advising that he wait until the courts ruled on the issue. Now, after the Jarecki decision, "they claim to have won, and I am again the subject of mirth and laughter."[44]

The political authorities resorted to the only strategy left open to them. They tried to persuade or shame delinquents into paying. Initially, Cermak limited his persuasion campaign to the ringleaders of the strike. He picked out names from ARET's letterhead and called them over the phone. He made almost no headway. Cermak's frustration welled to the surface. "If only the people who are holding back," he bemoaned, "could be made to see what great benefits will accrue all the way around if taxes are paid promptly." The effort to shame always accompanied efforts to persuade. Cermak castigated delinquents as wealthy individuals who, although financially able to pay, shirked their civic duty at the expense of ordinary taxpayers. The mayor compared tax delinquents who joined ARET to gangsters. In one run-in, he depicted ARET's Board of Directors as a "board of Racketeers." During the same week, he pointed to Pratt's $20,000 salary as evidence of a get-rich scheme. Pratt tried to brush off the charge with the statement, "I receive a substantial salary. I think I earn it. Mr. Sexton [the corporation counsel for the city] referred to me once as the exceedingly able manager of the association."[45]

Cermak coupled these accusations with threats of more tangible action. He talked of removing police protection from the property of delinquents and denying them other city "privileges" such as water service. In addition, he urged the press to deny advertising space to ARET. Cermak scored some points with this strategy. The daily newspapers refused to carry ARET's ads and two radio stations, WIBO and WCFL, canceled Pratt's radio broadcasts. ARET, which claimed that the stations had been coerced into breaking their contracts, quickly recouped when WLS and WBBM picked up the triweekly broadcasts.[46]

To reach ordinary tax delinquents, Cermak promoted a "pay-your-taxes" campaign. Kelly was one of the first to broach the plan. In January 1932, he appealed to teachers and business groups, like the Chicago Association of Commerce, to organize a drive to collect 1930 taxes then going into collection. The banks, in cooperation with the city government, formed "Pay-Your-Taxes Savings-Clubs" patterned after Christmas savings clubs. Members of the club paid their taxes in fifty installments over a specified period of time. At the end of this period, the banks would refund the interest to the taxpayer and turn over the principal to the city government.[47]

At a time when most of the media denied advertising space to ARET, the newspapers donated full page "Pay-Your-Taxes" ads to the city government's campaign. One ad, addressed to "Mr. and Mrs. Taxpayer," stressed three themes. First, it emphasized Cermak's record of economy in government and his pledge to do more if the taxpayers cooperated. Secondly, it equated tax collections with patriotic duty. Lastly and most conspicuously, it focused on the self-interest of taxpayers. One ad underscored the argument that taxpayers who paid promptly could save 12 percent in late penalties. The authors of the ad, of course, operated on the assumption, not shared by ARET, that effective tax penalties would quickly be restored.[48]

Local governments distributed posters throughout the city. Cermak came up with the slogan for one of the posters, "Take Your Trade Where The Taxes Are Paid," in the hope of inspiring a boycott of tax delinquents. Another poster, "This Property Is Now Paying Taxes" gave "patriotic" taxpayers, who followed Cermak's lead, a chance to show themselves. The *Chicago Herald and Examiner* carried an editorial praising those individuals who exhibited the latter "badge of honor" in their windows. It compared them to Americans who, during World War I, displayed Red Cross and Liberty Loan insignia.[49]

The Tax Striker as Anarchist

A poster bearing the slogan "Pay What You Think Is A Fair Tax" caught the eye of Mauritz A. Hallgren of the *Nation*. He sensed in this slogan dangerous evidence of civic impotence, or worse, anarchy. "This is not only a tax strike," Hallgren charged, "it is open revolt against government. One must consider the present state of affairs little short of anarchy when civic societies feel impelled to flood the town with posters calling upon the residents to 'Pay What You Think Is a Fair Tax! Pay Now! Keep Your Schools Open!' "[50]

Chicagoans hostile to the strike hardly needed a pay-your-taxes campaign to remind them of the analogies between anarchism and nonpayment of taxes. Charges of anarchy and treason permeated critiques of the strike. Carl Sandburg may have been thinking of ARET when, in 1932, he wrote for the *Chicago Daily News*, "Printed and spoken abuse of the government is seen and heard on all sides. . . . The viewpoint is anarchist." The *Chicago Tribune* asked whether participation in the strike constituted membership in anarchy and concluded that it did. Irvin A. Wilson, the president of the Chicago

Principals' Club, called the strike the "most dangerous form of terrorism and public disorder." Noting that Chicago's tax delinquency had reached 40 percent of levies, he charged, "Forty per cent citizenship is no less dangerous and perilous to the government of America today than it was in the days of Benedict Arnold."[51]

In general, strikers evaded the implications of anarchy but there were exceptions. When Elmer J. Schnackenberg, the Republican leader of the Illinois State Legislature, castigated the tax strikers as anarchists and public enemies, Millard J. Bilharz, a Chicago realtor and activist with ARET, caustically replied: "Apparently you would call those anarchists who participated in that little 'Tea Party' quite some years ago down in Boston. They also had a 'civic duty' to perform in the way of paying an unjust tax to the King of England. But did they? No! And more power to them. . . . The courageous patriots are those who will ignore your remarks, stand four square—and refuse to pay—thereby, by passive and active resistance, force an early correction before we are all sunk."[52]

ARET's leaders usually favored other tactics to deflect the anarchy charge. They went on the counterattack by publicizing the foibles and questionable character of local politicians. When Edwin J. Kuester happened on a copy of Fletcher Dobyns's muckraking biography of Cermak, *The Underworld of American Politics*, Pratt instantly saw the potential. Dobyns's book was a treasure trove of damaging material about the mayor's checkered background. It alleged Cermak's culpability in waste, corruption, and favoritism toward organized crime during his long political career. Essentially, ARET tried to sidetrack accusations of anarchy by exposing the crookedness of those who made the charge.[53]

Retrenchment and the Sargent Committee

In March, Cermak announced spending reductions that included job layoffs and salary cuts. He also had a suggestion as to the culprit responsible for such actions. Cermak predicted that "we shall be obliged to cut still more, not because we don't need the workers, but because people don't pay their taxes." At about the same time, the newly formed Committee on Public Expenditures (CPE) put still more pressure on Cermak. The CPE had a powerful chairman in Fred Sargent, who was also president of the Chicago and North Western

Railway. He made "retrenchment, and then more and more retrenchment" his credo.[54]

The CPE was an unofficial offshoot of the Strawn Committee. Sargent had been a member of the executive committee of Citizens' Committee. He depicted participants in the CPE as motivated by "their love of the city and their desperation as taxpayers." Members of the CPE included directors of four leading (and tax-warrant holding) banks: the First National, the Harris Trust and Savings, the Continental Illinois, and the Northern Trust. Sargent maintained that the banks "positively will not lend money for any municipal function which does not have our active support." In response to these pressures, Cermak enacted other economies in July, including a $15 million reduction in the budget of the Board of Education. Taking account of retrenchments put into effect both before and after the formation of the CPE, Chicago's city budget declined by 35.4 percent between 1930 and 1933. Critics assailed the cuts as destructive slashes enacted at the behest of a big business dictatorship.[55]

Compared to the efforts of other cities, Cermak's economies were quite impressive. Chicago's 35.4 percent reduction was 13 percent higher than the average percentage decline in spending for all cities over 100,000 in population. Ironically, though often portrayed as bearing the brunt of economies, the schools more than held their own. Between 1930 and 1933, school costs in Chicago declined by 28.1 percent (7.3 percent less than the overall spending reduction). These reductions gave local taxpayers short-term but, in the end, marginal relief. Increased payments for debt service canceled out the tax-reducing potential of many of the spending reductions.[56]

This may partially explain why ARET concentrated most of its resources on court litigation. When ARET's leaders did address the economy question, they promoted even more reductions. Bistor proposed a 32 percent slash (on top of the Sargent and Cermak retrenchments) in the 1932 budget. In March 1932, John J. Mangan, a member of ARET's Board of Advisors, supported a reduction of 60 percent! Mangan regarded the strike as the best way to guarantee a reduction in costs and force politicians to "relinquish the powers they have built up through governmental machinery and the allotment of jobs . . . which have no natural part of government. The only time the politician understands the people mean business is when the money is shut off. So shut the money off!"[57]

Closing the Public Schools

The debate over spending reductions put once unthinkable options on the table. Well-known individuals toyed with the ultimate economy, closing the schools. With the publication of the *Report of the Survey of the Schools of Chicago* in May 1932, the controversy boiled over. The Board of Education commissioned a study, dubbed the "Strayer Report" after its author, prominent educator George D. Strayer. Strayer raised a stir when he aligned himself with advocates of school closing. He did not base the recommendation on the need for economy—precisely the reverse. Strayer saw school closure as a device to shock the public into realizing that they could no longer "emasculate" the school system. According to the *Report*, "the schools should be closed and an appeal made to the citizenry of Chicago in the name of the children of the city to take the actions essential to the adequate financing of the schools."[58]

Cermak condemned the report, promising the "schools will never be closed as long as I am mayor." By contrast, Haley and Agnes Clohesy, the president of the Elementary School Teachers' Union, lauded Strayer's proposal. Like Strayer, they supported *temporary* closure as a way to scare the public away from the "wrecking" campaign of retrenchment. That Haley and Clohesy even considered this option attests to the desperation of teachers. From May 1931 to May 1933, Chicago's public school teachers received only four months of pay.[59]

Almost as soon as the smoke generated by the Strayer Report cleared, the teachers who advocated closing began to have second thoughts. They began to wonder whether such precipitate action could backfire against the teachers, rather than help them. At a mass meeting of the All-City Publicity Committee (an organization of teachers), a teacher named Mrs. Larkin was alarmed by one prospect in particular. She feared that closure might result in a massive and permanent switch of allegiance away from the public schools. "There are plenty of other schools in the city," Larkin observed, "for all the children to go to if we do [close the schools] and they will go. . . . There are private schools, there are Lutheran parochial schools and there are Catholic parochial schools."[60]

Many of ARET's leaders were perfectly willing to let the schools close temporarily, but not for the reasons outlined by Strayer.

Though he had ten children, Peter Foote, who headed one of ARET's branch offices, called for shutting down the schools to save money. Like other tax resisters, Foote demanded that government costs deflate as fast as had the private economy. Tongue in cheek, he commented, "Let them [school age children] learn to sew on buttons and other sensible things at home for a while."[61]

Still more disconcerting for the teachers, other leading Chicagoans shared Foote's sentiments. Herbert Simpson, for instance, promoted school closing to get a temporary dose of economy. He assailed the teachers' chronic threats to close the schools as a "third degree" bluff that taxpayers should call: "I have two children in the public schools now; I suppose I place as high value on education as anyone. But if closing the schools for six months or a year is the price we have to pay for the abolition of corrupt, incompetent and extravagant government, I should say without any hesitation, let us close the schools."[62]

ARET's leadership never challenged government schooling per se. The sticking point between them and the teachers involved another issue. The teachers considered the schools an essential government service no less important than courts and police. Individuals like Simpson and Foote, on the other hand, regarded tax-financed education as a secondary service of government and thus a primary target for retrenchment during a depression. For these reasons, among others, the teachers' support for closing the schools had faded rapidly by the last half of 1932.

Cermak Goes to Washington

In June 1932, accompanied by Fred Sargent and D. F. Kelly, Cermak went hat in hand to Congress to appeal for a subsidy. Testifying before the House Banking and Currency Committee, Cermak foresaw disaster unless Congress acted before 1 August, when the city government's money was due to run out. Committee members greeted his dark picture with stony skepticism. Several congressmen inquired why they should lend money to a city that the bankers considered a poor credit risk. Others wondered why Cermak had not been able to put down the strike. Kelly's answer to the latter question did not remove these doubts. "Give us the money," he testified, "and we will show up the tax slackers and the tax dodgers." Not even Cermak's most apocryphal statement could sway them. He told the committee to send "money now or militia later." They did neither. Frustrated and empty handed, he returned to Chicago and ruefully accused Washington of "fiddling while Rome burns."[63]

Four weeks later, the odds shifted once again in favor of Cermak. The Supreme Court of Illinois dealt ARET a blow by overruling Jarecki's decision in the Cesar case. This decision left the properties protected by the Jarecki ruling once again legally subject to sale and forfeiture. The court's opinion focused on the practicalities rather than the legalities of uniformity. It maintained that a ruling for strict uniformity could be used as an excuse for an unscrupulous assessor anywhere in Illinois to prevent government, both local and state, from functioning. The ruling underscored a problem that dogged ARET no end. When forced to choose between literal enforcement of the uniformity article or protecting the power of government, the courts invariably opted for the power of government.[64]

Hayden Bell, the state's attorney for Cook County, predicted that the ruling would destroy confidence in the strike. The press and other city officials exuded like-minded optimism. As had become their habit, enemies of the strike again spoke too soon. The lawyers who had brought the Cesar suit immediately vowed to appeal to the United States Supreme Court. ARET's leaders pledged to do the same with the Bistor case, which had also been recently overruled by the Illinois Supreme Court.[65]

To plead their case, they retained a member of the U.S. House of Representatives, noted constitutional lawyer James Montgomery Beck. During his tenure in Congress, Beck had built up a deserved reputation as a particularly aggressive tax cutter and enemy of big government. If the case reached the highest court, Beck planned to charge Illinois with violating the Fourteenth Amendment, which protects individuals from having their property taken without due process.[66]

Although still supremely confident in statements to the press and public, ARET's options had undeniably narrowed. If the U.S. Supreme Court turned down this appeal, there would be nowhere else to go. It would then come down to an unpalatable choice of either giving up or completely changing strategy. Beneath the outward optimism, ARET's leaders suspected that victory was unlikely. Beck, for example, equated bringing the Bistor case to the higher court with "holding a hot poker from the wrong end."[67]

Prosecutors examining the tax delinquency rolls as they prepare their case against Chicago's tax strikers in 1932. *Left to right:* Assistant State's Attorney John E. Pedderson, Assistant State's Attorney Louis E. Geiman, County Attorney Hayden N. Bell, John C. Connery, and Assistant State's Attorney James Clansey. (*Chicago Tribune*)

Nevertheless, for the foreseeable future, ARET remained a powerful stumbling block for local officials. The most effective short-term aid for the city government came from another source. In July, Cermak's persistence with Washington finally paid off. The Reconstruction Finance Corporation (RFC) advanced Illinois a loan of $3 million. Loans of $6 million and $5 million followed soon thereafter, with most of the money going to Chicago.[68]

The Cesar decision and infusion of RFC aid boosted the confidence of municipal creditors. Leading bankers, led off by Melvin Traylor, purchased more warrants before the city's coffers were to go dry in early August. Even so, the banks kept Cermak on a short leash. They set a maximum credit limit of $10 million to $12 million on further purchases. Traylor reiterated the necessity of suppressing the strike. "The whole situation goes back to the fact," Traylor argued, "that you can't run a government unless the people pay their taxes."[69]

These words to the contrary, the combined interests of the warrant-holding class necessitated that Traylor keep the credit flowing. As in Detroit and other municipalities, the banks had become so dependent on tax money that it had become too late to bow out. In Chicago, for example, debt service ate up over one-third of the annual tax collections. Holders of this debt ranked ahead of schools as the largest single tax-dependent group.[70]

Even if the bankers needed the city government as much as it needed them, Cermak still chafed under the restrictions. After testifying before Congress, his determination to quell the strike redoubled. More than anyone, Cermak abhorred Chicago's distinction for having the largest tax strike in the country if not in American history. In the months ahead, he would go to extreme lengths to break the back of illegal tax resistance.

CHAPTER 4

Breaking the Chicago Tax Strike

By the last half of 1932, ARET had scaled the pinnacle of its popular support. Its membership had surged to about 30,000. Antistrikers generally lumped strikers and delinquents together. They depicted these defaulters in two ways. Occasionally, they pictured at least some of them as dupes who had been bilked by wealthy taxpayers into joining a hopeless cause. Much more often, critics of the strike dismissed tax delinquency as a conspiracy of the wealthy out to defend their investments. Hayden Bell alleged that 95 percent of the common people had paid their tax bills. By contrast, he tagged delinquents as "investors and people of large means who were caught out on a limb." William J. Bogan, the superintendent of schools for Chicago, claimed that "61 percent of the tax delinquents are rich men whose bills total $10,000 or more; only 4 percent of the delinquents are in the $300 or less class."[1]

We do not have a comprehensive, much less reliable, study of Chicago's tax-delinquency roll. Even so, the high percentage of unpaid taxes, 53.4 percent in 1931–32, makes it hard to swallow these blanket equations of tax delinquents with rich men. Fortunately, as concerns ARET's membership, this riddle can be solved. In one of its court suits, *Reinecke* v. *McDonough*, ARET listed its entire membership as colitigants. The list, over 7,000 pages long, not only featured the names of members but also their assessments, tax bills, and the locations of their properties. Although the original document has apparently been lost, an index listing about 26,000 members still exists. Taking a random sample of this list and comparing it with official assessment records and the *City Directory* revealed a good picture of ARET's membership.[2]

The results called into serious question the stereotype of rich tax-dodgers propagated by Bell, Bogan, Cermak, and others. First,

ARET's members worked in a diverse cross section of occupations (see Table 4-1). The membership, nonetheless, differed notably from the general work force in Chicago. Using the chi-square test, I found a marked divergence between the occupational patterns of ARET's membership and the city as a whole. As detractors of the strike maintained, ARET's membership did draw heavily from proprietors. Proprietors constituted 17.2 percent of the membership as compared with 5.4 percent for all Chicagoans. Contrary to allegations by opponents of the strike, however, few of these businessmen were wealthy speculators. They were mostly small shopkeepers and other petty proprietors. Only seven of the thirty-one businessmen in the sample listed occupations in building or real estate. After that in frequency were restaurant proprietors, grocers, and owners of laundries. The rest included a druggist, the owner of a photography studio, the owner of a tailor shop, and the president of a plumbing firm.[3]

Despite this high representation of proprietors, ARET as a whole did not fit the petit bourgeois label. Skilled blue-collar workers constituted the biggest single group of members. Indeed, skilled workers joined ARET in numbers disproportionate to their percentage in the general population. Like the proprietors, they worked in a wide spectrum of pursuits. Of the fifty-four skilled workers in the sample,

Table 4-1

Occupational Distribution for the Population of Chicago
and for the Membership of the Association of Real Estate Taxpayers

| | Percent of Group | |
Occupational Group	Chicago, 1930	ARET, 1928–29
Proprietary	5.4	17.2
Professional and managerial	9.7	15.5
Clerical and sales	27.9	21.6
Skilled	27.0	30.0
Semiskilled and service	16.5	10.5
Unskilled	12.3	5.0

carpenters, painters, and tailors totalled six each. Next were plumbers at five and machinists at four. The balance came from an array of occupations and included electricians, station engineers, and mechanics.

This occupational schema did not do justice to the number of women, at least 26 percent of the members, who belonged to ARET. Significantly, only 14.2 percent of these women joined with men in double memberships. Most seem to have been unmarried. Women identified in the *City Directory* listed "widow" more frequently than they did an occupation. This makes it safe to surmise that these women depended heavily on pensions, inheritances (including real estate holdings), or taking in boarders for their livelihood. Considering the tenuous quality of these investments and undertakings, female real estate owners had ample motivation to become strikers.[4]

The assessment records bore out the relatively modest backgrounds of ARET's members. Unfortunately, the Office of Assessor organized these records by address and not by the name of the taxpayer. This made it almost impossible to tell either the total value or the number of real estate parcels each member owned. According to the press, one suit brought by 30,000 members listed 56,000 parcels. If these aggregate figures accurately reflect their real estate holdings (and we have no reason to believe they did not) each member owned on average a modest 1.86 parcels. Averages, however, can be misleading. I found the assessed value of residences the best available barometer of wealth. Using addresses culled from the *City Directory*, I used the assessment records to tally only those residences both owned and occupied by individual ARET members.

Each assessment listed the values of both the land and the improvements. Readjusted to reflect the traditional underassessment of Chicago's real estate, these figures worked out reasonably well as an estimate of market value. The median value of residences owned by ARET's members was $7,178 against a median value of $6,639 for owner-occupied homes in Chicago at the time of the assessment. These figures probably overstated the comparative residential wealth of ARET's members (marginal though it was). The figure for ARET encompassed all owner-occupied residences including undoubtedly a number of multiple-family homes and apartment buildings. The median value for Chicago, on the other hand, included only one- and two-family homes.[5]

Map 4-1
Residential Location of Members of the
Association of Real Estate Taxpayers in Chicago

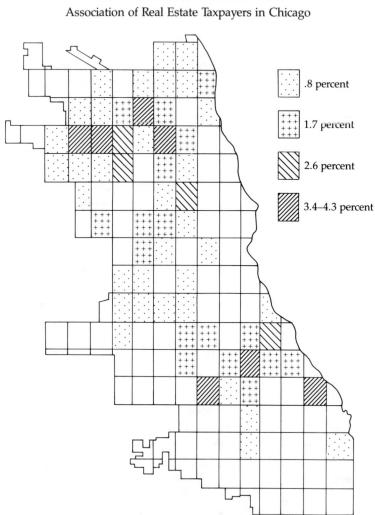

.8 percent

1.7 percent

2.6 percent

3.4–4.3 percent

Note: The map is divided into the grid format used by *Olcott's Land Values Blue Book of Chicago*, 1932. Each square in the grid shows the percentage of ARET's members residing there. Only those members with owner-occupied residences were included in this sample.

ARET did not recruit its membership from any one particular area (Map 4-1). Pratt's radio campaign, fortified by a financial war chest and extensive organizational network, had done well in attracting taxpayers throughout Chicago. Considering the frequent appearances of German, Slavic, Italian, and Greek names in the membership roll, ARET's recruitment success in ethnic neighborhoods is scarcely cause for surprise. Foreign-born Americans had the same chance as natives to own their homes. Members of some nationalities, among them Poles, northern Italians, and Bohemians, owned homes in greater percentages than native-born Americans.

The "black belt" of the South Side was conspicuously underrepresented. ARET never excluded blacks—blacks just did not own much real estate. Less than 10 percent of Chicago's blacks owned their homes in 1930, compared to the citywide average of 31.4 percent. Neither, however, did ARET recruit many members from the so-called gold coast area north of the Loop, so attempts to pigeonhole the strike as a movement of upper-crust taxpayers are dubious.[6]

The taxpayers who joined ARET were not so very different from other Americans of the 1930s who resorted to direct action. In 1935, Alfred M. Bingham, the leftist editor of *Common Sense*, characterized social unrest of the 1930s as a "revolt of the middle-classes." Under this rubric, Bingham placed groups ranging from the Farmers' Holiday movement to the followers of Father Coughlin. One year earlier, the writers of *Rebel America* arrived at much the same conclusion: "The militancy for the first three depression years had been, primarily, the militancy of the American middle and professional classes fighting against extinction. Only a small proportion of both rural and urban insurrectionists were looking for either Mr. Foster's proletarian dictatorship or Mr. Thomas' confiscatory capital levy. . . . Like the workers, they had no program but they were ready to support anything which seemed to offer change and relief."[7]

Like middle-class rebels elsewhere, ARET's members probably saw themselves as plagued by what could be characterized as relative deprivation (a term that historians have borrowed from social psychology). One historian defines it as "the discrepancy between what people believe they are entitled to and what they actually manage to obtain." Many of the entrepreneurs and blue-collar workers in ARET's rank and file had only recently moved up into the middle class. They had won a modest measure of security by acquiring a home or a small business. Now, the tax man endangered these small but hard-won gains.[8]

The content of Pratt's radio talks had surefire appeal for these middle-class taxpayers. They could empathize with Pratt's salvos against tax spenders and banks earning 6 percent interest on tax-anticipation warrants. His recurrent theme that the banks evaded personal property taxes on intangibles while owners of real estate paid the cost of local government must have galvanized them still further. Taxpayers in distress did not have to strain too hard to accept Pratt's opinion as to the culprits.

Pratt's populist rhetoric should not be mistaken as a mere propaganda ploy to reach the small taxpayer. The prosperous real estate operators who led ARET could also relate to his message. People like Bistor believed themselves equally threatened by banker, bureaucrat, and politician. Several members of ARET's executive committee, after all, had once been on the same middle-class level. The community of interest existed on yet another level. Though misleadingly posed by Cermak and others, the characterization of ARET's membership as speculators had some merit. The term might, for example, fit a plumber who had acquired a small apartment building or an extra parcel of land during the 1920s.

Give Me the Biggest Wrench You Have

As ARET's power grew, its opponents stepped up their campaign to break the strike. An almost insurmountable task awaits the historian trying to paint a coherent picture of these efforts. Much of the time (throughout 1931 and early 1932, for example), antistrike activity generated more smoke than substance. As usual, threats were never in short supply. Cermak made clear his readiness to go to almost any lengths to destroy ARET. When the time came for concrete action he and the rest of the city administration betrayed their befuddlement. At least within memory, Chicago had never faced a puzzle like this. City leaders had institutions, or at least precedents, to cope with a host of other social problems ranging from natural disasters to labor strife. In this crisis, they had to be innovators.

Initially, opponents of the strike gambled most of their hopes on an expanded pay-your-taxes campaign. In July 1932, Joseph B. Mc-Donough, the county treasurer of Cook County, floated a trial balloon that school board employees act as "visiting campaigners" to collect taxes from delinquents. McDonough's announcement greatly pleased the All-City Publicity Committee, which had supported the idea for quite some time. The committee had been appointed in the spring of 1932 by delegates from all 350 Chicago schools. In May, it had launched a campaign to place "car cards" with the slogan "pay your taxes" in all of Chicago's transportation vehicles. It also advertised a theme song entitled "Be Fair to Chicago's Boys and Girls! Pay Your Taxes Now." The committee hoped to make the slogan and theme song so familiar to Chicagoans "that the various opposed interests will not dare to attack further that foundation of all democracy—free and full education for the child."[9]

McDonough's proposal gave the teachers a golden opportunity to turn their publicity for tax collection into an all-pervasive operation. By August, the All-City Publicity Committee had a detailed plan ready for presentation to McDonough. Mary L. Leitch, the chair of the committee, pledged that a minimum of 10,000 teachers would donate their time to serve as special collectors. She also asked that the teachers be sworn in as unofficial deputy collectors. Leitch's comments evinced a sophisticated understanding of the psychology of taxpaying. "It's a selling job—this collection of taxes," she explained, "You must make it easy for the customer to buy. You must break down the sales resistance, and there is resistance to paying taxes. . . . There is a mental complex we must look for."[10]

Once they had a chance to look over the committee's plan, McDonough and other local politicians started to get cold feet. Swearing in the teachers to serve as deputy collectors presented difficulties because of the prohibitive expense of bonding requirements. Hayden N. Bell, the county attorney for Cook County, warned of racketeers posing as teachers to collect money for themselves.[11]

To solve the impasse, McDonough proposed a compromise. Under this plan, the teachers would still go to the taxpayers' homes, where they would make their sales talks. Then, the teacher would escort the taxpayer to an official collector. Ultimately, even this compromise fell through. Leitch was adamant that teachers be authorized to collect money, touting their automatic entrée into the homes of taxpayers. "We want to capitalize on [sic] sociological effects of asking for taxes," Leitch maintained. "If we are not deputies our work will be futile."[12]

Though largely unspoken, another, but equally salient, reason for the downfall of the tax-collection plan paralleled the controversy over school closing. The unorthodox strategy of having teachers take on the role of tax collectors always ran the risk of backfiring. Margaret Haley, for one, vehemently opposed the idea, branding it "dynamite." The teachers worried that much of the public held them in low repute. William J. Bogan, the superintendent of schools for Chicago, noted ruefully, "one serious cause for the unhappiness of the teachers is the growing suspicion that they and their work are not appreciated. The public in general appears to be apathetic. Some sections are hostile." Countering this sentiment had been the basis of the committee's formation. To have put teachers in the field as tax collectors would have invited still more resentment from taxpayers.[13]

The teachers did not limit their activity against the tax strike to pay-your-taxes appeals. They took care that the mechanisms of legal force would back up any campaign of persuasion. On 11 July, a mass meeting of teachers met to consider what steps to take against those taxpayers who ignored appeals to civic pride and patriotism. Among other demands, the gathering endorsed prosecution of tax strikers for criminal conspiracy. They won support from a powerful ally. Three days earlier, Hayden Bell had sent a letter in defense of the idea to one of the teachers' representatives. Bell wrote that an organized strike is "always immoral, always criminal, as it brings loss and suffering to public workers, and tends directly to the embarrassment and overthrow of government."[14]

The teachers got their wish. On 13 July, State's Attorney John A. Swanson announced that his office had launched an investigation of ARET. Swanson made headlines by calling Pratt, Bistor, Teninga, and other members of ARET to the witness stand. The final results did not bring much comfort to opponents of the strike. Swanson uncovered no evidence sufficient for prosecution. He concluded that ARET's affairs had been honestly handled. Only Pratt received a salary, and that money had been approved by a legally constituted finance committee. To say the least, the investigation did not intimidate ARET. According to the *Chicago Herald and Examiner*, Pratt laughed at the inquiry and said, "We are standing pat and nothing can be done about it."[15]

Swanson compounded the disgruntlement of antistrikers by rejecting the charge of criminal conspiracy as impractical. Such tactics, he maintained, would win sympathy for ARET's leaders by making them martyrs. Swanson could only manage a contempt suit. The suit charged that ARET had violated its nonprofit status by practicing law for the profit of its 30,000 members. Ironically, this accusation directly contradicted Cermak's claim that taxpayers gained no monetary benefit by joining ARET. Although Cermak continued to press for a criminal conspiracy prosecution, the state's attorney had high hopes for the contempt proceeding. Swanson inspired a round of applause from a mass meeting of principals and teachers when he vowed that litigation brought by his office would "wipe out the Association of Real Estate Taxpayers, and wipe it out of business with one stroke of the pen."[16]

In October, local authorities jubilantly predicted ARET's demise when the United States Supreme Court refused to consider the Bistor case. On hearing the news, Bell exclaimed that the "tax conspiracy has been broken." Optimism gave way to a stiffened attitude after it became clear that ARET's detractors had again jumped the gun. Shortly after the Supreme Court's decision, ARET circulated a bulletin that promised to start the process all over again in the lower courts.[17]

Tensions reached a high pitch. Sometime during this period, Pratt received a kidnapping threat against his son. As a precaution, his wife and son checked in at the Palmer House under the alias of "Prather." Every time Pratt ventured into the Loop, a member of ARET followed to provide security. Apparently, someone offered Pratt a lucrative job and a trip to Europe if he would resign from ARET. "I told him," Pratt recalled, "to go to—Europe, if he so chose."[18]

In the immediate months ahead, leading opponents of the strike showed remarkable ingenuity in hatching plans to wipe out ARET. Cermak even wrote a letter to the Federal Radio Commission asking that local stations have their licenses revoked for obstructing government by broadcasting Pratt's speeches. By this time, the city administration could count on thorough support from the press and leading business, professional, and government employee organizations. The All-City Committee cheered the legal drive against the strike and called for still tougher action.[19]

Fred Sargent proposed that the state and local governments cut off strikers' water and police protection, and even take away their legal standing in court. He saw no value in defending the civil rights of willful nonpayers. Strikers must pay their taxes, Sargent demanded, "if they are to continue to claim the rights of American citizenship."[20]

Cermak liked what he heard. He convened a meeting of the city council to translate these proposals into law. On 26 October, the city council passed a lengthy ordinance that followed Sargent's ideas nearly to a T. It authorized the city government to turn off water to strikers with bills over $10,000 and to revoke permits for switch tracks, driveways, electric signs, and all other use of government property upon, under, and over streets and sidewalks. Cermak and the council defended this law on the grounds that it removed government-granted privileges.[21]

To enforce this ordinance, the city council created the Chicago Emergency Commission or, as the press dubbed it, the "tax war board." Cermak appointed Bell, Chicago's corporation counsel William H. Sexton, and the commissioner of public works, Colonel Albert A. Sprague. The mayor also reserved slots for the Chicago Association of Commerce and the CREB. Though no supporter of the strike, J. Soule Warterfield, the president of the CREB, repudiated membership in the commission. Warterfield vowed that the CREB would "not be a party to a campaign of coercion or intimidation, nor will they [sic] countenance the use of extra legal practices."[22]

In contrast to Warterfield, Sprague accepted his duties with enthusiasm. Sprague demanded, "Give me the biggest wrench you have. I'll be pleased to turn off water to buildings owned by tax strikers." The commission zeroed in on Jacob Kesner, the vice-president of ARET, as the first target of the new law. To all appearances, it could not have found a tax striker more vulnerable to attack. He owed far more money than any other ARET member (an accumulated total of $660,000 for 1928, 1929, and 1930 taxes). A campaign against Kesner also seemed well suited from the standpoint of public relations. He owned thirty properties, all of them in the Loop, thus fitting the city's favorite stereotype of the rich tax dodger. On 10 November, the city council voted to revoke Kesner's permit, previously granted, for use of a canopy in front of one of his buildings. This vote empowered the commission to remove the canopy if it so chose.[23]

The media exploited the controversy over Kesner's canopy for all it was worth. Kesner and Cermak fought a spirited verbal tug-of-war. Kesner appealed to Cermak to revoke the order. Cermak responded by giving Kesner a lecture on citizenship that the newspapers printed in full. In private, Kesner revealed that he did not care much one way or another about the canopy. Edwin J. Kuester recalled that the canopy "didn't amount to a row of pins" to ARET and Kesner. They seem to have been rather amused by the whole matter.[24]

The Kesner tiff ended as a fiasco for the city administration. Sprague balked at enforcing the removal. Apparently neither the city government nor the commission had done its homework properly. When Sprague finally got around to inspecting the site, he discovered that the bronze canopy had been riveted into the steelwork of the building. Only a blowtorch could remove it and that would leave the building perceptibly scarred. Only two weeks earlier, Sprague had been eager to do battle with the strikers. Now, he pulled back from a fight. When asked when he would take down the canopy, Sprague replied, "The blood of the martyrs is the seed of the church." The commission, created with such fanfare, soon faded into oblivion.[25]

These clumsy acts of official coercion may have impressed the newspapers, but the fight with the highest stakes remained in the courts. Cermak had been disheartened by earlier failures to pursue a criminal conspiracy investigation, so his hopes must have brightened when a "coalition grand jury" agreed—in the wake of the Bistor decision—to try again. Following in Swanson's footsteps, the grand jury investigation looked into the charge of criminal conspiracy. Also as before, it summoned Pratt, Bistor, and other key ARET leaders to the witness stand. Cermak predicted that it would unearth criminality (including misappropriation of funds) of a scope so grand to "amaze the people of Chicago."[26]

The results, announced in November, did not fulfill the mayor's sensational scenario. Like its predecessor, the grand jury found no cause for prosecution. Even though given a clean bill of health, however, ARET's reputation had been irretrievably sullied. All through the investigation the media had played up Cermak's accusations. The conclusion of the inquiry, by contrast, received comparatively little attention. The *Chicago Tribune* highlighted Pratt's salary, frequently referring to him as a "$20,000 a year executive." Especially in 1932, the trough of the depression, the constant refrain about Pratt's salary could only harm ARET's credibility.[27]

ARET had fallen into a rut. Its only response to changed conditions was to file a new round of tax objections. ARET's lawyers and leadership stuck determinedly to a strategy of litigation that, by all the signposts of adverse court decisions, promised to lead to a dead end. The basis of the new tax objections was also more of the same. The suits relied exclusively on the charge that real estate owners had been overtaxed because of a nonassessment of personal property. The whole episode gave Bell another chance to allege that the suits would benefit only "big men" who "want to save their investments at the expense of government." He added, "If one or the other must fall—investment or government—it must be the former." The media widely publicized Bell's characterization of ARET. When Ferre Watkins, ARET's lawyer, countered by pointing out the modest background of the litigants, the press largely ignored him.[28]

From the standpoint of both propaganda and practicality, the political authorities reaped their greatest success through the traditional tax sale. On 14 November, Edmund Jarecki, the same judge who a year before had handed real estate taxpayers their greatest victory in the Cesar case, summarily dismissed all of ARET's objections. Adding extra sting to ARET's defeat, Jarecki entered a judgment for sale of the 56,000 properties owned by the objectors. He singled out these properties because they belonged to "genuine strikers." James Bistor and Jacob Kesner were among those strikers hit in the early wave of tax sale judgments. All the while, Jarecki left the door open to repentant delinquents. He announced a tempting 50 percent reduction in accumulated penalties for all taxpayers who came into court, received judgment, and made partial payments.[29]

There Will Be Bloodshed

These suits weakened but did not destroy ARET. The strike's demise came from within. Unbeknownst to the public, two factions had struggled over ARET's leadership since at least February 1932. Pratt and Bistor led the dominant bloc, which controlled five of twelve votes on the Board of Directors. Kesner spoke for an opposing faction of four directors. Directors George F. Koester, Thomas D. Collins, and Earle A. Shilton made up a swing group.[30]

Lack of documentation and the passage of fifty years have obscured the basis of this factionalism. Some who had knowledge of the struggle cited an ethnic dimension. Indeed, the Kesner faction included three Jews while the Pratt-Bistor group was exclusively non-Jewish. Although ethnicity may have contributed to the fray, it stands up inadequately as a general explanation. The Kesner group included one non-Jew, Edward M. Bertha, while another Jew, Shilton, belonged to the swing faction.[31]

Personal animosity appears to have been the real root of the division. Factional disputes turned around questions of organizational control rather than ideology or ethnicity. Kesner and his followers tried, for example, to take over the finance committee. Since the finance committee disbursed all funds, those who controlled it controlled ARET. At another point, the Kesner group proposed changing the vote requirement for control of the Board of Directors from a simple majority to two-thirds. Such a revision would have given Kesner's faction veto power over all decisions.[32]

All of these coups failed. Then suddenly, in 1933, the tables were turned. On 18 January, an ally of Kesner proposed that ARET establish a newspaper. For the first time, the swing vote joined with Kesner's faction and the measure passed. When the time came to appropriate money for the newspaper, ARET's treasurer James D. Stover, a backer of Pratt, refused to issue the check. To settle the matter, the Pratt camp took its case to the general membership. They garnered 600 signatures (more than the bylaws required) on a petition for a meeting of all the members (the first ever).[33]

The general membership meeting had the power to decide not only the leadership of ARET but also what policy it should follow for the upcoming 1931 taxes. The Pratt-Bistor group wanted to carry forward the strike. Kesner and his allies did not. Despite a move by the now dominant Kesner wing to suspend office operations (thus firing Pratt) and cancel the general membership meeting, plans went ahead anyway. The instigators scheduled the meeting for 14 February at the Chicago Coliseum.[34]

The reasons for the swing group's defection were even less clear than the basis of the earlier factionalism. Some Pratt supporters suspected behind-the-scenes dealings involving Henry Horner, newly elected as the first Jewish governor of Illinois. This opinion rested mostly on circumstantial evidence. Kesner long had been a political backer (and close friend) of the governor. In addition, Charles Schewrin, Kesner's ally on the Board, had worked for Horner's election in 1932. Years later William Waller, Jr., a member of the Pratt group, still complained that Kesner and his supporters had "sold out to the politicians."[35]

By this time, members of the two factions were no longer on speaking terms. At one tense meeting, they almost resorted to blows as one member from each group tried to take control of the minute book. Also, for the first time, the general row between the factions spilled over into the press, doing further damage to ARET's already precarious reputation.[36]

Interfactional strife heightened as the 14 February membership meeting approached. The authorities did their best to widen the rift. Bell branded the meeting a conspiracy against government compara- ble to a "crew of gunmen who plot to rob a bank." He suggested that the police commissioner register all participants at the door. Lee J. Lesser, a member of the Kesner faction, predicted that the meeting would result in bloodshed.[37]

Lesser may have anticipated bloodshed but he also probably ex- pected the membership meeting to vote against his faction. The Kes- ner group later claimed that Pratt had once bragged, "I am the Asso- ciation of Real Estate Taxpayers." Regardless of whether Pratt ever made this statement, as a description of the facts, it rang true. Pratt's radio speeches, more than any other single factor, had transformed ARET from a small band of well-off real estate operators into a broad- based organization of 30,000 members. If anyone had a better shot at swaying the votes of the general membership, it would be the media- conscious Pratt rather than the heretofore shadowy Kesner.[38]

Unfortunately, we will never know for sure. On the day of the meeting, a local judge issued an injunction calling it off. The decision resulted from an eleventh-hour petition by the anti-Pratt forces. They alleged that the general membership meeting would result in "riot- ing and breach of the peace." Their petition also accused the Pratt faction of extravagance in the use of funds and of plotting to start a radical third party. The strikers denied these allegations and charged that ARET's enemies in government had exploited the petition as a pretext to break the strike. "It was all a set up," Kuester asserted. "They [the anti-Pratt faction] had the political group and all the judges. They had no trouble to find a judge to do their bidding."[39]

Unaware of the injunction, 5,000 of ARET's members showed up at the Coliseum anyway. They encountered locked gates, a squad of deputy sheriffs, and nearly 200 policemen. The injunction effectively muzzled members of the Pratt-Bistor faction. It closed off access to ARET's funds and forbade them (in their capacity as members of ARET) to call any other meeting or to give speeches over the radio.[40]

Pratt and his allies assailed the court for violating their right to free speech and assembly. It was all in vain. By the end of the year, ARET had passed into receivership. The Illinois Supreme Court inflicted the final blow by fining ARET for practicing law without a license. In October 1933, Pratt truthfully observed, "The Association of Real Estate Taxpayers is dead."[41]

Mopping Up

To obliterate the last remnants of the strike and prevent its recurrence, politicians at both the local and state levels enacted a series of laws. In April 1933, Governor Horner signed the Skarda Act and the Graham Act. The Skarda Act was an attempt to reinvigorate the largely moribund tax-sale machinery. It authorized any local judge of competent jurisdiction to appoint receivers for income-producing tax-delinquent property. The receivers had the power to take charge of the property and ensure that a certain percentage of the assets went to taxes. Several other states that had tax-delinquency problems modeled their own tax-receivership laws after the Skarda Act. The effectiveness of the strike had been predicated on ARET's ability to bring suit without paying any taxes. The Graham Act, which became law the same month as the receivership law, removed this possibility by requiring taxpayers to pay 75 percent of their taxes before lodging an objection in court. The state government enacted a third law that prohibited incitements of taxpayers to strike. All parties concerned made quite explicit the strike-breaking intent of these laws. The *Chicago Tribune*, for example, dubbed the Skarda Act a tax strike bill.[42]

The remnants of ARET, a short-lived group called the Real Estate Defense Committee, cooperated with the CREB to oppose all three antistrike laws. After the demise of the committee, Pratt and Bistor pursued national careers that underscore the continuity of the tax strike with later movements, especially those marked by a distrust of centralized political control and powerful elites. Bistor eventually became chairman of the Honest Money Founders, a small group on the inflationist right that attacked the Federal Reserve's "money monopoly" and "international bankers." Pratt had a much longer public career. In the late 1940s, he organized the National Physicians Committee for the Extension of Medical Service. The committee played a major role in derailing Harry Truman's government-subsidized health insurance plan. In the 1950s, he promoted General Douglas MacArthur for president.[43]

The Tax Strike in Perspective

Compared to efforts in other American cities, did the strike bring relief to Chicago's taxpayers? The answer really depends on the starting baseline. Total general property tax collections from 1930 to 1933 increased by a bone-crushing 66.6 percent in Chicago even while collections fell an average 9.8 percent for all cities of over 100,000 in population. When taken in context, the figures for Chicago are misleading. Nineteen thirty was the last year of the "tax holiday" period when the city had to rely almost exclusively on revenue from sources other than property taxes, like license fees.[44]

If the tax holiday is accounted for, a different picture emerges. Yearly collections of general property taxes in Chicago between 1929 and 1933 averaged only 72.4 percent of the level of collections in 1928. By contrast, general property taxes elsewhere yielded a yearly average of 102.3 percent of what they had paid in 1928. For this reason, the question deserves an answer of a qualified yes. I emphasize qualified because the massive tax increases from 1930 to 1933 came at a time when Chicago's taxpayers were least able to pay. Between 1933 and 1940, the general property tax actually declined by a marginal .9 percent in Chicago while it increased 10.8 percent in all cities over 100,000. If taxpayers as a whole are considered, however, the divergence takes on a new meaning. Between 1933 and 1940, the *total* local tax load for Chicago increased 15.4 percent as compared to 12.3 percent for all cities over 100,000. Clearly, these general property tax reductions came at the expense of other taxpayers.[45]

This raises a harder question. What percentage of Chicago's tax delinquency is attributable to the strike? ARET's membership alone accounted for nearly 10 percent of the unpaid taxes for 1928, 1929, and 1930. Certainly, ARET's 30,000 members are evidence of many other willful tax delinquents too wary to open themselves to prosecution by signing legal petitions. Hayden Bell argued that 75 percent of all tax delinquents possessed the financial ability to pay. An authority on municipal government, Charles Merriam, professor of political science at the University of Chicago, made a similar estimate. Merriam guessed, "If at any time now the gentlemen [ARET] who decide to lift the ban on the payment of taxes would do so, I suppose 80 to 85 percent of the tax money could come in and we could go ahead and relieve the tax situation for this year." Real estate operators and members of taxpayers' groups, on the other hand, argued just as forcefully that economic impoverishment, not willful resistance, was responsible for most delinquency.[46]

A simple division of the delinquency rolls into taxpayers able and unable to pay obscures critical subtleties. It entirely omits taxpayers caught somewhere between the two extremes. Many individuals, though hard pressed, could pay at least part of their taxes but instead put priority on other bills. The disintegration of the tax sale system in Chicago, and most other parts of the country, could hardly fail to make an impression. With money so tight, taxpayers had every reason to ask why they should not take care of first things first. Viewed from this perspective, support of government seemed far less relevant than more immediate needs like meeting mortgage payments or putting the children through school.

The demise of the strike seems to have had a profound short-term impact on this middle group. The hyperbole from the media and politicians over the Skarda and Graham acts evoked renewed fears of coercive government power. Many people regarded the tax sale as a paper tiger, but it was hard to be quite so sure about the untried Skarda Act and its imposing receiverships. Bistor and Kesner, among other members of ARET, saw their properties fall into receiverships under its provisions.

In the months following the Skarda Act, the real estate tax-delinquency rate receded by nearly two-thirds. The drop was far larger than the decline in the rest of the country. Significantly, in contrast to the nationwide trend, Chicago's tax-delinquency rate edged up again in subsequent years. This happened, according to a critic of the Skarda Act, because financially embarrassed taxpayers, who had been briefly intimidated, finally perceived that the Skarda Act was ineffective.[47]

When evaluating the strike's impact, the limitations of poring over the nuances of the tax-delinquency roll become apparent. Those in power feared the strike not so much because it was attractive to some of the delinquent taxpayers but because it represented an organized movement. In other parts of the country, willful delinquents usually stood alone. Politicians could brand them as antisocial slackers and make the charge good. In Chicago, delinquents could join a mass organization that gave their behavior a sense of moral legitimacy. ARET broke the government's monopoly on tax information. It gave taxpayers a rare source of alternative options.

Nevertheless, tax resisters were disorganized when compared to their adversaries. The organization nearest to ARET in sympathy was the CREB. The CREB may have backed ARET's political, and even legal, program but it could not stomach the illegality of organized nonpayment. Chicago's other wealthy business interests generally kept aloof, but often opposed the strike. The Chicago Association of Commerce (CAC), the leading representative of the wealthier business interests, stayed conspicuously silent during the controversy.

Part of the reticence of these businessmen was because of their investment portfolios. Many of them had assets that were legally defined as personalty rather than realty. They found ARET's demand to tax intangibles and other forms of personal property highly unattractive. The subversive implications of a tax strike gave them additional pause. In illustration of this point, Kuester recalled that wealthy nonrealtor businessmen dubbed ARET's leaders "silk hat reds." Moreover, in 1930 and 1931, many of the larger businesses of Chicago had been quite susceptible to Strawn's warrant-sales campaign. In their new role as municipal creditors, these businessmen now had an added stake in stable tax collections.[48]

If the CAC kept its distance from ARET, the Chicago Federation of Labor (CFL), at least in the early stages of the strike, proved much more supportive. ARET, after all, drew its membership disproportionately from skilled blue-collar workers. This class of workers had always been the backbone of organized labor in Chicago. Even when the strike was at its height in February 1932, an article in the CFL's *Federation News* praised ARET as "a legitimate organization of citizens who have recognized the futility of individual protest." The CAC's magazine, *Commerce*, never carried ARET's ads. The *Federation News* prominently featured ads for John Pratt's radio talks. The organized teachers, on the other hand, virtually declared war on ARET.[49]

Strategies

Though ARET's emphasis on personal property taxation brought immediate dividends, it did not hold much promise for long-term success. Personal property taxation, even at the 1 percent rate which ARET promoted, seemed unlikely to produce enough money to satisfy the expanding wants of local government. In 1934, Clarence Heer, a widely acknowledged authority on taxation, predicted that enactment of the 1 percent limit on the general property tax rate would result in a 35 percent reduction in government spending. This reduction would have come in addition to the earlier economies of Cermak and Sargent. To have obeyed the uniformity clause of the Illinois constitution by allowing a 1 percent rate would have meant political suicide for many who were dependent on tax money.[50]

ARET's leaders miscalculated by gambling everything on litigation. In a fight like this, the checks and balances of government could be shunted aside. As dependents on tax money, politicians and jurists alike shared much common interest in destroying ARET, and virtually none in protecting it. When ARET neared the end of its legal rope in October 1932, Bell himself asserted: "Such citizens [tax strikers] stand wilfully opposed to government. They would not have much legal standing in court. It would be natural for governments to favor those who are not opposed to government."[51]

Even at this late date, Pratt clung doggedly to the legal strategy. He pointed out that the courts had invariably ruled on technicalities and had never addressed the merits of ARET's case. Although his point was well taken, Pratt never really asked the key question: How could the strike's defeat in the courts have been otherwise? ARET particularly erred in not formulating a fallback strategy. Consequently, when litigation failed, it had no other recourse than to go to court again.

ARET, and the massive taxpayers' revolt it led, embodied a distrust of big government and centralized institutions. Like so many other organizations evoking this sentiment in the 1930s, ARET lacked a well-articulated program. It called for reducing government's size but avoided concrete proposals. ARET's broadsides for economy usually, but not always, consisted of vague attacks on government extravagance and corruption. Considering the far-reaching ramifications of its tax-reduction program, such a strategy had obvious shortcomings. Had ARET been more forthright, it might have stood a better chance of winning more support from elements of the business community and the press who were friendly to tax reduction.

ARET's biggest blind spot was its inability to frame a convincing defense of nonpayment. For a while, its leaders could take refuge in trumpeting the questionable legal basis of tax levies. When the courts ruled against this premise, strikers were left without an alternative defense of nonpayment. Adverse rulings left them at a still greater loss to answer the allegation that the logic of the tax strike led to anarchy. Nevertheless, for the greater part of its existence, ARET had remarkable success. Pratt and Bistor, and the organization they built, managed to hold off the tax collector for nearly two years. They presided over what may have been the biggest concerted tax strike since the aftermath of the Revolutionary War.

CHAPTER 5

Selling the State: The National Pay Your Taxes Campaign

The antagonists of Chicago's tax strike could, if so inclined, seek reassurance (dubious though it might be) from one fact. They did not stand alone. Throughout the first half of the 1930s, nearly every part of the country faced a profound breakdown in enforcement of the general property tax. The sanction of the tax sale became a hollow threat in the depression era. Economist Harley Lutz noted that the tax sale's usefulness for motivating taxpayers to pay "exists only when delinquency is the exception, and it becomes entirely futile when taxes are in default on thousands of parcels since there is obviously no bona fide market under such conditions and the only result is to pile up penalties on a tax load which can not itself be carried." When Carl Chatters and Walter Harris of the Municipal Finance Officers' Association grimly announced in the November 1933 issue of *Municipal Finance* (the voice of the tax collector) that "tax sales will bring little help to tax collectors in 1933 or 1934," they only put into words what had long been baffling reality for their readers. Frequently, the system was so vitiated that taxes ceased to be taxes in the commonly accepted meaning of the term. In actuality, though not in the eyes of the law, general property taxes often became discretionary payments rather than coercive levies.[1]

Economic impoverishment kept many taxpayers from paying. Others defaulted for ideological as well as economic reasons. Harold Buttenheim, the editor of the *American City*, for example, traced willful tax delinquency to a "budget-slashing complex which has exalted tax-relief to the pinnacle of civic virtue." In the same vein, Charles Merriam targeted the "common opinion that all government is necessarily weak, ignorant, corrupt and contemptible" as the culprit. A recurring theme united the analysis of Buttenheim, Merriam, and other foes of tax revolt. They all agreed that willful tax delinquency arose as the logical culmination of radical agitation for tax reduction and budget slashing.[2]

Henry Traxler, the city manager of Janesville, Wisconsin, took up this question from the vantage point of an embattled municipal official. In "Why Pay Taxes?" a widely reprinted article in the July–August 1933 issue of the League of Wisconsin Municipalities publication *Municipality*, Traxler wrote: "Daily they [the taxpayers] have been told that money paid in taxes is just that much money withdrawn from circulation and that the only solution toward recovery of property was to cut the tax load and balance the budget." He especially denounced ruthless anti-big-government propaganda because it led perforce to "breeding the thought of 'why pay taxes' at all."[3]

While thousands of Americans at the local level failed to send in their taxes, there was general reluctance to take part in organized nonpayment campaigns. Even so, taxpayers' threats to go on strike cropped up with enough frequency to keep local politicians, bankers, and bureaucrats on edge. They had before them the uncomfortable reminder of Chicago. References to Chicago's strike not only found their way into national journals like the *New Republic*, the *Nation*, and the *Forum*, but also into both sides of taxation debates at the state and municipal level. Chicago became an object lesson for the taxpayer, either as an illustration of the need for restraint or, more provocatively, as a model for rebellion. Julia O'Keefe Nelson, who turned her position as school commissioner from the sixth ward of Atlanta into a platform for tax and spending reduction, warned the city's school bureaucrats that they risked "Chicago's desperate plight" unless "taxes are almost immediately heavily cut." She characterized Atlanta's taxpayers, like their counterparts in Chicago, as "seeing red" in "every section of the city, north, south, east, west, among every class. . . . They are forming plans to arouse every ward, parade the streets, picket the courthouse, and city hall, refuse to pay taxes!"[4]

Authors of New York City's agitation for tax revolt in early 1932 turned to Chicago as a source for inspiration. Others, just as eager to forestall a fate like Chicago's for New York, took a different tack. George S. Horton, president of the Brooklyn Real Estate Owners' Association, counseled against the "hysteria" of the tax boycott, "which would throw your city into the bankruptcy Chicago is already experiencing."[5]

Peter Grimm, president of the Real Estate Board of New York, agreed with Horton and with Charles Berry about the unlikelihood of a strike. He dismissed comparisons with Chicago. Grimm had a point. New York City had relatively low tax delinquency by Chicago's standards, and though New York's taxation machinery did not shine with honesty and efficiency, it never approached the corruption and venality of Cook County's tax racket. Grimm noted another telling difference between the two cities. New York's taxpayers never had much success in litigation but (at the time he spoke) "the taxpayers' strike in Chicago is upheld in the courts." Grimm, however, qualified his comments with an observation obviously intended for the city's complacent politicians. "For just as surely as disaster has overtaken in Chicago," Grimm predicted, "so will the time come in New York City, if we longer continue without regard for the ability of the taxpayers to pay."[6]

Bankers and Reformers

Nationally, Chicago's tax strike had implications that key interest groups found hard to ignore. For municipal bond dealers, the term "tax strike" gave off the unsettling odor not only of anarchy but, worse still, repudiation. To Sanders Shanks, the editor of the *Bond Buyer*, the bible of the municipal bond business, the Chicago tax strike represented both an opportunity and a threat. Shanks feared that a nationwide tax strike like that of Chicago would naturally follow from anti-big-government propaganda. He complained, "All we hear is the cry: 'Cut the budget—State, City and town. Force economy on the local politicians. If necessary to do this don't pay your taxes. Let the public treasury run dry and the politicians will come around.' "[7]

Still, Shanks saw reason for hope. Chicago's teachers had provided a worthy model for defenders of taxation. He cited with approval the "pay-your-taxes" slogan that the teachers had chanted at a recent rally: " 'Pay Your Taxes!' Here is a new slogan which might well be broadcast by everyone who is constructively interested in municipal financial problems. The Chicago school teachers, in putting these words on the front page of the metropolitan newspapers, have started something that may mean a great deal to municipal credit."[8]

Shanks moved quickly to put teeth into this proclamation. In less than a month, he convinced the National Municipal League (NML) to form a national campaign to promote taxpaying at the local level. NML placed the endeavor under its Committee on Citizens' Councils for Constructive Economy (CCCE). Adopting the slogan of Chicago's teachers, the new group called itself the National Pay Your Taxes Campaign (NPYTC). Joined by Shanks—who became secretary of the new organization—Thomas H. Reed, the head of CCCE, took over the chairmanship of NPYTC.

At first glance, Shanks's background did not fit him for this new role of civic activist. He was born in Brooklyn in 1891 and in 1914 became a reporter on the *Bond Buyer*, a weekly trade paper devoted to the municipal and state securities market. The *Bond Buyer*, founded in the late nineteenth century by Shanks's grandfather, William F. G. Shanks, remained largely a family affair in the 1930s. An uncle held a directorship on the paper during much of Sanders Shanks's tenure. After joining the staff of the *Bond Buyer*, Shanks moved up rapidly, becoming secretary, treasurer, and with the onset of the 1920s, editor.[9]

More than any other factor, Shanks owed his foray into municipal reform to the dismal state of the municipal bond market. "Today," Shanks wrote in the same editorial in which he praised Chicago's teachers, "the municipal securities market is badly shattered. . . . The city which can sell bonds or notes is today the exception, not the rule. It is no longer 'news' when a default occurs." He tempered this pessimism with the consolation that municipal bonds as a class had declined less markedly than most other investments. Shanks depicted the relative strength of the municipal bond market as "not illogical." Municipal bond dealers, in having a priority claim over the extractive power of government, enjoyed an enviable advantage over their fellow businessmen. Shanks never tired of reminding *Bond Buyer* readers that municipals, unlike other investments, "are actually a first lien on the bulk of the property in the debtor community."[10]

With equal force, Shanks cautioned that the rise of the tax striker threatened to transform this heretofore unchallenged legal privilege into a de facto legal fiction. Frank H. Morse of Lehman Brothers, who, like Shanks, had only recently started to explore the terrain of municipal activism, echoed these fears. "If tax strikes become general," Morse concluded, "we would have in the municipal bond market the equivalent of what happened in 1929 in the stock market."[11]

Shanks gave NPYTC's ads and news a prominent place in the pages of the *Bond Buyer*. Few salesmen could hope for a more receptive audience to hear their pitch. One full-page ad in the *Bond Buyer*, typical of NPYTC's ads in that publication, carried a mammoth headline: "PAY YOUR TAXES!" Under the headline followed three paragraphs of copy, the first three lines of which read: "Municipal bond men do not need to be told of the necessity for paying taxes. Fundamentally their business depends on tax payments. It is for this reason that municipal bond men throughout the entire country should make every effort to encourage prompt payment of taxes by those who can and should pay them promptly." The ad went on to warn against "demands for lower budgets [from which] has come a considerable amount of misleading propaganda urging taxpayers not to pay their taxes."[12]

The close connections that Shanks and the rest of the *Bond Buyer*'s staff had forged with the banking community paid off handsomely for NPYTC. The publisher and president of the *Bond Buyer*, Charles Otis, was also publisher of the prestigious *American Banker*. He guaranteed Shanks an invaluable entrée into the higher echelons of finance. Members of NPYTC's national committee came to include representatives of some of the biggest banks, bond dealers, and investment houses in the country: John S. Linen of the Chase National Bank, Frank Morse of Lehman Brothers, Henry Hart of the First Michigan Corporation, and E. Fleetwood Dunstan of Bankers Trust, who also represented the Investment Bankers' Association of America. The national committee's roster also boasted the membership of David Wood. By Wood's own account, clients of his law firm (Thompson, Wood, and Hoffman) held more than $1 billion worth of municipal, county, and state securities (more than those of any other firm).[13]

Thomas Reed, the chairman of NPYTC, more than compensated for the sparse reform credentials of Shanks and the members of the national committee. He exemplified municipal reform as few other men could. Reed, a veteran of civic-reform crusades dating back to the Progressive Era, possessed that rare combination of experience as a politician and impeccable reform credentials. He was born into a well-off Boston family in 1881 and received his LL.B. from Harvard in 1904. After completing postgraduate work at Columbia, Reed embarked on a long career in academia, first as professor of government at the University of California from 1909 to 1922 and then at the University of Michigan between 1922 and 1936. During the 1920s, he built up a reputation as an authority on municipal government, writing several books in the field.[14]

While in California, Reed threw himself into the stormy world of progressive politics and municipal government. In 1911, he went through a brief stint as executive secretary to Governor Hiram Johnson, a Republican. One year later, Johnson ran as Theodore Roosevelt's vice-presidential candidate on the Progressive third party ticket. As the Progressive Era drew to a close at the federal level, Reed gained his first real taste of administrative experience as a city manager in San Jose, California, from 1916 to 1918. During the 1920s and 1930s, he strengthened his credentials as an expert on municipal government by working as a consultant to a number of local governments. These forays into the hard realities of government do not seem to have harmed Reed's reputation in academia. In the early 1930s, his colleagues elected him chairman of the Committee on Policy of the American Political Science Association.[15]

Reed took a back seat to none in denouncing tax resisters and extremist budget cutters. He liberally peppered his speeches and writings on the subject with words like "hysteria" and "anarchist." While still a professor of government at the University of Michigan in 1932, Reed strongly criticized that state's proposed 15-mill limit on the general property tax. In a speech to delegates at the 1932 convention of the Michigan Municipal League, Reed predicted that the limit "would plunge the state, and every city and village and township and school district in the state, into the most terrible situation of uncertainty and distress imaginable." He faulted the proponents of the amendment for their single-minded strategy of tax reduction, finding it to be "not constructive" and "not . . . statesmanlike." "It is hysterical, it is unreasonable, it is silly to start out on a program of tax reform in Michigan," he charged, "by destroying your present sources of revenue *before you put anything else in place*."[16]

Reed's campaign against those who sought cuts in taxes and spending caught the eyes of NML's leaders, who asked him to chair their new Committee on Constructive Economy. He came still further into the limelight at the President's Conference on the Crisis in Education, in January 1933. When delegates at that conference formed the Citizens' Councils for Constructive Economy (CCCE), they asked NML's Committee on Constructive Economy—and hence Reed—to take over the helm.

Dedicated to a "constructive" alternative to "destructive" budget and tax slashing, CCCE had been formed in response to a suggestion by Carl Milam, the chairman of the American Library Association. The membership of CCCE's central committee read like a who's who of individuals and groups most potentially imperiled by tax strikes and government retrenchment. They included, in addition to Milam, Milton Porter of the National Education Association, Harold Buttenheim, Clarence E. Ridley of the International City Managers' Association, and Louis Brownlow of the Public Administration Clearinghouse.[17]

Reed took care to give academia a major voice on CCCE's central committee. The committee included two prominent administrators, Charles R. Judd of the University of Chicago, and John K. Norton of Columbia University, in addition to Charles Merriam, widely regarded as America's leading political scientist. In all, CCCE claimed a constituency of 15 million people. When Reed united CCCE and NPYTC three months later under his chairmanship, he brought together a potent and diverse coalition that ranged from Bankers' Trust to the National Education Association.[18]

Civic reformers, bureaucrats, and bondholders extolled the values of good government but they also acknowledged other justifications for the alliance. In July 1933, the *Public Administrators' News Letter* praised what it regarded as a trend among bankers and businessmen to abandon the slogan "REDUCE TAXES" in favor of the more constructive "PAY YOUR TAXES." The *News Letter* took full account of the reason for this turnabout. "No doubt," it observed, "the not-too-distant possibility of wholesale municipal bond defaults has had something to do with the wide-spread adoption of this slogan by various banking organizations and business groups."[19]

Reed could not resist the temptation to needle Frank H. Morse of Bankers' Trust good-naturedly when they appeared together on a radio show. After Morse pronounced himself in favor of government reform, Reed exclaimed: "Somebody wake me up. I must be dreaming. Here is a hard-boiled Wall Street banker trying to keep up with the Joneses in municipal reform. Wonders will never cease."[20]

The pragmatic advantages when investors like Morse "get religion" about reform did not escape Reed's notice: "The investor . . . can talk turkey to politicians. 'No reforms, no loans!' What an eloquent speech is that. All the best lectures on citizenship and government pale into nothing along side of it."[21]

It would be hard to find a coalition more free of acrimony than that between CCCE and NPYTC. The banker-dominated NPYTC adopted CCCE's platform in toto and spirited arguments for municipal reform graced the pages of the *Bond Buyer* and the *Investment Banker*. More than a Pollyanna-like enthusiasm for municipal uplift was behind this conversion. As Howard P. Jones, the secretary of CCCE put it, "Holders of municipal bonds are beginning to realize that their chances of getting their money back with interest are decidedly dependent upon the administration of the government that issues the bonds." For all intents and purposes, CCCE and NPYTC amounted to one organization dedicated to a single overriding goal: invigorated tax collections. All parties to this coalition agreed on constructive economy as the means to attain this goal.[22]

Destructive versus Constructive Economy

CCCE's identification with constructive economy may give a misleading picture of its origin. Those who participated in CCCE's formation did not act from a crusading zeal to slash the size of government. Instead, they expected CCCE to stem or rechannel the tide of sentiment for economy then rising across the nation. As outlined by the *Bond Buyer*, CCCE emphasized protection of "the social and educational services of government from further destruction by indiscriminate budget slashing."[23]

When CCCE's supporters spoke of destructive economy, they had something quite specific in mind. According to Simeon Leland, the chairman of the Illinois State Tax Commission, advocates of destructive economy "demand the curtailment of governmental functions and expenditures not only in the hope of minimizing individual tax bills but also in the belief that the scope of public activities can be curtailed. . . . It is directed at the *amount* of expenditure rather than the *services* rendered."[24]

CCCE pledged to fight across-the-board spending reductions as one of the most dangerous species of destructive economy. Edward Hopkinson, the chairman of the Investment Bankers' Association's Committee on State and Local Taxation, approvingly quoted a report that denounced "horizontal and ill-considered cuts in public expenditures made in response to blind pressure for wholesale reduction of budgets." In an article for *Municipality* distributed in pamphlet form by CCCE, Harold Buttenheim denounced the popular and, in his opinion, "ruthless demand that 10, 15 or 25 per cent of the budget be slashed regardless of consequences." William Anderson, a professor of political science at the University of Minnesota, seconded these sentiments. In a pamphlet for CCCE, he upbraided taxpayers' groups that "oppose constructive changes and demand only that taxes be cut, and cut, and cut again." Anderson condemned this approach because it placed government spending on education, health, and relief on the same low level of legitimacy as other government services. Defenders of destructive economy, Anderson complained, could only reiterate their single-minded "boast of every and any cut as a step in the right direction."[25]

To Reed, Buttenheim, and Anderson, anyone who favored the placement of fixed limits on government expansion fell irrevocably into the camp of destructive economy. Thus they set themselves squarely against the recurrent demand of tax resisters that government deflate as fast as the private economy. Buttenheim noted the penchant of the "average citizen" for harping on the relationship between the tax burden and national income. Critics of high taxes, for example, often bolstered their case by pointing out that since 1890, taxes had risen twice as fast as the national income. Buttenheim, who did not deny the accuracy of this statistic, thought such figures "largely beside the point." Turning this argument on its head, he asserted that there "is no proof for the assumption that governmental costs, if honestly and efficiently expended, ought not to increase in greater proportion than the population or the national income."[26]

This distinction was at the core of the debate about destructive and constructive economy. For leaders of CCCE and NPYTC, constructive economy *never* entailed overall reductions or even fixed limitations on taxes and spending. Fred Fairchild, a noted public finance economist and municipal reform advocate, stressed that any reduction in taxes from constructive economy would be "relative not absolute." Fairchild chided cherishers of "the illusion that we are, even at the best, going to have lower taxes." Leland characterized constructive economy as reduction at the margin and not an attempt to "minimize government functions *per se.*" [27]

Local campaigns could draw on a panoply of periodicals and literature published or recommended by the national offices of NPYTC and CCCE. These included two newsletters, the *Citizens' Councils News Bulletin* and NPYTC's occasional *Current Tax Problems.* To these periodicals could be added countless others put out by municipal reform groups and professional organizations. At the behest of CCCE/NPYTC, local groups utilized leading national publications, such as the *National Municipal Review, Municipal Finance, Public Administration, Tax Policy,* and the *Bond Buyer* for ideological ammunition. NPYTC's *Campaign Manual* and the *Publicity Handbook* helped introduce local affiliates to the nitty-gritty of organizing. Basically, the *Campaign Manual* laid out a recommended organizational framework for individual pay-your-taxes chapters. It described ways in which local activists could mobilize the resources of key constituencies in the city. It urged that links be established with organizations representing the following important groups: the city employee, the local merchant, the local banker, the family, and the taxpayer. The *Manual* delineated methods of targeting campaigns to show how tax delinquency harmed specific groups and individuals. As another primary focus, it advised local chapters to form a series of subcommittees including a survey committee, canvassing committee, legislative committee, and publicity committee. The research committee, among its other responsibilities, had the task of uncovering the extent and composition of tax delinquency in the city.[28]

On the basis of this information, the canvassing committee would send a representative from its house-to-house division to approach taxpayers in arrears. The authors of the *Campaign Manual* recommended that the committee should be "the one most representative of all the co-operating organizations." It qualified this statement, however, by suggesting that the house-to-house division might try to recruit unemployed white-collar workers (no explanation for the omission of the blue-collar unemployed) to go door-to-door.[29]

The problem of holdouts inevitably arose. Here the board of interviewers, a division of the canvassing committee, swung into action. The board would call those taxpayers who did not respond satisfactorily to the house-to-house division into "proceedings." There it would talk to them at greater length. In contrast to the representative cast of the house-to-house division, NPYTC counseled that great care be taken when choosing the board of interviewers. It underlined the need to exploit the psychology (a term used often among pay-your-taxes supporters) of the holdout when selecting the board's membership. In the words of the *Campaign Manual*, the board "should include the city finance director or a representative of his office, and the city attorney or one of his staff, as well as several outstanding business men of high integrity commanding universal respect." NPYTC found the board an invariably successful method of motivating payment from holdouts.[30]

Pay-your-taxers knew that any successful campaign needed to make the publicity committee the centerpiece of attention. Organizers of NPYTC believed the publicity committee so crucial that they published a separate booklet, the *Publicity Handbook*, to describe its activities. In the opening section, "Aims of the Publicity Program," the authors of the *Handbook* did not shrink from calling the campaign propaganda, albeit "in the very best sense." More specifically, they depicted it as "propaganda for community action which is necessary to preserve the city's welfare and the future security of its citizens."[31]

The *Handbook* presented a step-by-step media campaign that local chapters could follow. It suggested two major phases: four weeks of preliminary "general educational work," to be followed by a four-week intensive effort. At the onset, the campaign was to be announced over the radio and in the newspapers. The *Handbook* outlined ways of persuading the newspapers to carry serial articles written by city department heads, bankers, and other civic leaders, each explaining how tax delinquency "harmed" their particular fields. It advised pay-your-taxes speakers to make the rounds of various civic organizations and, if possible, draw on their membership to recruit additional activists. The churches also had a part to play. "Get local ministers," the *Handbook* suggested, "to comment on campaign in their sermons on Sunday before campaign begins." Displaying posters and placing billboards in strategic places would complement such oral persuasion. To keep all eyes continually glued on the ultimate goal, authors of the *Handbook* urged the erection of a tax receipts scoreboard and poster in front of city hall.[32]

In essence, the intensive portion of the campaign was a redoubling of these tactics. NPYTC eschewed overt political biases. The *Handbook* stipulated that "political references and controversial subjects should be scrupulously avoided, here as throughout the entire publicity program." The same *Handbook*, however, advised that its local affiliates become involved in a whole series of "controversial subjects," each of which deeply divided the general public. It told public employees to use the pay-your-taxes campaign as an opportunity to point out how cuts in their salaries reduced purchasing power and thus worsened the economy. It also called on campaigners to stress the relative efficiency of government provision of services. In the matter of legislation, the *Campaign Manual*, employing the Illinois Skarda Act as an example, recommended that pay-your-taxers promote draconian, and politically divisive, tax receivership legislation.[33]

Newark: The Sale of the City

Of all the taxpaying campaigns launched in the early 1930s, the "sale of the city" drive in Newark, New Jersey, won the most national attention. For good reason, the 1935 editions of the *Publicity Handbook* and the *Campaign Manual* highlighted it as a model for other cities.

Newark's city government entered the depression in precarious financial shape. Like many of their counterparts in the 1920s, local politicians had increasingly indulged in that questionable, but apparently painless, practice of issuing tax-anticipation warrants. Initially, warrants had a limited expiration date covering only the period between tax levies. In addition to warrants, the city government also issued tax-revenue notes payable from past-due delinquent taxes. Even in the 1920s, all of these practices entailed some risk. Certainly the city's political authorities did not have much reason to take pride in their collateral. The annual tax collections on which city debt depended for repayment hovered around only 80 percent.[34]

The post-1929 collapse and subsequent tax delinquency caught the city government completely off guard. Tax delinquency reached historic highs, going from 25.3 percent in 1930 to 33.3 percent in 1932. Had these uncollected taxes been their only problem, Newark's politicians could probably have adapted to the changed situation without too much difficulty. They could, after all, be reasonably secure in the knowledge that other cities of similar size were contending with even higher rates of delinquency. These facts were insufficient to sway city leaders, however. Their actions only compounded Newark's financial difficulties. While other cities reacted to the depression by cutting back new borrowing, Newark's leaders issued $20 million in long-term bonds in 1930 and 1931. Unmindful of the consequences, they failed to make provisions for repayment. Thus, as Ralph Kloske points out, while "the country headed for the bottom of the depression, Newark had the highest ratio of net-bonded debt to population for any city of its size."[35]

After 1931, the city government, ever on the verge of default, stumbled from one fiscal crisis to another. Relief rolls mounted. Bankers and other investors grew reluctant to keep lending the city money and demanded substantial economies. Public employees, in turn, resisted attempts to impose layoffs and cut salaries. Yet something had to be done to stave off receivership. Finally, in July 1932, city employees agreed to salary reductions ranging from 1 to 15 percent. This belated concession was not enough. Sidestepping further economies or new levies as too politically risky, they chose the path of least resistance—an advertising campaign to collect back taxes. The campaign owed both its inception and its organization to Newark's director of public safety. Dubbed a "sale of the city" drive by its organizers, *Public Management* described the effort as "like the war bond drives" in that "the appeal was to community patriotism, a request to recognize community obligations, plus a reminder that payment of taxes is not voluntary with the taxpayer." Even the advertising trade journal *Printer's Ink* made mention of the campaign. The drive's pay-your-taxes sales pitch had—as this quote from *Public Management* reveals—an almost Orwellian pervasiveness:

> Trolley car and bus riders traveled in cars containing reminder posters. Airplane trailers described sky appeals by which the attention of an entire city was centered through a single aerial stunt. Milk bottles, gathered by housewives in the early morning carried the label, "Have you paid your taxes?" . . . Policemen and firemen were assigned to lists of taxpayers. . . . Telephone girls, otherwise unoccupied, were furnished with lists of taxpayers who received an unexpected prompting when taking down telephone numbers. Uncle Sam's mail service was utilized by the cancellation of every letter passing through the post office with the stamped query as to tax payment.[36]

Although organizers claimed that the campaign increased tax payments by one-third, in the end it turned out to be at best a holding action. Newark's tax delinquency in 1932 increased overall. Moreover, although the drive may have been at least partly responsible for persuading local businessmen to advance loans in late 1932, the threat of default still loomed.

Shattering even these small gains, delinquency climbed to a record 35.2 percent in 1933. In September of that year, Reginald C. S. Parnell, the director of the city revenue department, announced plans for a tax drive to take place in October. Parnell did not refer to the 1932 campaign, but he apparently saw the need to go beyond a mere repetition. He placed the tax drive, unlike its forerunner which had been planned and carried out by the city government, under the control of private citizens. A broad-based privately run campaign, aided by local politicians and bureaucrats, promised to reach a wider audience.[37]

Parnell delivered a pep speech on 14 September to the organizers of the upcoming drive, who took as their name the Citizens' Committee for the Collection of Taxes (CCCT). "The city is facing a crisis," he proclaimed. "I am placing the fate of the city in your hands."[38]

Some of the most prestigious businessmen in the city and state signed up as chairmen of CCCT's committees, including Joseph H. Hurley of New Jersey Bell Telephone, Ronald Jump of the Mutual Benefit Life Insurance Company (cochairman of the educational committee), Elmer Hopper of the Murphy Varnish Company (chairman of the speakers' committee), and advertising executive Morris Scheck (chairman of the publicity committee). Topping off this list, F. Milton Ludlow of the Public Service Corporation, the city government's chief creditor, took charge of a special committee to target the larger delinquents. The drive's other business support was concentrated in the insurance companies. Nationally, and quite probably in Newark, insurance companies owned more state and municipal bonds than any other sector of the economy except for banks.[39]

CCCT forged a remarkably intensive campaign, reaching down to the neighborhood level. It appointed forty-two district chairmen, each assisted by a vice-chairman. The district chairmen directed the activities of nearly 2,500 solicitors of whom teachers, numbering 500 strong, made up the largest contingent. District chairmen supplied their subordinates with lists of delinquent taxpayers. Solicitors were expected to collect a certain number of tax-payment pledges to be followed up later by the city's department of revenue.[40]

Comparisons with the wartime liberty bond drives abounded. Stanley S. Holmes, president of the Newark Chamber of Commerce, even speculated that if "the people of Newark were alive to the consequences of this drive, it would bring more enthusiasm than any of our wartime campaigns did." CCCT's drive also paralleled another effort that invited its own comparisons with World War I mobilization, the National Recovery Administration (NRA). The campaign's slogan, "Don't let Newark down—Pay Your Taxes," complemented the NRA's self-consciously patriotic motif, "We do our part." The linkage could be even more direct. During school exercises for the NRA, teachers implored students to put pressure on their tax-delinquent parents, "to keep the schools going."[41]

The publicity committee—run by a professional advertising executive—demonstrated a keen knack for catching the public eye. It brought the newspapers, who printed "pay your taxes" ads free of charge, squarely behind the drive. The *Newark Evening News*, for example, praised CCCT's campaign as "not only a civic duty but a measure of self-protection." The media reported that clerics in "practically every church in Newark" would, on the Sunday before the drive began, solicit their congregations to pay taxes. One of the few exceptions was the Reverend Marple Lewis of the Washington Baptist Church, who refused his cooperation. Lewis equated the drive with "sustaining political machines." "The pulpit," he asserted, "is not a throne for any ecclesiastical system or a place for over-lord dictatorship, nor is it a place to debate doubtful theories or to air political propaganda."[42]

CCCT staged parades, complete with attention-grabbing gimmickry. One parade featured the services of a police dog, Santa von Schulhaus, who wore a card around her neck reading, "Don't Let Newark Down. Pay Your Taxes." According to the press, Santa, whose mother "saw service" in World War I, recently had marched in an NRA parade. CCCT propaganda flooded the city. Campaigners set out to distribute 5,000 posters, 25,000 placards for store windows, 100,000 buttons, and 5,000,000 stamps for letters and envelopes. In addition, they gave the movie theaters "pay your taxes" color slides.[43]

W. Paul Stillman, president of the National State Bank, cau-

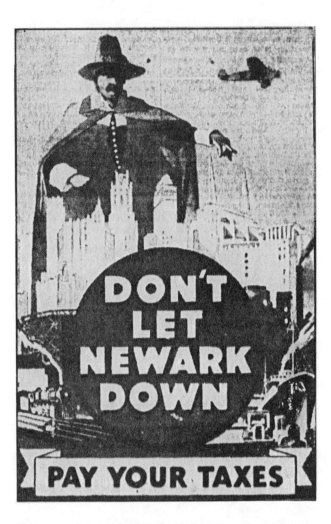

Poster used in Newark's Pay Your Taxes Campaign in 1933 (*Newark Evening News*, 28 September 1933; courtesy Newark Public Library)

tiously hoped that pay-your-taxes propaganda could convince delinquents to pay up. "If the people of Newark would only take time to consider the many services which the city renders to them," he suggested, "they would not withhold the payment of their taxes where possible." CCCT took out newspaper ads that played up apocalyptic scenarios. Each ad pictured a mock newspaper front page from a taxless future. One carried the headline: "NEWARK FIRE DEPARTMENT ABOLISHED FOR LACK OF FUNDS . . . CITY IN CHAOS."[44]

CCCT tried hard to instill guilt in tax delinquents who continued to resist. It branded them as selfish holdouts who sponged off patriotic citizens. Supporters of CCCT compared unpaid tax bills to other forms of debt. "Paying your bills is an old-fashioned virtue," argued Chester I. Barnard of the New Jersey Bell Telephone Company. "It is still a virtue and always will be as long as people want to look themselves in the face in a mirror."[45]

What motivated Newark's willful tax delinquents? Nonpayers sometimes acted out of the belief, often well founded in the past, that holding out would force the city government to reduce penalties or forgive back taxes altogether. Holmes dismissed this hope as a wild dream and warned that anyone who held it would "one day wake up to find that his interest charges on his tax bill make a fancy price for his dream." Implicitly, Newark's politicians had already demonstrated that taxpayers' reluctance could in fact be rewarded. The city government had lowered penalties and had even encouraged CCCT to incorporate the alternative of installment payments as an inducement to tax delinquents.[46]

Other delinquents simply resented the political uses of high taxes and saw resistance as their only recourse. The *Newark Evening News* described such people as believers in the theory that "paying taxes in these times is just sending good money after bad, to be thrown away by politicians." When willful delinquents rejected CCCT's entreaties, the threat of force, always lurking behind campaign publicity, came out into the open. In one case, a resister tore up the identification card of a tax-drive solicitor and ordered him out. Another tax delinquent told a campaigner, "Why should I pay my taxes? Nothing will happen to me if it don't!" In response to these incidents, Parnell issued an icy edict: "In such cases I have asked the tax drive committee to turn over to me the debtor's name and address together with the solicitor's report. When the time comes for stringent action I can promise that these people and any others who express defiance will be singled out for prompt action to the full extent of law."[47]

When the drive drew to a close in late October, CCCT pronounced it a resounding success. Parnell agreed. He gave the highest kudos to the solicitor who "went forth as an apostle of good-will" to build "a new attitude upon the part of the public towards city officials." Approximately 15,000 taxpayers (about 40 percent of those in arrears) signed pledge cards. In monetary terms, these pledges totaled $5 million; exactly the minimum goal Parnell had set at the beginning of the drive. According to the city government, tax payments for October and November ran substantially ahead of collections for the same months of the previous year. Even so, this did not prevent Newark's rate of delinquency from rising above the 1932 level. Only in 1934 did tax delinquency start to register an annual decline, falling to 30.5 percent from its all-time high of 35.2 percent in 1933. Whatever the effectiveness of the drive, it would still be a long time before Newark's city government was able to rest safe from repeated fiscal crises.[48]

Strategies of Persuasion, Coercion, and Reward

Localities across the country repeated Newark's experience. Boston, Massachusetts; Trenton, New Jersey; Columbus, Ohio; Houston, Texas; and Memphis, Tennessee, were only a few of the places that carried out pay-your-taxes drives. With some local variations, approaches employed to convince delinquents to part with their money fell into four broad categories: ideology, the pocketbook, threats, and rewards.[49]

On the ideological front, pay-your-taxers mobilized against the tax resisters' class model. Resisters pictured government as the scene of perpetual struggle between invasive tax spenders and exploited taxpayers. This class framework dated back at least to Locke. In one guise or another, it found expression in the works of Jefferson and his more radical compatriots, Paine and John Taylor of Caroline. Taylor could have been quoting a tax-protest tract of the 1930s when he concluded that "a free form of government cannot last, if heavy taxes continue until the poverty of the payers, and the wealth of the receivers, have separated the nation into two orders far apart. Heavy taxes are both an effect and a cause of tyranny."[50]

In "The Other Side of the Tax Problem," an article distributed by CCCE and NPYTC in their campaigns, William Anderson, professor of political science at the University of Minnesota, tried to debunk the class approach. He described resisters as purveyors of a "render unto Caesar idea of government." According to Anderson, advocates of this approach held that "government and the people are as far apart as the poles, utterly opposed to each other, and that every increase of the power and the activity of government is a burden and an oppression to the people. The government is 'they' as distinct from 'us.' " In place of the class model, Anderson substituted what might be called a cooperative model of government. "It is their [the voters'] government," he asserted, "their organization for co-operative action."[51]

Critics of tax resistance frequently invoked the cooperative model. In a critique of the taxpayers' revolt, the National Education Association's journal *Nation's Schools* characterized government as "social cooperative activity carried on by the people collectively at a much lower cost than would be possible if delegated to the realm of private effort." A writer for the *American City* framed this theory in everyday terms. He portrayed government services as nothing more than community purchases "just as one individual may desire a car or a coonskin cap and thereupon set about to secure it."[52]

The theme remained consistent; only the nuances changed. Frank Morse of Lehman Brothers compared government to a club and taxes to dues, seeing the tax delinquent as a contemptible slacker ignoring the greater interests of the club. This argument overlooked the crucial distinction that club members, unlike taxpayers, could not be forced to join.[53]

More than one prominent foe of tax resistance wondered why taxpayers, often so meticulous about meeting private bills, balked when the tax collector came to call. A writer in the October 1934 issue of *Tax Policy* asked in frustration: "Is it too much to expect of citizens of a great democracy that they shall recognize their governmental obligations and pay their tax bills in as upright and self-respecting fashion as they pay for automobiles and chewing gum?" One of America's leading intellectuals, H. L. Mencken, the editor of the *American Mercury* and a friend of tax revolts, exemplified the perspective which *Tax Policy* criticized. According to Mencken, the average taxpayer did not view government as

> a committee of citizens chosen to carry on the communal business of the whole population, but as a separate and autonomous corporation, mainly devoted to exploiting the population for the benefit of its own members. . . . When a private citizen is robbed a worthy man is deprived of the fruits of his industry and thrift; when the

government is robbed the worst that happens is that certain rogues and loafers have less money to play with than they had before. The notion that they have earned the money is never entertained; to most sensible men it would seem ludicrous. . . . The intelligent man, when he pays taxes, certainly does not believe that he is making a prudent and productive investment of his money; on the contrary, he feels that he is being mulcted in an excessive amount for services that, in the main, are useless to him, and that, in substantial part, are downright inimical to him.[54]

Pay-your-taxers sometimes displayed a kind of Jekyll and Hyde outlook about taxation and government. At certain points, they pictured government as a spontaneous, almost voluntary organization (just like a club or business). This conception of government fit incongruously with their equally persistent demands that force be used against the resister. By positing this analogy between government and voluntarily financed institutions, subscribers to the cooperative model impaled themselves on the horns of yet another argumentative dilemma. Mabel Walker, the executive secretary of the General Welfare Tax League, the publisher of *Tax Policy*, characterized taxes as a "payment for goods and services, just as checks sent to the automobile dealer, the dress shop, the grocery store and the electric light company are." This statement seemed at odds with many others by Walker and allied civic reformers praising the superiority of government over private provision of services. After all, if government was just like private enterprise, what justified its increasing claim on the taxpayer's dollar and the use of force against those unwilling to purchase government services?[55]

Descriptions of government by pay-your-taxers often bordered on what historian Alan Wolfe called "epicanization" or "the process by which political figures, rather than being seen as public *servants*, are transformed into public *heroes*, generally of epic dimensions." Witness these comments from Thomas Reed at the 1932 convention of the Michigan Municipal League: "I believe that government affords the greatest single opportunity that is afforded in modern life for social service, that without a government . . . we can not live modern life. I say that government is a necessity of life, not to be classed with automobiles and radios or with diamond rings and sables, but to be classed with food and sleep and clothing of the necessary sort. We can't do without it."[56]

In addition to ideological appeals, pay-your-taxers used a set of arguments aimed at the pocketbook. The *Campaign Manual* emphasized that the taxpayer must be "made to feel that tax dodging is not only unpatriotic but costly." Foes of resistance hammered home their claim that dollar for dollar, government provided better service than private alternatives. NPYTC recommended that local affiliates use the publicity campaign to highlight how much the typical taxpayer paid for particular government services, like police, and then ask how much it would cost if provided privately. This would show, NPYTC claimed, that the individual taxpayer could never afford private alternatives "no matter how wealthy he might be."[57]

The gist of this argument was that government gave cheaper service because it used cooperative purchasing. Pay-your-taxers never really grappled with the question of why individuals needed the force of government to purchase services cooperatively—especially if the benefits were so manifest. Of course, tax resisters rarely addressed these questions either. As shall soon become clear, resisters could more than match pay-your-taxers in skirting the uncomfortable implications of an ideology.

The constant repetition of market analogies in local pay-your-taxes campaigns tended to cloud the issue still further. A poster used in the Memphis drive featured a smiling man (labeled taxpayer) buying a basket full of goods (each representing a separate government service) from an amiable grocer (labeled city government). Overhead read a caption: "Good merchandise Fairly Priced." Daniel Hoan argued for the superiority of tax-provided services on the grounds that private enterprise engaged in comparably more wasteful duplication. Hoan asked: "Do not six or eight milkmen pass our doors before we arise in the morning? Do not the shop-keepers protest that there are too many stores? . . . Without question there is much more duplication in private business than in government." This argument, although commonly used, failed to address a possible counterargument that private enterprise, unlike government, operated in the context of a competitive market where consumers were free to take their business elsewhere, and were not forced to pay for goods they did not agree to purchase.[58]

Morris Tremaine, the comptroller of New York, maintained that a tax strike would increase the cost of government tremendously by making municipal bonds less marketable. Tremaine estimated that a

Poster used in 1934 for the Memphis Pay Your Taxes Campaign (*United States Municipal News*, 1 October 1935)

tax strike "would double or triple the cost of borrowing money" for local governments. By refusing to pay taxes, he concluded, the "tax striker is really striking at himself by destroying the credit of his municipality, and in so doing, impairing the value of his own real estate and increasing the cost of government." Although this kind of argument had greatest appeal to bondholders eager to keep up the credit rating of their political lenders, civic reformers also took it to heart. The National Municipal League sponsored a scholarship in which it asked high school and college students to answer the question: "My Town—What Can I Do to Boost Its Credit?"[59]

Pay-your-taxers always cautioned that the sanctions of force be credible enough to pose a threat to willful delinquents. E. Fleetwood

Dunstan of Bankers' Trust, chairman of the Municipal Securities Committee of the Investment Bankers' Association of America, looked on NPYTC's efforts as essential "to establish the principle that every citizen able to pay his local taxes should do so, voluntarily if possible, under compulsion if necessary." Advocates of government reform tenaciously clung to faith in the possibilities of efficient administration to solve massive social problems such as tax delinquency. At a time when the depression most severely pinched taxpayers' incomes and property values, Carl Chatters, the executive director of the Municipal Finance Officers' Association, could still maintain that "the failure of tax-collecting officers to perform their duties . . . must be set down as the most common and most inexcusable cause of local real estate tax delinquency."[60]

With the breakdown of traditional procedures like the tax sale, new techniques of coercion had to be developed. The *Campaign Manual* touted the selective foreclosure of a few flagrant cases as always having "a wholesome effect on other tax delinquents." It also urged local campaigners to seek laws denying business and professional licenses to delinquents and to obtain the help of mortgage holders who had an interest in their property. Daniel Hoan pioneered with one of the more ambitious innovations when he created Milwaukee's Division of Tax Enforcement, with 175 employees.[61]

Conditions in the depression era also necessitated that these new forms of coercion be coupled with a new set of selective inducements. Most tax experts recognized the limits of blanket or overly severe applications of force. Public finance economist William Shultz pointed out the utter futility of laws allowing delinquents to be jailed, which were still in force in certain New England states. Shultz and other leading experts based their objection to criminal penalties on practicality rather than morality. According to Shultz, "Juries persistently refuse to convict a person indicted for tax evasion, when such conviction would make him liable to a jail sentence, feeling that the punishment is too severe for the offense."[62]

Experts and reformers frowned on nonselective remission of penalties even more than on draconian severity. The *Campaign Manual* warned that a recent spate of cancellations of tax penalties threatened to destroy the morale of taxpayers and stimulate "the hope that future laws will be passed giving even more concessions." In 1936, Wade S. Smith of NML recalled that in the early part of the decade legislatures had granted a "mass of indulgences undermining the morale of the taxpayer who pays promptly while extending to delinquents, without distinction as to their real needs, every opportunity to continue delinquent under the pleasantest circumstances which can be devised."[63]

Smith blamed this trend on public hysteria and the legislative lobbying of real estate and taxpayers' associations "generally lacking in knowledge of tax theory." Carl Chatters called it a vicious tendency that began in 1931 and reached high tide in 1933. By the end of 1933, twenty-one states had lowered or canceled penalties and some had reduced the principal. Furthermore, many other states had extended redemption periods and postponed tax sales.[64]

Tax experts feared that if penalty rates dipped as low as the going interest rate, taxpayers would see delinquency as a cheap way to "borrow" money temporarily. Taxpayers who engaged in this practice did so with the intention of paying off their penalties before the expiration of the redemption period (usually two or three years after the initial delinquency date). As historian Robert P. Swierenga has demonstrated in his book *Acres For Cents*, this practice had a basis in precedent. In the late nineteenth century, Iowa's taxpayers lapsed intentionally into temporary arrears, prompted by tax penalty rates that ran at or under interest rates in the private credit market.[65]

Although pay-your-taxers expressly rejected penalty reduction, they embraced other inducements to delinquent taxpayers. Many local tax drives incorporated installment payment of taxes into their campaigns. The installment method had much to recommend itself. Howard P. Jones of CCCE liked this method because taxes broken down into monthly payments "wouldn't hurt so much." Nor did the installment plan have the mark of an untried innovation. By the late 1920s, the practice had become familiar to a large segment of American consumers. Most of all, advocates liked the discretionary aspect of installment payments. Unlike uniform penalty reduction, only those taxpayers willing to pay could participate. To encourage installment payment of taxes, pay-your-taxes campaigners in Memphis, Newark, and many other localities followed the example of Chicago and formed taxpayer clubs. Residents of Memphis could, for example, open a club bank account in which they would pay taxes in ten equal installments. In return, the bank would issue the taxpayer a receipted tax bill along with a 1.5 percent discount in reward for prompt payment.[66]

Robber Barons, Anarchists, and Slackers

Inducements and sanctions were complemented by strategies to discredit tax delinquents. Pay-your-taxers often depicted the average delinquent as a rich and selfish businessman. E. Fleetwood Dunstan charged that "it is the large taxpayer who is most guilty of the delayed payments." The *National Municipal Review* concluded that "in general, it is the big fellow who isn't paying his taxes." Usually, subscribers to this view based their conclusions on studies showing that in many localities, vacant lots made up the single largest proportion of tax-delinquent parcels of property. For example, Carl Chatters blamed vacant property for being a primary cause of tax delinquency. Leonard White, America's leading authority on public administration, bolstered Chatters's allegations by quoting statistics on the vacant lots in St. Petersburg, Florida.[67]

Proponents of the vacant lot theory frequently cited a voluminous study of real estate tax delinquency completed by the U.S. Bureau of the Census in 1933. The study—which included a detailed breakdown of tax-delinquent properties in a number of leading urban areas—revealed a median delinquency of 31 percent for vacant property against 18.2 percent for single-family dwellings. A simple reading of these statistics fostered a misleading impression, because (as in Detroit) vacant lots usually accounted for an insignificant portion of total tax collections. Nothing very malevolent was behind the high percentage of delinquent vacant parcels. It was merely another legacy of the collapsed building boom of the late 1920s.[68]

Unfortunately, we know comparatively little about how much, in monetary terms, different categories of property contributed to tax delinquency. The U.S. Bureau of the Census study, for example, never addressed this question. What we do know from the few local studies conducted during the period counteracts the stereotype of rich tax dodger. Ironically, Carl Chatters, before he took on the role of pay-your-taxes activist, had tried to discredit this caricature. Writing in 1930, Chatters, then director of finance for Flint, Michigan, observed that tax delinquency in his city "is common to all classes and that probably the greatest amount of unpaid taxes in dollars and cents is represented by houses falling within the valuations of $1,000 to $4,000—in which group would be included the homes of most of the working people and middle class people of the city." A study of tax delinquency in Detroit found that the "delinquent tax sale is but a cross-section of the general tax roll—there is no one group more than any other responsible for the delinquency."[69]

Nonetheless, pay-your-taxers invariably asserted that significant numbers of taxpayers, regardless of economic class, could but would not pay taxes. An editorial in the July 1933 issue of the *National Municipal Review* may have voiced a view extreme among tax experts (although not by much) when it claimed that the majority of tax delinquents "in most communities can pay if they will." The same editorial writer speculated that a "check-up would certainly show that most delinquent taxpayers continue to run their automobiles and attend the movies and to do a thousand and one other things that cost money but which may be far less essential than keeping the local government going."[70]

Tax delinquents were also accused of being unpatriotic or lacking in civic loyalty. To Chatters, for one, the percentage of tax collections in a community was "a composite index of its civic pride." Historian William Leuchtenburg has described how backers of the New Deal often invoked wartime language and analogies. Following Newark's lead, the "analogue of war," as Leuchtenburg calls it, became a fixture of the pay-your-taxers' lexicon. The *Campaign Manual* stressed emulation "of the 'war psychology' publicity of the World War, when the enthusiasm of the whole nation was centered upon a single aim." Chatters hoped for a day when "the delinquent taxpayer becomes as unpopular as so-called 'slackers' were during the World War. The citizen who tries to break down government in peace time by organizing a tax strike is a greater enemy to civilization than many who conscientiously avoided war service." In answer to the "merciless and universal" attack on government, Clarence A. Dykstra, the city manager of Cincinnati and a popular figure among civic reformers, praised taxes as "sinews of war with which we fight the battle of those who believe in law, order, decency, public health, sanitation and welfare." Harold Buttenheim extolled "martial virtues and the impelling force of wartime patriotism" as one way to undermine tax resistance and other societal ills.[71]

These appeals had an interesting corollary. Like their compatriots in Chicago, pay-your-taxers elsewhere usually assailed tax resisters for inciting anarchy. A 1934 issue of *Tax Policy* recalled that in 1933 partisans of the taxpayers' revolt had put forward "anarchistic and lawless proposals for deliberately withholding taxes." Charles

Merriam also detected the black flag of anarchy in the crusade of the tax resister. "There is no one, with the exception of the professional anarchist," he wrote in an article for *Minnesota Municipalities* in 1932, "who really wishes to be entirely rid of organized government. But the attitude of many persons who are carrying on a crusade against waste in governmental expenditures is exactly the same as those who are against all government."[72]

In their use of the anarchy analogy, pay-your-taxers unintentionally followed in the footsteps of Revolutionary Era psychologist Benjamin Rush, who discussed societal "diseases" like "anarchia" (an excess of liberty) and "revolutionia" (Toryism). Like Rush, they repeatedly applied the terminology of mental illness to mass social phenomena. In 1933, a report of the American Municipal Association entitled "Anarchy through Economania" claimed that "there are a great many people with whom the need for economy has become such an obsession or mania that they have become violent and destructive opponents of all government . . . anarchists or as they are now called economaniacs." According to the report, economania, once a minority view, had with the depression become the manifestation of popular hysteria. If not stopped, the association feared, this trend would "destroy the progress of decades," as embodied by the expansion of government since the Progressive Era.[73]

There was more to allegations of anarchy than rhetorical hyperbole. To be sure, even the most extreme of tax strikers would have rejected the association out of hand. For the most part, they saw themselves as productive citizens and pillars of the community. Yet, the anarchy analogy had a certain logic that tax strikers could not easily dismiss. By tax refusal, they had implicitly challenged the ultimate basis of state power: coercive taxation. Without such power, the state would, as pay-your-taxers pointed out, cease to be a state. In this vein, Henry Traxler observed in his article "Why Pay Taxes?" that "they [tax resisters] are destroying the faith of a people in government. To destroy the faith of a people in government is to destroy the very government itself."[74]

To drive home this point, opponents of tax resistance painted a decidedly unflattering picture of an imaginary world with greatly reduced or nonexistent government. They presented this low tax or anarchist world as the inevitable culmination of tax strikes and destructive economy. The American Municipal Association (AMA) challenged the tax resister: "Try sending a messenger across the continent with a letter for three cents! . . . Try buying your own roads!" *Nation's Business* editor Merle Thorpe, and a few other "economaniacs" had, in fact, seriously argued for privatizing the U.S. Postal Service and certain other government functions. AMA dismissed schemes for privatization as absurd, and saw it as self-evident that only government could provide these services. An article in the *National Municipal Review* ventured an especially alarmed prediction about life without taxes: "Water would cease to flow from faucets. Sewer pumps would stop. . . . Millions of school children would roam the streets. Criminals and lunatics would break from their cells."[75]

The specter of anarchy evoked by Reed, Merriam, and others bore but faint relation to the anarchism of Kropotkin, Emma Goldman, and Alexander Berkman. In the shorthand of the pay-your-taxers, anarchism translated into an excess of rugged individualism or as Harold Buttenheim put it, the fruition of "the 'lazy fairy' method." In essence, they objected to a form of individualist anarchism. Ironically, this strain of anarchism, which had been represented in the nineteenth century by the likes of Benjamin Tucker and Lysander Spooner, had, by the 1930s, gone into almost total eclipse.[76]

Not only tax strikes but other forms of resistance, like the tax limit, evoked analogies to anarchism. Shortly after voters in the state of Washington approved a 40-mill limit in 1932, the *National Municipal Review* published an article entitled, "Taxpayers Strike in Washington." According to a resolution of the American Municipal Association, tax-limitation laws threatened the very existence of government. Reed predicted that a tax-limitation amendment then on the ballot in his own bailiwick of Michigan would "plunge the state into virtual anarchy."[77]

During the first three years of the depression, good-government reformers were caught off guard by a wave of tax resistance and "destructive economy." Since the late nineteenth century, they had grown accustomed to regarding the urban political machine as their major nemesis. Now, an unprecedented taxpayers' revolt necessitated a temporary change in emphasis. New strategies and alliances had to be forged to deal with the threat that tax resistance posed to the municipal-reform and rationalization edifice that they had taken so long to build. By the end of 1933, municipal reformers had largely agreed on what these strategies should be. Along with other critics of the tax revolt, they put into place a plan of counterattack. Resisters could tap existing anti-big-government attitudes in American society and often, but not always, had the advantage of popular support. Against these advantages civic reformers matched three decades of professional expertise and commitment to a strong (and legally unrestrained) taxing system. As we shall see, these could be powerful weapons when deployed in the fight against tax resistance.

CHAPTER 6

Selling the State through Radio: "You and Your Government"

In late 1932, a coalition of municipal reformers, academics, and government employees took to the national airwaves to sell the virtues of a far more active state. From 1932 to 1936, these groups cooperatively produced a radio series entitled "You and Your Government." Thomas H. Reed, the head of CCCE and NPYTC, was yet again the central player. He brought additional good tidings to these groups through a third organizational hat he wore. He chaired the Committee on Civic Education (hereafter referred to as the Committee) of the National Advisory Council on Radio and Education (NACRE). NACRE had been formed in 1930 with financing from John D. Rockefeller, Jr., and the Carnegie Corporation to promote educational programming. The Committee traced its genesis to an offer of free evening air time by John Elwood, educational director of the National Broadcasting Company (NBC). Elwood put only one restriction on the offer: NACRE had to use the slot for a radio show on civic education.[1]

To discuss Elwood's proposal, NACRE leaders met in November 1931 in the boardroom of the Carnegie Corporation. There they formed the Committee and selected Reed, then head of the Committee on Policy of the American Political Science Association, as chairman. The executive committee, also elected at the meeting, had a leftist and civic-reformist bent. Members included historian Charles Beard, socialist educator George S. Counts, Albert Meredith, chairman of the American Council on Education, Charles Merriam, and Murray Seasongood, the former reform mayor of Cincinnati. Seasongood was also president of the National Municipal League (NML).

Except for the nebulous requirement to promote civic education, Reed had carte blanche over the choice of speakers and format.[2]

With Reed at the helm, "You and Your Government" offered CCCE and NPYTC an invaluable publicity outlet. Committee literature repeatedly billed the series as "Impartial, Non-Partisan Broadcasts." In the *Listeners' Handbook*, the Committee assured readers that the "addresses will not be propaganda for any theory, cause, party, or 'ism.'" The programs did fit the nonpartisan mold: the Committee counted members from both parties among its leadership, and Reed, despite his enthusiasm for the New Deal, classified himself as a "good old Massachusetts Republican." The selection of program topics, however, cast doubt on the pledges of impartiality.[3]

The initial installments of "You and Your Government," which ran from April to November 1932, concerned the upcoming general election and included a good mix of speakers from the Republican, Democratic, and Socialist parties. After the election, evenhandedness became a much rarer commodity. We should not be surprised by this apparent schizophrenia. The programs after Series I focused on the local and state issues that the Committee's leaders *cared* most deeply about. To them, controversies of a federal and partisan nature took a back seat at least until the mid-1930s.

Even some of the titles in the series—"Constructive Economy in State and Local Government" and "Constructive Economy," to name two—meshed uneasily with the claims of impartiality by the Committee. Much the same can be said for titles of individual programs. These included "Tax Dodging by Constitutional Amendment" (a critique of constitutional tax limitation), "Tax Paying Made Easier," and "Taxation for Prosperity" (a defense of increased taxation).

In its retrospective on "You and Your Government," *Four Years of Network Broadcasting*, published in 1936, NACRE grouped the 270 people who had appeared in the series into the following categories: 97 as academic and quasi-academic persons, 94 as public officials, and 79 as business and professional. Well represented were people whose careers were linked closely to maintaining a steady flow of tax collections.[4]

The academics who appeared were generally not strangers to government service and civic reform. Reed, of course, was a veteran of these pursuits. Professor Joseph H. McGoldrick of Columbia University, one of the more frequent guests, not only had been active with NML but also had served as comptroller of New York City. Harold W. Dodds, the president of Princeton University, was a former president of NML. Charles Merriam had once been a city alderman in Chicago. Professors Fred Fairchild, Simeon Leland, and several other guests had served on tax commissions.

Academe had an obvious claim to participation—this was, after all, an educational series. The predominant civic-reformist and leftist perspective also had a certain logic. In a speech before NACRE, for example, NBC journalist William Hard tried to answer potential objections. He pleaded guilty to accusations from conservative elements that the speakers on "You and Your Government" leaned to the left but claimed extenuating circumstances. "The radio company," he declared matter-of-factly, "is not concerned. Under its theory of operation, it takes the American academic world as it is. . . . It has no 'responsibility'—except that of lending facilities of utterance to American academic thought as America itself has formed it."[5]

Again, in light of the mission of civic education, the heavy representation accorded political officialdom made perfect sense. In contrast to academics and professional government officials, who lined up against tax limitation and reductions in tax penalties, a considerable number of politicians supported such measures. West Virginia's far-reaching tax-limitation law, for example, won the backing of the Republican and Democratic candidates for governor. Ohio's tax limitation, though no less controversial, received unequivocal support from the incumbent governor and three former governors.[6]

These facts could have easily escaped the attention of anyone who relied exclusively on "You and Your Government" for education on taxation issues. Not one of the politicians and bureaucrats in the series spoke up for tax-resistance causes like tax limitation, the election rather than appointment of assessors, or reduction of tax penalties. Those politicians who addressed these issues on "You and Your Government" supported NML's goals of civic reform and rationalization.

The professionals and businessmen on "You and Your Government" further fortified the perspective presented by the other guests. Of the nineteen businessmen who appeared, nine were bankers, most specializing in various facets of municipal lending. Four of the other businessmen came from the insurance industry, which, as mentioned previously, owned more municipal bonds than any other single class of business except banks. Like the show's other guests, these businessmen fully supported NML's political program.[7]

From the beginning, the series drew criticism both from executives at NBC and from listeners. After surveying a list of upcoming "You and Your Government" speakers, a disgruntled NBC executive penned a confidential memo to educational director John Elwood. It read in full: "Practically all of these people live off tax money, why not give the 'guy' who pays a chance?" Howard P. Jones, the secretary of the National Municipal League, read a similar letter over the air from a listener: "From your radio talks I have formed the opinion that you are more interested in the tax eater than in the taxpayer. The tax striker's method may be a crude way of getting what we want, but I can see no other way by which America can be kept a government by and for the people."[8]

These complaints contained more than a grain of truth. Nowhere in the series appeared leading critics of high taxes like Adam Schantz, head of the National Association of Real Estate Boards' Committee on Taxation; Merle Thorpe, editor and publisher of *Nation's Business*; or Robert McCormick, publisher of the *Chicago Tribune*. Their absence made questionable the committee's pledge that "speakers have been selected for their ability to set forth the theory and practice of government irrespective of party argument or political creed." Thomas Reed, one of the two authors of this statement, constantly reiterated that taxpayers' leagues grew like mushrooms during the depression. Nevertheless, though he controlled the booking of speakers, not one representative from a taxpayers' organization appeared on the "You and Your Government" show.[9]

No elaborate conspiracy theory is needed to explain this. Reed was quite candid about the protaxation slant of the series. In his 1932 report to NACRE, Reed promoted "You and Your Government" as an effort to preserve America's endangered democracy from the menace posed by the taxpayers' revolt. He singled out a proposed law to limit real estate taxes that was then on the ballot in his home state of Michigan. Although Reed portrayed the limitation as "the most destructive kind of folly that could possibly be proposed," he sullenly, and accurately, foresaw that it would be approved hands down by the voters "because the hysteria of the people over their tax burden is so excessive." For these reasons, he trumpeted "You and Your Government" as a wonderful opportunity to channel sentiment for economy into constructive ends. "We can't," Reed warned, "leave it to the ignorant movement of the mass of people who feel sore and hurt, but do not know exactly what it is that has hurt them. We have to give it intelligent direction." Reed made it quite clear that these statements represented not only his own opinion but that of the Committee in its official capacity.[10]

Was Reed consciously deceptive in pledging objectivity in one breath and then, in another, trying to sell "You and Your Government" as a crusade against the tax revolt? Probably not. By all indications, Reed did not view these two approaches as contradictory. He was from an old-school progressive tradition that supported the special role of the expert in government. Unlike previous generations of reformers, Reed owed most of his credentials in municipal reform to university training. If anyone had a claim to the title "municipal expert," it was Reed. Given his training, it was second nature for him to conclude that the findings of the scientifically trained expert had a legitimacy above the bromides of novice tax resisters. Because the experts condemned tax-resistance measures, there was, in Reed's view, no further possibility of productive debate. Thus, at the pinnacle of the taxpayers' revolt in 1932, Reed could make this recommendation to NACRE: "How can we do that better [forestall tax resistance measures like the limitation] than by a group of political scientists, let us say, formulating a program of reform. They can readily agree as to what substantial reforms should be made in state and local government. These are *not controversial questions* in any real sense of the word."[11]

Reed could not see the sense of refighting old battles. To him, the progress of civilization had long ago refuted the old anti-big-government doctrines. An expanding democratic government, which he believed by its nature to be beneficent, and civilization depended on each other. He simply could not understand why tax resisters held to a philosophy that, to him, seemed so irrelevant to the modern age. The people guided by expert opinion now had the tools, namely the powers of government, to solve age-old injustices. Given this outlook, it should be no surprise that he asked, Why be afraid to use them? Reed took it for granted that the facts gathered by experts demonstrated the need for more government. It was only a matter of educating the public.

Reed could scarcely have asked for a better vehicle than "You and Your Government" to carry forward this message of civic reform to ordinary Americans. Broadcasts ran every Tuesday evening from 8:00–8:30 P.M. (eastern standard time), truly a prime-time slot. Less than a year later, much to the consternation of the Committee and NACRE, NBC moved "You and Your Government" up to 7:15–7:45 on the same evening. Nonetheless, though a bit jarred by the time change, the producers never complained that the network had "shunted [them] into an 'inconspicuous' time." Even with the change in time, the show had the enviable position of following the highly popular "Amos 'n' Andy."[12]

According to CCCE, most of the production expenses for the series came out of the pockets of the same investment banking group that underwrote and led NPYTC. Due to NBC's generosity, the cost of the airtime itself, worth over $1 million during the run of the series, presented no obstacle. Besides sending out regular advance stories to the newspapers, NBC tried to persuade affiliates to carry the show. This raised a few difficulties, because many of the local stations could, and often did, sell this valuable airtime to local advertisers. Despite this handicap, "You and Your Government" enjoyed a wide national market. At its peak, over forty stations, mostly members of NBC's blue network, carried the series. The program reached markets in key urban areas including New York, Chicago, Boston, St. Louis, Baltimore, Cleveland, Los Angeles, and New Orleans.[13]

Beyond this, NBC drew the line on sinking further money into promoting, or paying for, the programs. This reluctance arose partly from a natural inclination to shift depression-strained resources into profitable operations. Of equal importance, many in the network distrusted the motives of NACRE and the committee. Their suspicions went beyond those already noted about the tax-spending biases of those organizations. Many of these critics looked on NACRE and the Committee as a Trojan horse intent on fostering government control of radio. They argued—with much accuracy—that support for private ownership of radio broadcasting among most NACRE and Committee members ranged from lukewarm to nonexistent. Though he usually portrayed himself as a believer in private ownership, Levering Tyson, the chairman of NACRE, alienated many NBC executives by heaping praise on government-owned operations like the BBC. At the same time, he found little good to say about the efficacy of private broadcasting and charged that it fostered "blatant and nauseating commercialism."[14]

When NBC switched the time slot for "You and Your Government," Tyson warned that it courted disaster with influential members of his organization. In a letter to Richard C. Patterson, the executive vice-president of NBC, Tyson declared that the network could "not afford to treat such people in that manner. Broadcasting's position in this country at present is not overly secure." He noted that because of "You and Your Government," many influential members of the Council who had supported government ownership had become convinced that "the American system is and can be workable." Now, according to Tyson, NBC risked the undoing of this precarious good will. "It will be perfectly apparent to these individuals," he suggested, "that American radio will always be relegated to the pure [sic] commercial, and that all the public service for which the medium itself gave such promise is mere bunk."[15]

If NACRE and the Committee wanted to promote "You and Your Government," they knew that the onus lay on them to come up with the necessary resources. In this undertaking, they had the good fortune of being able to draw on the talents of a myriad of well-placed organizations. Reed persuaded many allied groups to carry ads for the series in their newsletters and distribute program information to members. The United States Office of Education also became involved. It informed 18,000 school superintendents about the series. This cooperation brought additional publicity because many teachers required group listening among their students. Often, these teachers incorporated "You and Your Government" into the curriculum and asked students to write essays.[16]

No group gave more help than the National Municipal League. NML cosponsored every show after Series V and printed and distributed transcripts in book form. In all, over 1,200 groups and individuals cooperated in this campaign to distribute transcripts. This did not even include the broadcasts reprinted in NML's publication, the *National Municipal Review*. CCCE and NPYTC, operating out of the offices of NML, benefited immeasurably from this consolidation of effort. In fact, many of the transcripts distributed by NML contained the imprimatur of CCCE opposite the title page.[17]

Pay-Your-Taxes Players

The Committee exploited this publicity opportunity to the fullest. It tried hard to make the shows accessible and entertaining to ordinary citizens. In one of the segments, the Committee went so far as to present a play, "A Voice in the Dark." In *Four Years of Network Broadcasting*, NACRE described the broadcast as an effort "to encourage taxpaying, constructive as contrasted with indiscriminate economy, and the formation of the Citizens Councils." The cast of characters included Levering Tyson, who played the mayor of a fictional town, and Howard P. Jones, the secretary of CCCE, who, appropriately enough, acted the part of an agitator from the citizens' councils.[18]

The plot centered around a running debate between the Mayor and the Voice, played by "You and Your Government" announcer Alois Havrilla, over what to do about the problem of tax dodgers. The Voice, who represented the Association of Evicted Unemployed, blamed tax delinquency on the wealthier taxpayers of the city. "From the viewpoint of public welfare," the Voice advised the Mayor, "there's no discernible difference between the gangster who ignores criminal laws and the tax dodger who does the same thing with a different set of laws." Needless to say, the Mayor did not dispute the validity of this comparison. The Mayor did, however, seem disturbed when the Voice criticized him for hiring political cronies in order to win votes. The play climaxed with the formation of a citizens' council, the inference being that it would expose the tax dodger and, at the same time, recommend needed reforms for the city.[19]

Besides Jones, the founding members of this local citizens' council included the Voice and a patrolman, who came complete with an Irish brogue. Though later judged a sorry performance by NACRE, at least a few members of citizens' councils praised the play highly. "The skit hit our situation so well," wrote an unidentified "citizen of a small town" to the *Citizens' Councils News*, "that I want to use it. Our Schools could run the rest of the year if one party alone would pay his past and present taxes, and he is able to do so—runs [*sic*] hotel, restaurant, movie, etc. and is president of the Taxpayers' Association of this county."[20]

The Committee did not repeat its brief foray into drama. The other programs, though presented as roundtable discussions or interviews, were similarly, if less obviously, well prepared. Before each show, the discussion leader, usually Reed, sent out an outline to the guest speakers who then, in turn, prepared their own material. The leader then revised the submissions and refashioned them into dialogue. After that, the guests, reading from the script, which had been retyped for them on individual cards, went through two rehearsals before the show aired. According to Reed, "By this careful preparation a greater appearance of spontaneity can be given to a discussion than by allowing relatively inexperienced radio speakers to try to be extemporaneous."[21]

While Reed primarily justified advance scripting as necessary to give the programs polish, it had other virtues. The guests on "You and Your Government" shared a common ideological dedication to "constructive economy" and invigorated tax collections. Boosters of the program, like Katherine Ludington of the National League of Women Voters, completely missed the mark. Ludington, whose organization sponsored several shows, portrayed the "You and Your Government" format as one "in which both sides of a subject are presented simultaneously while the program-producing organization itself remains strictly neutral." Though ideological unanimity between guests and producers was a boon in certain respects, it could also make for deadly dull programming. Advance scripting solved this problem by creating debates and controversy where they heretofore had not existed.[22]

One of these choreographed debates, "Reducing the Public Works Budget" (changed to the rather incompatible "More Money for Public Works" when reprinted in the *National Municipal Review*) was broadcast in September 1933. In reality, the participants, Donald C. Stone, representing the Public Administration Service; Carl Schneider, the president of the International Association of Public Works Officials; and Alfred E. Roche, the commissioner of public works for Troy, New York, all supported more spending on public works. Essentially, the debate consisted of Schneider and Roche arguing in favor of expanded public works while Stone acted as a devil's advocate for the contrary point of view. A less discerning listener may have believed Stone to be a genuine opponent of increased public works, especially since the panelists did not see fit to indicate otherwise.[23]

At the onset, Stone lambasted public works in terms befitting a tax resister. "Everyone knows," he told his copanelists, "of the inefficiency of government and the crooks that are in office. Do you recall the old saying 'The politicians loaf, but the public works?'" For the rest of the show, Stone played the part of the flustered economaniac checkmated at every turn by the superior arguments of the opposition. Stone brought up examples of graft and scandals in public works that he had read in the newspapers while Roche and Schneider parried that such stories did not represent the norm. As Roche put it, "The public doesn't know of the long hours many of their officials put in after closing time. Scandal is news, Stone; hard conscientious work is not a subject for headlines." He also argued that dollar for dollar, citizens received more from taxes than money spent on other purchases. Schneider defended public works in almost Keynesian terms detailing to Stone the countercyclical advantages to be reaped from increased appropriations. He counseled Stone that "we haven't taxed enough in the past, taking the country as a whole. We have saved too much." As the debate closed, Stone confessed that, as a result of these arguments, he had been converted over to the opposition: "I am beginning to see that I may have been wrong in my demand for reducing public works services . . . perhaps we may *save* by spending *more* through our public works departments. As the old saying goes, we cannot afford to be penny-wise and pound-foolish."[24]

These and many other "You and Your Government" broadcasts concentrated on winning over the public to the goals of NPYTC and CCCE. "You and Your Government" further tied together the local affiliates of these two organizations into a common ideological network. Both NPYTC and CCCE promoted group listening and acted as conduits for disseminating program transcripts. In its first year of operation, CCCE distributed a grand total of 390,000 pieces of campaign literature, including 350,000 transcripts of "You and Your Government" programs. Most of all, "You and Your Government" gave added respectability and legitimacy to the goals of NPYTC and CCCE. It made it easier for people like Reed to picture these organizations as transcending petty political debates at the local level. "You and Your Government" helped those who wanted to narrow the debate over economy and taxation to a "constructive" parameter. Similarly, it served to consign the numerous advocates of radical reductions in spending and taxes (and tax strikes) beyond the bounds of respectable discourse.[25]

CHAPTER 7

The Doldrums Set In:
The Decline of the Tax Revolt

By the end of 1933, the effectiveness of the tax-resistance movement had started to wane. Writers on the tax revolt in publications for municipal reformers and government employees had adopted a new upbeat tone. The focus had shifted noticeably from the previous siege mentality. Howard P. Jones applauded what he saw as a reversal in citizen psychology. He observed that from " 'How can we cut the cost of local government?' the question has been turned to 'How can we keep local government going?' "[1]

Even Reed, ever the dour pessimist about the tax revolt, praised the return to "saner and sounder views." To him, this portended a broader shift in the taxpayers' conception of government. "There is less talk than a year ago," he commented with satisfaction, "of taxes being a mere drain on the community's resources . . . and of government being a necessary evil to be reduced to the lowest terms." William Allen White, the editor of the *Emporia Gazette*, encapsulated the reborn self-assurance of supporters of good government. He acclaimed signs that the day of the amateur resister had passed. "The term 'tax striker,' " White wrote, "is not so popular as it was three years ago, and tax cuts are coming to have an unpleasant connotation."[2]

Most of all, civic reformers extolled the winning of new allies from the business community. According to the *National Municipal Review*, "The tide is turning. Conservative business and financial leaders are lining up on the side of the maintenance of essential local governmental services as opposed to indiscriminate cutting and slashing. 'Pay Your Taxes' has become the slogan and symbol of the passing of hysteria." Welles A. Gray, of the finance department of the United States Chamber of Commerce, spoke for this new breed of businessman. In 1932, Gray delivered a crowd-pleasing speech to the convention of the International Association of Comptrollers and Accounting Officers. He branded the tax strike as "too dangerous a weapon for any group to invoke" and inveighed against taxpayers' groups who wanted "to solve the budget problem with an ax." He urged local businessmen to steer clear of these extreme policies and cooperate with local officials. Gray emphatically endorsed the interventionist state. "They [tax resisters and destructive budget reducers] forget that many public services and functions which were unnecessary, or perhaps not thought of even as little as ten years ago, are today absolutely indispensable."[3]

These words would have been anathema to businessmen like Merle Thorpe, the editor and publisher of *Nation's Business*, the official organ of the Chamber of Commerce. He represented the dwindling hard-core anti-big-government wing of the organized business community. Thorpe often quoted the radical Jeffersonian dictum "That government is best which paves the way for its own resignation." The praise he heaped on the tax revolt (although he stopped short of backing tax strikes) made him a bane to reformers.[4]

Despite the confident proclamations from good-government elements and their business allies, the "destructive" side of tax revolt could not be completely disregarded yet. The successes of the tax-limitation movement carried over from 1932—albeit with reduced force. During 1932 and 1933, sixteen states and numerous localities adopted property tax limitations. An additional three states put homestead exemptions on their statute books. In 1935, Jens P. Jensen, a prominent public-finance economist, recalled that during these years in "proportion to efforts made [for tax limitation] the batting average had been high."[5]

The NAREB's national committee on real estate taxation fostered the homestead exemption movement. For its day, the NAREB's campaign to exempt all homes under $5,000 was a brilliant strategy to win over middle-class voters. Municipal reformers sensed as much and attacked this new form of tax protest vigorously. *Tax Policy* characterized homestead exemption as part of "a racket that is sweeping the country." Strangely, the homestead exemption movement did not really gain momentum until after the tax revolt's climax in 1932. The NAREB would have probably enjoyed still greater success had it latched onto the exemption strategy in 1931 or 1932.[6]

With the onset of 1934, Adam Schantz maintained that the number of states adopting the overall limitation, the most radical species of tax-rate restriction, would double in number from the current seven. Later events did not bear out his prediction. Voters rejected four proposed overall limits in 1934. Not one was approved at the statewide level. Mitigating these losses somewhat, three states enacted homestead exemptions. In addition, the electorate in the state of Washington voted to extend the overall limitation adopted in 1932.[7]

The years 1935 and 1936 put to rest any doubts about the trend away from tax revolt. Of over 100 limits proposed in 1935, only three became law—none of the restrictive overall variety. A writer in the *National Municipal Review* accurately summed up the tax-limitation movement's successes in 1935 as negligible. He also asked with hopeful caution, "Is it a warranted conclusion that the tax limitation epidemic has lost its virulence?" Any lingering doubts of good-government reformers were assuaged when voters defeated five out of six limitations in 1936. Three states enacted homestead exemptions but these proved more a feeble last hurrah than the start of a new offensive.[8]

The Federal Role

Federal policy helped to undermine those limitations still on the books. The Public Works Administration (PWA), headed by Harold Ickes, led the way. Under PWA rules, a locality had to put up 55 percent of the construction cost for a project to get federal financing. Since most projects required long-term borrowing, the PWA made federal funds contingent on the provision of reasonable security by the local government. Localities "hampered" (a term used often by PWA officials) by strict debt and tax limitations found it difficult to get loans.[9]

The PWA's legal division went out of its way to help local politicians evade or otherwise circumvent limitations. Frequently, the PWA's lawyers drafted the model legislation for these purposes. The legal division recommended that local and state governments seeking to sidestep limits resort to two methods in particular. First, it promoted the creation of authorities able to borrow money or issue bonds outside the stipulations of local limits. Secondly, the PWA touted (and greatly speeded a trend towards) the use of general revenue bonds. These were bonds which local governments could float for "self-sustaining" projects. When all else failed, the PWA manipulated its loan policy to exert pressure on local governments. It used a local tax-limitation law in Cleveland as a basis to restrict loans for public works. The PWA also, for a time, refused money to Indiana because that state operated under a stringent real estate tax limitation.[10]

In 1935, Harold Ickes evaluated the PWA's role in opening up loopholes in tax and debt limitations. He recalled that "endless as these obstacles [debt and tax limitations] seemed to be, the staff managed to overcome them or get around them, and each time a new obstacle was encountered a new way out was discovered by those who were determined to drive the program through." The American Municipal Association, a leading good-government opponent of limitations, wasted no time in utilizing the PWA's good offices. In 1933, it appointed a special committee to cooperate with the efforts of the PWA's legal division to weaken tax and debt limitations.[11]

The receding tax delinquency rate paralleled the decline of the tax-limitation movement. After reaching its zenith, 26.3 percent in 1933, the rate of uncollected taxes for all cities over 50,000 in population dipped to 23 percent in 1934. Thereafter, it continued to ebb slowly and steadily. Tax-collection revenue rose in every region of the country.[12]

Many of the pay-your-taxers were quick to claim credit for the downward trend in tax delinquency. The *National Municipal Review* outdid itself: "Surely we have travelled far since the drinking song of Robert Burns' day, 'The De'il Fly Away with the Exciseman.' It must be a relief to one invaluable but sorely tried branch of our public service to feel that the Lord is on the side of the tax collector at last! . . . Who ever dreamed that a time could come when paying your taxes would appeal to the imagination?" Doubtless, pay-your-taxes campaigns told part of the story—but it is impossible to say how much. The general nature of the decline, encompassing many states and cities without such campaigns, points to the contribution of other factors. Even many pay-your-taxers carefully noted this.[13]

They extolled a reversal of the trend toward granting "indulgences"—such as postponement of penalties—to delinquent taxpayers. Reed, for instance, applauded the end of the "sentimental orgy"

of eased laws. For pay-your-taxers, the drive toward tougher legislation was more than a simple holding action. It meant going on the
offensive. They succeeded in getting major laws enacted with teeth
in them, such as the Skarda Act, to punish delinquents by imposing
tax receiverships. The *Municipal Finance News Letter* spoke for most
tax reformers when it predicted that the act "should effectively break
the Chicago tax strike." To spread the word, the *News Letter* reprinted
the full text of the law. Within a year, Iowa, New Jersey, Ohio, and
other states had adopted receivership laws explicitly modeled on the
Skarda Act. Subsequent experience, at least in Illinois, did not bear
out the enthusiasm for receiverships. The receivership proved a
costly and ponderous device that invited corruption and abuses of
power. It worked best as a scare tactic. Even this soon wore off when
tax delinquents came to understand the difficulties of enforcement.[14]

The "carrot" strategy probably did more to bring in additional
collections than the punitive receivership. At the beginning of the
depression, the installment method of tax collection had still to reach
the experimental stage. By 1933, it had become commonplace.[15]

The upturn in the economy ranks as the most obvious factor in
improving tax collections. The beginning of a slow improvement in
the real estate market by 1933 also should be stressed. Beneath the
simple rubric of economic recovery lay the hand of the federal government. It would be hard to overemphasize the importance of federal policies.

The Home Owners' Loan Corporation (HOLC) filled a role in
stemming tax delinquency analagous to that of the PWA in undermining tax limitation. The HOLC was established in 1933 to subsi-
dize homeowners by providing low interest mortgage loans. The law
creating the corporation included an amendment, added at the behest of good-government reformers, to advance real estate owners
immediate cash loans to pay off back taxes. Loans could be given in
cash only for tax payments and repairs. The HOLC amortized repayment of these loans over a fifteen-year period at 5 percent interest.
As a condition for getting *any* loan, a borrower was required to use
part of the money to clear all outstanding tax arrears. Between 1933
and 1935, the HOLC lent over $200 million for delinquent taxes, all
of which flowed into state and local treasuries. An average of 7.4
percent of every dollar lent went for this purpose.[16]

In 1935, Lehman Brothers polled 106 city governments asking
for their explanation of the downturn in tax delinquency. The ma-

jority of respondents cited the HOLC's loans more than any other single factor. Thirteen listed it as the only reason. David Hoan typified the enthusiasm of urban politicians when he lauded the HOLC for its "invaluable help in reducing tax delinquency." Almost immediately after the passage of the act, NPYTC incorporated the HOLC's loan program into its campaign repertoire. NPYTC's *Campaign Manual* urged local chapters to coax delinquents by pointing out that loans from the HOLC would be available upon payment of back taxes. The HOLC brought down tax delinquency in two ways. It improved the economic condition of the delinquent, thus motivating payment. In addition, it tied the delinquent's fortunes to the state. Resisters found no place in the HOLC's loan program.[17]

The HOLC, and later the Federal Housing Administration (FHA), also helped undermine tax revolt more indirectly. Between 1933 and 1935, the owners of one-tenth of all nonfarm owner-occupied residences obtained HOLC mortgages or other loans. Historian Kenneth T. Jackson has demonstrated how the selective loan policies of the HOLC and the FHA speeded suburbanization, racial segregation, and the depopulation of the inner city. Federal housing policy left another legacy. Intentionally or not, it quieted taxpayers' discontent by defusing the conditions that bred rebellion. Those homeowners who were major beneficiaries of government largesse had little reason to bite the hand that fed them. The HOLC's programs, in effect, co-opted the potential leaders of tax-resistance movements. The real estate industry staffed many of the agency's local offices and virtually monopolized its appraisement services. Additionally, the HOLC usually assigned the management of defaulted properties to real estate firms.[18]

Co-opting Resistance

In 1931, economist Richard Ely wrote, "Every real estate organization in the United States finds in taxes a paramount interest, foreshadowing everything else." By 1933, this statement was no longer completely true. Issues of federal policy, like the HOLC, had begun to replace, and by the middle of the decade, supersede taxes as a policy concern for the organized real estate industry.[19]

Writing in late 1933, H. L. Mencken—no friend of taxation—evaluated the weakening of tax rebellion. Although he did not specifically mention federal housing policy, his comments could have aptly served as a description of the HOLC's impact on resistance. He recalled the earlier years of the depression when the "taxpayer, confronting the appalling cost of interest and amortization, began to yell for relief; worse, he began to refuse to pay his tax bills. . . . There ensued a sort of reign of terror for public job holders." Mencken maintained that the New Deal or "this new doctrine that every freeborn American deserves his whack at the public treasury" had coopted tax resistance and budget cutting. "That nightmare," he concluded, "is now over, and politicians believe in God again, and if not in God, then at least in the New Deal. It has delivered them."[20]

Another reason for the erosion of tax resistance may seem at first paradoxical. Arguably, the tax revolt had brought relief to some taxpayers. The relief was largely limited to general property taxes. The percentage of the national income devoted to state and local taxes fell from 16.6 in 1932 to 12.3 in 1939. Real estate owners had always borne most of this burden.[21]

Other evidence demonstrated that even for payers of general property taxes this relief was quite hollow. First, for taxpayers in general, including many who owned real estate, federal tax increases canceled out reductions at the local and state levels. Taxes at all levels of government took 21.5 percent of the national income in 1932. After a brief but slight decline, the percentage rose again to 19.9 in 1939. Never again would the low taxes of the 1920s be repeated— or even approximated. At the end of the decade, even local and state taxes had doubled their predepression share of the national income. According to these statistics, tax resisters completely failed to achieve their objectives. At best, they held off even greater tax increases.[22]

When the conditions that gave rise to resistance were mitigated, the internal weakness of the tax-revolt movement provided the coup de grace. Resisters lacked a strong ideological rudder. True, they shared a general suspicion of the centralized and expansive state. Simeon Leland, a member of the Illinois Tax Commission and a former staff worker for the Strawn Committee in Chicago, exaggerated only slightly when he characterized the tax revolt as "in part, the product of an individualism which desires to deflate government on the ground that public expenditure is necessarily unwise—a belief which harks back to the days when Say expressed the notion that government expense is a loss to society. . . . Such an attitude has roots in early American traditions where opposition to taxes without representation was really objection to any taxes at all." Merwin K. Hart, of the New York State Economic Council, linked his group's campaign for tax reduction to the struggle for "individualism, as opposed to collectivism." He pictured the council as a defender of "the right to hold property," calling it "one of the most sacred of human rights." The *Washington Taxpayer* recalled that before the adoption of Washington's real estate tax-limitation law, "with the deadly certainty of creeping paralysis private ownership of property was being made an impossibility by the insidious but sure method of constantly increasing taxation." Beyond these general precepts, the resistance program (if it can be called such) lacked depth and specificity.[23]

The tax rebel of the 1930s focused almost entirely on limiting the means of government expansion. Many resisters believed that restricting the government's power to tax would *by itself* bring reduced government. They paid almost no attention to the question of ends. Resisters often waffled and contradicted themselves when it came to proposing specific alternatives to those government programs put in peril because of tax limitations. The *North Dakota Taxpayer*, for example, editorialized against state and local governments' accepting "free money" through federal aid projects as "robbing Peter to pay Paul." Apparently not aware of the inconsistency, the *Taxpayer* published another editorial supporting federal enactment of the Missouri River Diversion program. With some exceptions, resisters lacked a clear societal vision, not to mention a transition program to achieve that vision.[24]

Resisters did have the raw material for a transition program. Nathan MacChesney, for example, publicized a sophisticated critique of the cult of the expert. Adam Schantz showed a highly perceptive understanding of the political economy of bureaucratic expansion. Resisters, in general, advanced a persuasive, if undeveloped, class analysis of tax spenders versus taxpayers. Perhaps these and other ideas could have been the building blocks for a more cohesive ideological vision and ends-oriented program. The potentialities, however, remained unexploited.

For a time, instigators of the tax revolt could justly claim success in achieving a series of short-term goals to relieve the taxpayer. Until 1933 and 1934, they won enactment of numerous tax-penalty abatements and tax limitations at both state and local levels. The label short-term (short-term in the sense of not leading to overarching long-term goals) merits emphasis. Pay-your-taxers had a good case when they assailed the vagueness of their adversaries' ultimate objectives. Resisters were long on calls to slash spending but they never really formulated concrete examples of where and how this could be achieved. The Washington State Taxpayers' Association, for instance, lauded tax reductions made possible by the passage of the real estate tax-limitation initiative. When the time came for suggesting specific spending cuts, however, it emphasized two rather cosmetic proposals: an anti-nepotism bill and legislation to restrict the use of government-owned automobiles. Unlike some latter-day foes of the interventionist state, the leading lights of the tax revolt in Washington State and elsewhere failed to develop specific proposals for privatizing government services. Amorphous calls to abolish fads and frills and government extravagance had limited mileage. The weakness of such a superficial stance often came back to haunt resisters after the enactment of tax limitations and homestead exemptions. Almost invariably they shied away from the opportunity to put forward proposals about what services of government should and could be reduced.[25]

Resisters did not deserve all of the blame for these ideological and strategic shortcomings. By and large, they were political novices. Most of the tax-revolt organizations sprang up, often on an ad hoc basis, during the depression. Rapid growth produced side effects including political naïveté. "Taxpayers as a group," conceded Lawrence Holmes, Schantz's colleague in the NAREB's tax-limitation campaign, "are not shrewd political strategists. Their opposition usually is." Resisters had neither a national organization to coordinate their efforts nor even a clearinghouse for the exchange of information. Try as it might, the NAREB never filled this void. As a trade organization for realtors, it could never have more than a limited influence over the disparate organizations representing taxpayers. To be sure, the NAREB's property owners' movement enjoyed some success. This too had limits. The division's close relationship with the NAREB restricted the effectiveness of populist appeals to the average taxpayer.[26]

The Expert and the Amateur

Municipal reformers and their allies in government, by contrast, had long track records of activism in issues related to government. The National Municipal League, the premier reform organization, dated back to 1895. Many of the state leagues and professional associations for government employees traced their origins to the Progressive Era. During the 1910s and 1920s, a long list of universities, including Stanford and the University of Chicago, established programs of public administration. These programs enshrouded the old doctrine of municipal expertise with a cloak of academic prestige.

The founding of the Public Administration Clearing House (PACH) in 1930 provided an information exchange service for the leading good-government and municipal professional organizations. The PACH, itself a member of CCCE, included representatives from the American Municipal Association, the Municipal Finance Officers' Association, and the American Public Welfare Association. Not surprisingly, resisters came up short when they faced what historian Kenneth Fox has called this extensive "network of individuals, organizations, university programs, research bureaus, and private consulting firms."[27]

Owners of real estate might be so hard pressed during a crisis like the depression as to be driven to confrontational—even illegal—forms of rebellion. When prosperity reappeared, however, these erstwhile rebels invariably returned to the more immediate demands of their careers. For civic reformers and other pay-your-taxers, on the other hand, the distribution of tax money was a central question during both good times and bad. They had an ongoing interest in stable tax collections. Good-government advocates and municipal professionals not only had superior organizational experience and resources—they had much more. Unlike most resisters, they had a highly developed philosophy of municipal government and a programmatic strategy to implement it. Simply put, those who led the fight against resistance *knew* what they wanted. Merle Thorpe lamented this barrier. "The development of a class consciousness among those who constitute the personnel of the public service," he observed, "is at once easy to understand. How to make 120,000,000 people tax conscious is one of the most important issues of our day."[28]

To make sense of the tax struggles of the 1930s, it behooves us to explore the worldview of advocates of good government. "Constructive economy" and civic-reform ideology were of a piece. The tenets of the constructive economy program had been part and parcel of municipal reform since the turn of the century, including merit hiring, centralized purchasing, consolidation of overlapping governments, and elimination of elective offices. On the surface, these goals seem to have been first and foremost procedural—namely, to perfect the machinery of government. A closer look reveals a larger agenda: expanded spending on welfare, public health, and schools, and more regulation to protect the "public interest." Achievement of any of these would be impossible without an efficiently functioning government.

Reformers had convicted the boss and the seeker of radical tax and budget cuts as guilty of the same crimes. The machine's greatest sin had been inefficiency. Inefficiency, reformers believed, led to weakened government. A former alderman and key leader of Chicago's clean government element, Charles Merriam, saw no hope for building "an effective government on the sands of the spoils system." More specifically, people like Reed and Merriam preached against the machine not only because it fostered corruption but because it stole scarce tax dollars from the constructive side of government. Resisters, they claimed, did the exact same thing—albeit in a different guise.[29]

The American Municipal Association and the National Federation of State Leagues of Municipalities phrased it succinctly in a joint report. They charged that across-the-board salary reductions coupled with the "popular tendency to assign to public employees the role of villain in the tragedy of present economic conditions" destroyed the incentives behind the merit system and thus perpetuated the machine. According to a speaker at the 1932 convention of the International Association of Comptrollers and Accounting Officers, an emphasis on tax and budget rollbacks led to a "tendency to *drive out, and keep out*, those individuals who are best qualified to govern well, and too frequently invites in the inefficient, spoilsman, grafters and racketeers."[30]

The doctrine of the expert had a pivotal place in the constructive economy program in particular and reform doctrine in general. Historian Samuel P. Hays long ago noted that trust in the highly trained and nonpartisan expert lay at the root of municipal reform ideology during the Progressive Era. "Progressive professionals," observed Arthur S. Link and Richard L. McCormick, "tended to equate justice with the application of their expert methods, both because of the specific benefits conferred and because scientific techniques seemed inherently impartial. . . . No progressive trait has been more enduring than the tendency to entrust experts with social controls in the hope that they will achieve for us what Lippmann called 'mastery' over the forces of change." If anything, this faith in expertise reached new heights in the early 1930s. Municipal professionals and reformers belonged to a general consensus that the expert needed a free hand to carry out the mandates of government rationalization. The machine had interfered with the expert by encouraging cronyism. The resister did it by placing limits on government through budget and tax reduction.[31]

Charles Merriam warned that "hurried hacking at budgets with dull axes in inexperienced hands will not take the place of scientific planning in terms of modern science and social ideals, conducted by America's greatest talent." During the crest of the tax revolt, an article in the *Oklahoma Municipal Review* deplored the fact that the expert had been a target of tax reduction campaigns. "The average citizen," it observed, "notes with satisfaction that teachers' pay has been slashed . . . that policemen and firemen will receive no pay that week and that great numbers of them are being fired. 'Serves them right,' he exults, 'they're all a bunch of crooks and grafters; they ought never to be paid.' In his mind there is no distinction between the politician and the technician."[32]

Defenders of political expertise had never found taxation policy a pliable object of reform. Despite their best efforts, the elected local assessor remained the mainstay of the system. Much to the annoyance of reformers, resistance to professionalism made sense to the average assessor, usually a part-time official. Voters put a premium on lower taxes and cared little whether their assessor had mastered the finer points of the assessment manuals prepared by the professionals. *Tax Policy*, the journal of the civic-reformist Tax Policy League, reflected its readers' disapproval of the amateur assessor: "The ballot box is a poor gauge of a man's fitness to appraise property. Too often it merely reflects his leniency in overlooking taxable wealth."[33]

Since tax reformers could not abolish elected assessors, they did the next best thing. They sought to check the assessor's power through the use of a state tax commission. By 1931, the vast majority of states had created tax commissions, often at the behest of municipal reformers. Employment opportunities in great number opened up for the still relatively small corps of public finance professionals.

Many leading academicians in the field, including Harold Groves of Wisconsin and Robert Murray Haig and Simeon Leland of Illinois, were able to put theory into practice as members of tax commissions.

By the 1930s, tax commissions could be counted on to stand as bulwarks against tax-resistance campaigns. The commissions strongly opposed the movement to put constitutional or statutory limits on taxation. Adam Schantz, the leading spokesman for limitations, accurately observed that tax limitation "is damned by most state tax commissioners. . . . It is applauded by a mass who owns property." The Illinois Tax Commission put aside nonpartisanship and threw its weight against a proposed statewide real estate tax limitation in 1934. In a special report published by the commission, member Simeon Leland sounded the tocsin against the proposal. He wrote, "All of those interested in the continuance of adequate public services or in the welfare of governments should unite to oppose this [tax-limitation] movement—a movement led, incidentally, by those having a vested interest in the reduction of property taxes."[34]

As a tax commissioner, of course, Leland arguably had his own vested interest to defend. Opposition to tax limitation, however, had roots which coexisted with and often transcended crude self-interest. The academic and civic-reformist backgrounds of people like Leland, Reed, and Merriam encouraged an ideological mind-set against politically imposed restrictions on government's tax-raising power.[35]

Tax Policy, for example, described constitutional tax limitations as the result "of popular clamor rather than of expert opinion." One seeks in vain to discover kind words from the recognized experts in academia, much less in good-government circles, for statutory and constitutional restrictions on taxation. Public finance texts of the period uniformly denounced tax-limitation laws. Indeed, the authors disparaged any attempt to write taxation principles or procedures into state constitutions. This opposition to constitutional restraints on taxation extended to uniformity clauses (requiring property to be assessed and taxed at the same rate) and by the early 1930s also included proposals to exempt homesteads from taxation. In his text *Public Finance*, Harley Lutz spoke the conventional wisdom about public finance when he recommended, "The best constitution is that which makes no reference to methods or forms of taxation, leaving these subjects wholly to the will and discretion of the legislature." In much the same vein, *Tax Policy* proposed that state constitutions should contain "only one brief reference to taxation, to-wit, 'The Legislature shall provide by law for a system of taxation.' The electorate that is afraid to trust its representatives and must hedge them about with all sorts of constitutional restrictions deserves no sympathy."[36]

Good-government reformers who staunchly defended constitutional limits to protect freedom of the press stridently objected when resisters tried to impose analogous restrictions on the taxing power. The intensity of opposition seems hard to reconcile with the fact that almost all tax reformers conceded that real estate owners paid an excessive percentage of the total tax bill. The answer to this riddle becomes more apparent when fuller account is taken of the overall philosophy of most tax experts.[37]

Civic reformers believed that the tax expert, because of superior training, deserved a completely free hand. In his comments on a proposed tax limitation in Michigan, Reed bluntly concluded: "We have got to take and cut the unnecessary things out from among the necessary things, and it takes a skill and understanding to do that. It can't be done by some taxpayers' organization, which has sprung up over night and headed by some individual in the community who never took any interest in government before. It has to be done by the trained public servants of the community. . . . It is an operation which must be gone at with the skilled surgeon's knife." *Tax Policy* complained that under some limitations there "seems to be little left for local budget-makers to do and budget-making becomes an empty gesture."[38]

To the modern reader, this doctrine may appear rife with antidemocratic implications. Good-government reformers did not see it that way. As heirs of the Progressive Era, they regarded experts in government service as neutral agents of democracy, well equipped because of their training to carry out the collective will of society dispassionately and efficiently. The voters, through their elected representatives, had hired experts. Hence, it would be a needless waste to prevent these officials from using their years of training to the fullest advantage.

The good-government advocate looked on public administration as a scientific discipline subject to unbiased and predictable rules of operation. Merriam asked, "Must we conclude that it is possible to interpret and explain and measurably control the so-called natural forces—outside of man—but not the forces of human nature?" Given their philosophy, it is easy to understand why good-government reformers perceived tax resisters—and others who wanted to restrict the expert's autonomy—as spokesmen for a pecuniary, fanatic, or misinformed special interest. In their view, the trained government official was a scientist, who, like all scientists, functioned best if left unhindered.[39]

In particular, Reed, Merriam, and others found it hard to comprehend the tax-limitation movement's profound distrust of what economists Geoffrey Brennan and James Buchanan called the "in-period" (or the period of government operations between elections) political process. Good-government reformers always insisted that public officials deserved a free hand in the in-period. To be sure, the taxpayer had a legitimate role to play, but it was as voter (and perhaps informal advisor) never as policymaker. Tax protest leaders like Adam Schantz came under attack precisely because they sought to constrain government during this in-period. To Schantz, the tax limitation fulfilled "the SAD (yes, I mean sad) need for the people to protect themselves by constitutional mandate when elected representatives no longer serve them."[40]

Thus, though reformers usually agreed in theory that real estate owners paid an excessive percentage of local taxes, they viewed with still greater alarm the prospect of a permanent closure of the tax planner's flexibility through legal limitations. "The imposition of maximum rates for any particular tax," wrote Brennan and Buchanan in language that could describe the fears of tax reformers during the 1930s, "will result in a diversion of fiscal pressures toward those taxes that may not fall under the rate limit constraint. However, any rate limit on one tax from among the allowable set available to government must reduce the total revenue potential collectible by government from the whole set." Moreover, replacement taxes took time to enact and entailed a whole set of sometimes insurmountable political obstacles. At least in an embryonic sense, resisters understood this issue. Merwin Hart predicted that if New York passed a real estate tax limitation, the "state in its efforts to find the [replacement] money, will meet such resistance from every group it proposes to tax that people will at last understand government is costing far more than they can afford. Real retrenchment will then begin."[41]

Tax experts did not want their options narrowed by tax limitation. If a replacement tax had to be enacted, they wanted a leading part in planning and implementing it. Harold D. Smith, the director of the Michigan Municipal League, clearly summarized the perspective of civic reformers on the timing of replacement taxes: "It would seem to be a much better approach to relieve the burden on real estate by *first* securing new sources of revenue. It appears that the minority groups advocating tax limitations at this time cannot be constructive in their point of view and first advocate new sources of revenue because this would seem to be inconsistent with their policy of tax reduction." Smith's characterization fit Schantz's views perfectly. Schantz unfailingly advised resisters to avoid talk of replacement taxes until after the enactment of a real estate tax limitation.[42]

Smith, however, greatly overestimated the consistency and depth of the views espoused by resisters in general. Most of them lacked a well-thought-out philosophy of either taxation or strategy. They showed an even weaker grasp of the spending side of the equation. Because the promoters of the tax rebellion had nothing remotely resembling a think tank, they turned by default to groups like CCCE for research, rationale, and facts. As CCCE's founders had envisioned, the strategy of co-optation proved a powerful weapon against the tax rebellion.

The Lure of Good Government

The constructive-economy approach offered temptations that taxpayers' organizations found hard to resist. A frontal attack on specific government services brought with it predictable political risks. Promoting the efficient *delivery* of these functions, on the other hand, was a different story. Who could object to reducing waste and getting more bang for the buck? Even a Socialist like Daniel Hoan found little to challenge in such goals. If constructive economy was, at least in the short run, the path of least resistance, in the long run, it helped cripple tax revolt. What may have been safe politically proved uninspiring to potential recruits. Even under the best of circumstances, not many people could be expected to charge the ramparts for centralized purchasing.

Only a few supporters of tax rollbacks and reduced government understood the strategic disadvantages of the constructive-economy approach to achieving these goals. One of the more thoughtful and exceptional was journalist Garet Garrett, a writer for the *Saturday Evening Post*. Until his death in 1954, Garrett fought a continuing rearguard struggle against the mounting power of the state. In June 1932, he addressed the economy question in a highly perceptive piece, "Insatiable Government," for the *Saturday Evening Post*. Garrett scrutinized the issues at hand with a penetrating and, despite his very real biases, dispassionate style.

Garrett pointed to an apparent paradox. Logic told him that those groups dependent on government would also be the most eager to expand its power. Yet the facts seemed to tell a different story. "The higher you go," he discovered, "the more sympathetic the representatives of government are to the taxpayer's demand for economy in the budget and efficiency in the bureaus. They move his mind that way. If he is wanting facts, or examples, or propaganda, he will be supplied with them by the representatives of good government themselves—by the good-government bureaus and by the municipal leagues supported by government."[43]

On closer scrutiny, Garrett discerned no contradiction at all. He noticed, first of all, that the good-government economizers picked their targets selectively. Primarily, they went after the political machines. Crusades against the boss helped the good-government cause in two ways, according to Garrett. First, these campaigns had always been popular and thus more effectively channeled proeconomy sentiment away from attacks on the "good" aspects of government. Secondly, and equally important, reducing the power of the machine set the stage for still greater government expansion. Garrett downplayed the "predatory, parasitic, more or less shameless forces" of political corruption as contributors to the growth of the state. "Corrupt government," he argued, "tends to limit and defeat itself. It is much easier to extend what we call good government."[44]

Garrett emphasized that, second only to rooting out the machine, municipal reformers wanted to centralize local government. Advocates of good government usually justified the abolition of duplicative local government as an economy and efficiency measure. Centralization, they often claimed, would cut costs and thus reduce taxes. Garrett rejected this argument as a delusion. Centralization may have led to efficiency of service delivery but it also speeded the expansion of government. "Such competition [among local governments]," he wrote, "is embarrassing and unscientific from the common point of view of government seeking revenue. It is well known that a cow milked by a few expert hands in a regular manner will give more milk than the same cow milked in a haphazard manner by the neighborhood." Efficient and streamlined delivery of services only made the extension of government more palatable to the voters.[45]

Garrett bemoaned the decline of American individualism, associating it with the spread of statism. Nevertheless, true to the observational tone of the article, he steered clear of detailed advice as to alternatives. Garrett did warn believers in low taxes and low spending that they could never get smaller government through good-government economizing. He maintained that the only effective way to achieve permanent economy, that is to halt the growth in spending, was to propose the elimination of government services instead of merely focusing on modes of delivery. Putting exclusive emphasis on perfecting government efficiency "will be only like pruning the tree, for lustier growth hereafter, unless we settle what public credit is for in principle and limit in a drastic manner the ferocious growth of government."[46]

Time and again, the literature of municipal reform and public finance confirmed Garrett's diagnosis. Promoters of "constructive economy" repeatedly emphasized that their program would facilitate extension of certain services of government. As the Tax Policy League put it, "Constructive economies are always desirable, as thereby the tax money of the citizens may provide a greater range and higher grade of community services." Appearing on a "You and Your Government" program, Harlow S. Person, of the Taylor Society, used words that could have been culled from Garrett. Person compared constructive economy to pruning a tree. "All government activities and expenditures are certain to increase," he asserted, "for which reason pruning in all its aspects is all the more important."[47]

Garrett disliked the good-government version of economy because it diverted more anti-big-government forms of resistance into safer (from an anti-tax-revolt perspective) channels. A cursory reading of civic-reform publications discloses this strategy as a guiding purpose of groups like CCCE. *"Turn public interest into constructive channels,"* implored the lead sentence of a joint report put out by several organizations including the American Municipal Association, Municipal Finance Officers' Association, and the International City Managers' Association. The minutes of the Executive Committee of CCCE illustrate the depth of this strategy: "Fear was expressed that influence [in the local Citizens' Councils] might get into the hands of the wrong group. The danger was, of course, present elsewhere—for instance, it was far from advisable in some cases for the taxpayers' groups to be the instigators of Citizens' Councils. Prof. Reed thought that the Committee should adopt the guiding principle that the impetus for starting Citizens' Councils for Constructive Economy should come primarily from the cultural and social groups and that the taxpayers' group should come in as cooperators. Mr. Milam added to this thought that the interest should be in social and cultural forces *and* good government."[48]

Although sentiment for tax revolt had largely waned by 1935 and 1936, the organized part of the movement lingered on for a few more years. According to an in-depth study by *Tax Policy*, there were still 1,159 taxpayers' groups around the country in 1938. Massachusetts alone had 200 local associations linked by a state organization, the Massachusetts Federation of Taxpayers Associations (MFTA). *Forbes* placed the membership of all the Massachusetts groups at 125,000.[49]

Repeated defeats of tax limitation, and the virtual disappearance of tax-strike talk, belied the superficial signs of organizational health in the tax-protest movement. The programs of taxpayers' associations increasingly steered clear of controversy. Sylvia Porter (later of investment management fame) found that taxpayers' organizations in 1940 emphasized unsubversive questions like the prices "of sewage pipes, and paper clips." The remnants of the tax revolt did not greatly trouble the officers of the National Municipal League. In 1936, NML voted to shut down CCCE on the grounds that (according to the league's biographer) the need for "combating harmful reduction of expenditures" had passed.[50]

World War II nearly extinguished the remaining organizations. In Massachusetts, for example, the number of local associations had declined from 200 to a mere 40 by the mid-1960s. During and after the war, the MFTA, originally a clearinghouse for the local groups, gradually abandoned efforts to retain a mass following. It became a quintessential exponent of constructive economy and embraced the "positive," that is interventionist and expanding, state. The MFTA (now called the Massachusetts Taxpayers' Foundation) still exists, but it operates primarily as a nonpolitical research group and rarely gets involved in lobbying.[51]

Other states and localities duplicated many attributes of the Massachusetts experience. If anything, the descent in tax-resistance fortunes elsewhere seems to have been more precipitous. Like the MFTA, the state groups that still survive long ago purged their programmatic agendas of "destructive" tendencies. Holdovers from the 1930s include the Wisconsin Taxpayers' Alliance, the Minnesota Taxpayers' Association, the California Taxpayers' Association, and the New Jersey Taxpayers' Association. Several of these groups that were started as "destructive" became "constructive" and now are purely research and nonpolitical organizations. By and large, they only faintly reveal their tax-revolt origins.

In 1932, Murray Seasongood asked, "Shall this [taxpayers'] sentiment be mobilized and directed toward an intelligent and discriminating economy which preserves the good while eliminating the bad . . . and actually makes government better, or shall it be left under uninformed or fanatical leaders in the newly-discovered cause of economy to . . . destroy essential services, and bring government itself into contempt?" Leaving aside Seasongood's value judgments, ensuing events confirmed his hopes and Garrett's fears. The forces of "constructive economy" had won.[52]

CONCLUSION

The taxpayers' revolt of the 1930s should not be dismissed as a fluke, aberration, or simple response to the stimulus of the depression. The United States not only originated out of a tax strike, but another tax strike—the Whiskey Rebellion of the 1790s—produced the new nation's first serious crisis. Resistance to high taxes has appeared under a variety of economic and social conditions. The tax-protest campaigns of the 1970s, for example, were not born of depression or even deflated real estate values. Although the precipitating role of the depression was crucial, it tells only part of the story.

The tax resisters of the 1930s tapped into anti-big-government sentiment that predated the depression. They did not have to face the problem of creating a constituency out of whole cloth. Tax revolts in American society, including that of the 1930s, have often reflected, and continue to reflect, persistent suspicions of expansive government, entrenched bureaucracy, and domination of political institutions by experts.

This continuity can also be traced forward in time through the New Deal period. Leading Americans who praised tax protests (although not always tax strikes) like Garet Garrett, H. L. Mencken, Merle Thorpe, and Robert McCormick became vocal critics of the Roosevelt administration. They were joined in this opposition by less well known local resisters, like Clinton Bardo, president of the New Jersey Taxpayers' Association, John Pratt and John J. Mangan, leaders of Chicago's tax strike, and Merwin K. Hart of the New York Economic Council, who fought FDR's policies for the same reasons they opposed high taxes. In their eyes, the New Deal embodied a dangerous expansion of central power that threatened the rights of the individual. Roosevelt's reliance on government intervention seemed only to bolster their old nemesis, the tax spender.[1]

For a long time, historians discounted the popular appeal of Roosevelt's opposition. At times, the literature treated movements against the New Deal in almost conspiratorial terms. George Wolfskill and John A. Hudson, in *All but the People: Franklin D. Roosevelt and His Critics, 1933–1939*, repeatedly portrayed FDR's opponents as a small, disaffected, sometimes paranoid, often selfish minority, caring primarily for money.[2]

Since the late 1960s, James T. Patterson and other historians have forced at least a partial revision of this stereotype. Patterson found that politicians dedicated to strict economy and limited government continued to win elections before and during the New Deal. "As tax revenue dwindled and unemployment increased," he wrote, "economy in government became a magic word . . . retrenchment dominated the governors' messages of 1931 and thereafter." Nevertheless, Patterson tempered his conclusions by picturing retrenchment-minded politicians as out of step with ordinary Americans. He concluded that voters would have preferred more interventionist policies. Otis Graham, Jr., endorsed Patterson's conclusions, pointing to the persistence of "reactionary and unrepresentative" state governments.[3]

In 1975, most of the contributors to *The New Deal: The State and Local Levels* noted the lasting sway of sentiment for economy in government after 1933. According to the editors, John Braeman, Robert H. Bremner, and David Brody, "traditional attitudes about the role of government, states rights, free enterprise, pay-as-you-go, and individual self-reliance continued to exert strong appeal." Elliot A. Rosen echoed these findings at the national level. "The individualist-voluntarist alternative to Roosevelt's statist proposals," he asserted, "remained potent even during the depression."[4]

Throughout the 1930s, politicians campaigning against high taxes and spending still fared well at the polls. Especially in 1932 and 1933, voters approved many tax-limitation laws at both the state and local levels. Tax strikes, and more often threats of tax strikes, became common fare from local taxpayers', real estate, and homeowners' organizations. Reliable estimates placed the number of taxpayers' organizations at well over 1,000. One, which promoted a tax strike in Chicago, boasted a broad-based membership that included significant numbers of blue-collar workers. Many civic reformers and public officials readily acknowledged the appeal of tax rebellion for the masses and the average voter. These estimates came mostly from foes of tax reduction campaigns who were in a position to know. Almost daily, they fought in local and state political trenches against the onslaughts of the economaniacs.

Historian Robert S. McElvaine has espoused the contrary view. He has argued that depression-era "leftist intellectuals were basically in tune with values of the public" and Congress "was more conservative [i.e., anti-big-government] than the electorate in 1933." Leftist intellectuals during the 1930s, such as Mauritz Hallgren, Stuart Chase, and Harold Buttenheim, would have disagreed with McElvaine's conclusions. They did not so quickly discount the strength and appeal of the opposition.[5]

One reason the persistence of these ideas during the depression era has been underrated is that historians have focused primarily on the period after 1933. There may well have been a shift in voter attitudes roughly corresponding to the onset of the New Deal in 1933. Here, some of the traditional explanations for the New Deal's popularity still make a good deal of sense. The economic recovery after 1933 and Roosevelt's charismatic leadership overwhelmed opponents of big government.

Certainly good-government reformers and other critics of the tax revolt exuded renewed confidence in the later months of 1933 and thereafter. They expressed nearly universal agreement that aggressive tax-reduction and anti-big-government convictions had begun to ebb—although by no means disappear. After 1933, tax limitations fared poorly and tax strikes even more so. A popular ideological swing toward government interventionism certainly provides part of the answer. In the face of their declining fortunes, tax resisters showed themselves unable or unwilling to formulate a concrete alternative. Their appeal to anti-big-government sentiment among voters rarely advanced beyond the superficial level. Moreover, subsidies to taxpayers—like the Home Owners' Loan Corporation—helped take the edge off critiques of an expanded state.

By contrast, the years between 1929 and 1933 seem less easy to classify. This is best seen as a period of ideological flux and uncertainty; when few options could be entirely ruled out. Sometimes in treatments of Roosevelt's 1932 election victory, historians leave the impression, perhaps unintentionally, that voters had somehow endorsed the interventionist policies of the future New Deal. But before his election, Roosevelt gave at best only a glimmer of his later policies. Campaign statements that foreshadowed the New Deal were issued alongside contradictory pledges to carry out the Democratic platform's pledge to cut government spending 25 percent. More than once during the 1932 campaign, Roosevelt accused Hoover of presiding over the "greatest spending administration in peace times in all our history." He also asked the voters "very simply to assign to me the task of reducing the annual operating expenses of your national government." At another point, Roosevelt blamed the Republican Party for "fostering regimentation without stint or limit."[6]

Americans may have wanted change in 1932 but it does not perforce follow that they desired more government intervention. To voters, change and innovation entailed a wide range of possibilities. In the state houses, the description "innovator" could encompass progressive interventionists, like Philip La Follette of Wisconsin, or economizers, like Harry G. Leslie of Indiana. There was nothing new in the association of innovation with hard-nosed budget slashing. Grover Cleveland, for example, built his career as a champion of retrenchment and producer of unending vetoes. The proposition that depressions automatically facilitate movements to expand government needs to be reexamined. If the 1930s give us any clue, it seems equally true that depressions also stimulate powerful movements in the opposite direction.

The tendency of historians, until recently, to underestimate popular suspicion of big government during the depression has a similarly misleading corollary, namely an unwillingness to take seriously the ideological concerns or good faith of these critics. McElvaine goes to the extreme of characterizing the anti-big-government view as "self serving for most of those who have subscribed to it."[7]

For many years, some historians came close to reading proponents of limited government out of the debate entirely. According to Graham, "the actual course of American history was making the conservatives look ludicrous and unreasonable." In the 1960s, the historical debate centered on whether the New Deal represented true reform or merely a conservative effort to save capitalism. Along these lines, Paul Conkin highlighted what he regarded as a "supreme irony." He asserted that the "enemies of the New Deal were wrong. They should have been friends." He wondered why these critics did not realize that FDR's policies served as an insurance policy for capitalism. Since both FDR and his opponents believed in the profit system, Conkin treated all the vitriolic dialogue between them as much ado about nothing.[8]

In a sense, Conkin's approach represents a leftist form of consensus theory. Debates about tax rates or government regulation between supporters of capitalism (be they FDR or Garet Garrett) become, under the logic of Conkin's approach, mere details of keeping the all-important system alive. Framed in this context, the real issues are those revolving around whether or not capitalism should survive. Intracapitalist debates are considered to be much less important.[9]

In general, the tax resisters of the 1930s and their later anti–New Deal incarnations lacked a focused ideological program. Nevertheless, a common set of assumptions about the proper nature of government constantly reappeared in their writings and speeches. Merle Thorpe, John Pratt, Adam Schantz, and many others who participated in the tax revolt and anti–New Deal causes looked on the issue of the individual versus the paternalistic state as timeless and relevant to any society. They saw these questions as worthy of consideration on their own terms and not merely as alternative strategies to carry out shared capitalist goals.

APPENDIX

A Note on Sources and Methods

Regrettably, there has been no significant attempt to preserve the source material of taxpayers' protest. The comparison with labor history is especially revealing. Newsletters of a myriad of unions, sometimes very obscure, have been preserved with diligence. Secondary literature, manuscript collections, and oral interviews abound for the interested researcher. The labor union official can draw on a rich folklore and tradition that historians have documented, fortified, and expanded.

Taxpayers' organizations in the 1930s also printed a bumper crop of newsletters. Most, despite listings in the *National Union Catalogue*, have been lost or thrown out. Interviews with the principals have been almost unheard-of, even though some, like Adam Schantz, are still alive. What struck me as especially telling is that the leading tax protesters of today, in organizations like the National Taxpayers' Union, know nothing of their precursors in the 1930s. By contrast, one would have to search long to find a major labor union leader who has never heard of Samuel Gompers or the sit-down strikes of the 1930s.

Fortunately, the Chicago tax strike seemed an exception to this generally frustrating absence of sources. As headline news, the strike received extensive (though often biased) coverage in the press. None of the strikers, at least to my knowledge, left behind manuscript collections of any consequence. Two members of ARET, Edwin J. Kuester and Ronald Chinnock, were available for interviews and proved extremely helpful. John M. Pratt's son, John T. Pratt, gave me much honest and evenhanded insight into his father's colorful background and character. Ted Diller, a lawyer who worked for the firm that defended ARET, was instructive from the legal angle. The manuscript collection of the Chicago Teachers' Federation, the strikers' chief organizational nemesis, included some eye-opening correspondence, broadsides, and verbatim transcriptions of meetings.

Court records proved the most valuable source. All of the court sources utilized are at the Illinois State Archives in Springfield. The evidence in *People of Illinois* v. *Association of Real Estate Taxpayers* included pamphlets produced by ARET and voluminous accounts of the strike's history. The index to the objections of litigants in *Reinecke* v. *McDonough* offered the greatest find. The index to litigants, about 26,000 names, is the closest facsimile to a complete membership list for ARET. I took a random sample of 550 names of individuals and business firms and then eliminated the 17 business firms from the sample.[1]

To find the occupational backgrounds of individuals listed, I turned to the *Chicago City Directory* for 1928–29. This posed a problem because of the time lag of three years between the *City Directory* and the index of litigants. In addition, the commonness of many names hampered a positive identification. Some of the litigants compounded this problem by listing initials rather than their full first names. My research method could be faulted because it imperfectly reflects changes in occupational mobility between 1928–29 and 1932. While this problem must be reckoned with, it should be noted that most, if not all, occupational mobility for this period was downward.

In the end I identified, with reasonable certainty, the occupations of 180 individuals. This figure did not include 13 women who listed "widow" instead of an occupation. To find skill ratings, I used the 1939 edition of the *Dictionary of Occupational Titles*, published by the United States Employment Service of the United States Department of Labor. I made one notable modification in my use of the *Dictionary*'s ratings. I collapsed the occupations listed under "Service Occupations" and "Agricultural, Fishery, Forestry, and Kindred Occupations" into the other categories. To get the skill ratings of these occupations, I turned to the 1932 occupational schema of Alba M. Edwards, a statistician for the U.S. Census.[2]

I identified the residential addresses of 226 individuals in the sample. To match the addresses with the assessed valuations, I used the 1931 published *Real Estate Assessment* for Cook County. By this method, I found the residential assessments of 116 individuals. Those assessments that matched addresses in the *City Directory* but did not list the name of a litigant were eliminated from consideration. This yielded a median assessment of $2,656.[3]

Despite its listed date, the *Real Estate Assessment* was not completed until the later part of 1932. At least according to its authors, the *Assessment* reflected the 26 percent decline in real estate values between 1930 and 1931. The assessor made it a uniform policy to value all properties at 37 percent of market value. Taking him at his word, I readjusted the median assessment to reflect 100 percent of market value. I found the median value for all one- and two-family homes in Chicago in *Census Data of the City of Chicago, 1930*. I then deflated the figure by 26 percent to compensate for the decline in market value between 1930 and 1931.[4]

NOTES

Introduction

1. For an excellent recent history of the Whiskey Rebellion see Slaughter, *Whiskey Rebellion*, p. 141. According to Slaughter, like the "American Country opposition," the Whiskey rebels supported "militias over standing armies, limited revenues, local administration, small government, extinction of the debt, and frequent elections."

Shays's Rebellion, the major internal crisis of the era of the Articles of Confederation, has often been characterized as an agrarian struggle against the payment of private debt. See, for example, Szatmary, *Shays' Rebellion*. Challenging this interpretation, Forrest McDonald persuasively argues that the Shaysites were first and foremost tax rebels. Forrest McDonald, "On the Late Disturbances in Massachusetts," in a volume of bicentennial essays by Forrest McDonald (Lawrence: University Press of Kansas, forthcoming).

2. Adams, *Secrets of the Tax Revolt*, pp. 73–86; Benson, *The Concept of Jacksonian Democracy*, p. 106; Leggett, *Democratick Editorials*, p. 4.

3. Yearley, *The Money Machines*, p. 250. Terrence J. McDonald and Sally K. Ward observe, "The nineteenth century public sector existed in the midst of a profoundly antistate ideology. 'Permission' for the local state to grow fiscally was given rarely and grudgingly." McDonald and Ward, *The Politics of Urban Fiscal Policy*, p. 29.

4. For more on tax-limitation campaigns during the late nineteenth century see Griffith, *A History of American City Government*, pp. 20–21; and Adams, *Secrets of the Tax Revolt*, pp. 185, 190, 219.

5. The dichotomy between tax spenders and taxpayers advanced by tax resisters in the 1930s strongly resembled one posed by antebellum political leader John C. Calhoun. Calhoun asserted that the state, by its fiscal action, creates two contending classes in society, the taxpayers [or more accurately the net-taxpayers], who "bear exclusively the burden of supporting the government" and the "tax-consumers" [or net-tax-consumers], who are the "recipients of their proceeds through disbursements, and who are, in fact, supported by the government." Accordingly, "the effect of this [government taxation policy] is to place them in antagonistic relations . . . every increase is to enrich and strengthen the one, and impoverish and weaken the other." Calhoun, *A Disquisition on Government*, pp. 17–18.

6. Brinkley, *Voices of Protest*, p. xi; and Ribuffo, *The Old Christian Right*.

For tax controversies at the federal level, see Leff, *The Limits of Symbolic Reform*.

7. Patterson, *The New Deal and the States*.

8. Connolly, *Legitimacy and the State*, pp. 69–70. Recent entries in the debate over legitimacy include Habermas, *Legitimation Crisis*; Wolfe, *The Limits of Legitimacy*; and Evans, Rueschemeyer, and Skocpol, *Bringing the State Back In*, p. 5.

As Dall W. Forsythe put it: " 'Extraction' is an ugly but necessary term that neatly summarizes the complex strategies governments adopt to assure themselves adequate flows of revenues. Once so stated, it seems quite obvious that rulers cannot develop a central state apparatus without some degree of capacity to extract revenues from the subject population." See Forsythe, *Taxation and Political Change*, p. 1.

Chapter 1

1. Kimmel, *Cost of Government*, p. 36; and *Tax Yields*, pp. 21, 25.

2. *Tax Yields*, pp. 21, 25; and Franklin, "Taxes, Taxes, Taxes!" p. 201.

3. President's Conference, *Home Finance and Taxation*, 2:103, 149–50.

4. Ibid.

5. Buchanan, *Fiscal Theory and Political Economy*, p. 62.

6. Strayer, *Report of the Survey*, p. 224.

7. President's Conference, *Home Finance and Taxation*, 2:104, 152.

8. Eyre, *A Study of Tax Delinquency*, p. 1; Advisory Commission, *City Financial Emergencies*, pp. 17–18; National Industrial Conference Board, *The Fiscal Problem in Missouri* (New York: National Industrial Conference Board, 1930), pp. 186–87; and President's Conference, *Home Finance and Taxation*, 2:110.

9. Wickens, *Residential Real Estate*, pp. 57, 296.

10. National Industrial Conference Board, *Cost of Government*, p. 61.

11. Kimmel, *Cost of Government*, p. 36; and *Tax Yields*, pp. 21, 25.

12. Bird, *The Trend of Tax Delinquency*, pp. 5, 22, 23; and *Proceedings of the National Tax Association* (1934), p. 378.

13. Wickens, *Residential Real Estate*, pp. 57, 296.

14. Allen, "Collection of Delinquent Taxes," pp. 397–404.

15. In Detroit, the value of tax titles purchased by private buyers plunged by a whopping 99 percent, from over $7 million to a meager $3,804. In contrast, the value of tax titles "bid in" (coming into possession of the city government) went from $498,791 in 1929 to over $23 million in 1932. Smith, "Recent Legislative Indulgences," p. 377; and Eyre, *A Study of Tax Delinquency*, p. 3.

16. McCormick, *The World at Home*, p. 93; and Buttenheim, "Are Local Expenditures Excessive?" p. 1.

17. Hallgren, *Seeds of Revolt*, p. 146; and Swierenga, *Acres For Cents*, p. 13.

18. "Tax Strikes a la 1934," p. 485; and "Taxation and Tyranny," p. 4.

19. "The Taxpayers' Revolt," p. 5; and "Help Forced on the Farmer," p. 15.

20. Hallgren, *Seeds of Revolt*, p. 138.

21. Ibid.

22. J. M. Setten to Henry Horner, 10 January 1933, Papers of Henry Horner.

23. *Journal of Proceedings of the Ohio State Grange*, p. 34; and Babcock, "Farm Revolt in Iowa," p. 372.

24. *National Real Estate Journal* 32 (19 January 1931): 51, *Chicago Real Estate Magazine* 8 (7 November 1931): 25.

25. *National Real Estate Journal* 32 (12 October 1931): 38, and 33 (November 1932): 74, 75.

26. NAREB, *Over-all Limitation*, p. 9; and *National Real Estate Journal* 33 (October 1932): 63.

27. NAREB, National Committee, *Bulletin*, 1 (1934): 3.

28. NAREB, *Over-all Limitation*, pp. 33, 13; Giovanni Montemartini, "The Fundamental Principles of a Pure Theory of Public Finance," in *Classics in the Theory of Public Finance*, ed. Musgrave and Peacock, pp. 137–51.

29. Ortquist, "Tax Crisis and Politics," pp. 118–19; and Leet and Paige, *Property Tax Limitation Laws*, p. 63.

30. *Proceedings of the National Tax Association* (1932), p. 14; Merrill, "The Taxpayer Looks at Government," p. 801; Reed, "The Role of Government," p. 210; Barrows, "A Challenge to Reform," p. 223; and Shultz, *American Public Finance*, p. 110.

31. Hoan, *City Government*, pp. 158, 159; Hoan, *Taxes and Tax Dodgers*, pp. 5, 15 (emphasis Hoan's); and *City Problems of 1933*, p. 70.

32. Barrows, "A Challenge to Reform," p. 223; and Jones, "Unrest," p. 470.

33. Steed, "Adventures," p. 16. Steed identified "Uncle Horace," a member of the league, as an Atlanta real estate operator in Steed, *Georgia*, p. 30. I have not been able to match with equal certainty any names of the other members of the actual league with the aliases Steed gave them.

34. Steed, "Adventures," p. 303; *Atlanta Constitution*, 8 April 1932, p. 1, and 10 March 1932, p. 8.

35. Steed, "Adventures," p. 16; *Atlanta Constitution*, 22 February 1932, p. 8, and 13 April 1932, p. 4.

36. Steed, "Adventures," 11 November 1933, p. 30.

37. Wisconsin Taxpayers' Alliance, Release for daily newspapers, 26 September 1932, Wisconsin State Historical Society, Library.

38. Leggett, *Democratick Editorials*. For Taylor see Harp, "Taylor, Calhoun," pp. 107–20; American Taxpayers' League, *Handbook*, p. 82; *North Dakota Taxpayer* 1, (May 1935); Carr, *School Finance*, p. 42; and *Illinois Teacher* (November 1931): 84.

39. West Virginia Taxpayers' Association, *The Tax Burden*; and Munro, "Taxation Nears a Crisis," p. 661.

40. Cline, "Economic Recovery and the Public Employee," pp. 471, 472.

41. *Iowa Taxpayer* 1 (6 July 1936): 3; *Oklahoma Municipal Review* 7 (May 1933): 70; and "The Financial Plight of the Cities," in National Municipal League, *The Crisis*, p. 5.

42. Merriam, "Reducing Government Costs," p. 147; and Frank, "Constructive Versus Destructive Economy," p. 314.

43. *Washington Taxpayer* 1 (May 1936): 4; *Wisconsin Taxpayer* 1 (1 February 1933): 4. The 16 December 1935 issue of the NAREB's *Confidential Weekly Letter* observed, "Leagues of Municipalities, Conference of Mayors, etc., are inveighing against us. . . . They would ignore our program if they did not feel certain that it would reduce the revenues which they receive. . . . Inci-

dentally, the money they spend in attempts to defeat our tax proposal is tax money."

44. Leet and Paige, *Property Tax Limitation Laws*, pp. 18–20.

45. *Proceedings of the Investment Bankers' Association of America* (1934), p. 121; and *Bond Buyer*, 25 November 1933, p. 33.

46. *Milwaukee Leader*, 24 August 1932, p. 10.

47. Ibid., 19 September 1932, p. 2, and 7 November 1932, p. 2.

48. *Milwaukee Journal*, 2 April 1933; and *Milwaukee Leader*, 28 March 1933, p. 4.

49. *Milwaukee Leader*, 28 March 1933, p. 1; *Milwaukee Journal*, 5 April 1933, pp. 1, 9; and Stachcowski, "The Political Career of Daniel Webster Hoan."

50. Fox, *Better City Government*, pp. 134–35.

51. Fine, *Frank Murphy*, p. 324.

52. Ibid., p. 355.

53. Ibid., p. 356; and Tickton, *An Analysis*, p. 9.

54. Fine, *Frank Murphy*, pp. 359, 356; and *Detroit Free Press*, 7 August 1932 (ATR enclosed broadside, p. 2).

55. *Detroit Free Press*, 7 August 1932 (ATR enclosed broadside, p. 2).

56. Fine, *Frank Murphy*, p. 357; and *Detroit Times*, 5 August 1932, p. 7. According to Eric Monkkonen, "Business interests throughout the city all united behind the mayor to defeat the budget limitation proposal, suggesting that the persons petitioning for tax reduction represented just who they claimed they did, small property owners." McDonald and Ward, *The Politics*, pp. 149–50.

57. Fine, *Frank Murphy*, p. 206.

58. Ibid., p. 297; and McDonald and Ward, *The Politics*, p. 147.

59. Fine, *Frank Murphy*, pp. 317–19.

60. Ibid., pp. 357, 358.

61. *Detroit News*, 3 August 1932, p. 6.

62. *Detroit Free Press*, 7 August 1932 (ATR enclosed broadside, p. 1).

63. Fine, *Frank Murphy*, pp. 357, 359.

64. *New York Times*, 25 March 1932, p. 19.

65. *New York Herald Tribune*, 22 March 1932, pp. 1, 2.

66. Ibid., 23 March 1932, p. 1; and *New York Times*, 24 March 1932, p. 23.

67. *New York Times*, 24 March 1932, p. 23, and 26 March 1932, p. 1, and 25 March 1932, p. 20.

68. *New York Herald Tribune*, 29 March 1932, pp. 1, 2, and 12 April 1932, pp. 1, 3.

69. Ibid., 9 May 1932, pp. 1, 4.

70. Ibid., 15 May 1932, p. 1, Sec. V, and 22 May 1932, p. 1, Sec. V.

71. Walsh, *Gentleman Jimmy Walker*, pp. 308–13; and *New York Herald Tribune*, 27 May 1932, p. 16.

72. Bird, *The Trend*, p. 21; and *New York Herald Tribune*, 24 March 1932, p. 32.

73. *New York Herald Tribune*, 18 March 1932, p. 32.

74. *North Dakota Taxpayer* 1 (July 1935); and NAREB, *Over-all Limitation*, pp. 19, 23.

75. *New York Times*, 25 May 1933, p. 29; and Traylor, *What Can Be Done*, p. 13.

Chapter 2

1. Simpson, *Tax Racket*, p. 3.
2. Merriam et al., *The Government*, p. 9.
3. Simpson, *Tax Racket*, p. 102; and Cook County Joint Commission, *A Study*, p. 33.
4. Simpson, *Tax Racket*, pp. 101, 104.
5. Murphy, "Taxation and Social Conflict," pp. 248–54; and Altman, "Chicago's Experiment, p. 21.
6. Murphy, "Taxation and Social Conflict," p. 255; and Simpson, *Tax Racket*, p. 124.
7. Stark, "The Political Economy," p. 167; and Stuart, *Twenty Incredible Years*, p. 402.
8. Altman, "Chicago's Experiment," p. 22; and Simpson, *Tax Racket*, pp. 126, 131–34.
9. Mayer, "When Teachers Strike," p. 122; and Simpson, *Tax Racket*, pp. 71, 58.
10. Simpson, *Tax Racket*, p. 67.
11. Yearley, *The Money Machines*; and Simpson, *Tax Racket*, pp. 70, 107.
12. Residential property had an average assessment of 32.6 percent, which ran a little under uniformity. Homes valued over $50,000 were assessed at 28 percent in contrast to 33.5 percent for homes under $15,000. Simpson, *Tax Racket*, pp. 71, 77; and Murphy, "Taxation and Social Conflict," p. 258.
13. Williams, *They Got Their Man*, p. 49; and Simpson, *Tax Racket*, pp. 143, 135.
14. Simpson, *Tax Racket*, p. 150.
15. Ibid., pp. 172, 174, 167.
16. Chicago's traditional reliance on short-term debt—an especially dangerous practice during depressions—surged. In 1926, short-term debt as a percentage of gross debt had stood at 25 percent. By 1931, it had climbed to 41 percent. Hardy, "American Privatism," p. 290; Simpson, *Tax Racket*, p. 187; Williams, *They Got Their Man*, p. 52; and *Chicago Tribune*, 22 November 1930, p. 12.
17. "Revolt of the Chicago Taxpayers," p. 6; and Simpson, *Tax Racket*, p. 184.
18. Simpson, *Tax Racket*, p. 184; *Who's Who in Chicago* (1931), p. 944; and *Chicago Evening Post*, 18 February 1930, p. 1.
19. Sutherland, *Fifty Years*, p. 61; Civic Federation of Chicago, *Bulletin*, 113 (December 1930); and *Social Register* (1930).
20. Sutherland, *Fifty Years*, p. 61; Simpson, *Tax Racket*, p. 186; *Chicago Evening Post*, 25 January 1930, p. 2; and 25 February 1930, p. 1.
21. Simpson, *Tax Racket*, p. 186; Murphy, "Taxation and Social Conflict," p. 367; and *Chicago Evening Post*, 27 January 1930, p. 1.
22. Comery, "A Study," p. 12.
23. Hoyt, *One Hundred Years*, pp. 475, 399.
24. Ibid., pp. 472, 379, 380.
25. Copy of ARET's Registration for non-profit status with the Secretary of State of Illinois, 9 May 1930. (Illinois State Archives in Springfield); *People of the State of Illinois* v. *Association of Real Estate Taxpayers of Illinois*, in the

Supreme Court of Illinois, *Abstract*, June Term, 1932, pp. 35–36, Illinois State Archives, Springfield.

26. *Who's Who in Chicago* (1931), p. 95; Bistor, Telephone interview; and Kuester, Interview.

27. Kuester, Interview.

28. *Who's Who in Chicago* (1931 and 1936).

29. Lindheimer, "Both Groups to Fight," pp. 5, 6.

30. Ibid., p. 6.

31. *People* v. *Association, Abstract*, p. 36.

32. Ibid., p. 37; *Who's Who in Chicago* (1945), p. 13; Pratt, Telephone interview; *Biographical and Genealogical History*, p. 658; and Allan, *Times Past to Present*, pp. 129, 140.

33. Pratt, Telephone interview; and Allan, *Times Past and Present*, p. 404.

34. *Grain Growers' Guide* 10, 28 November 1917, p. 20; and Pratt, Telephone interview.

35. Pratt, Telephone interview; and Kuester, Interview.

36. Kuester, Interview.

37. Pratt, Telephone interview.

38. Ibid.

39. Kuester, Interview.

40. ARET, *Today You Must Choose*, p. 9; ARET, *The Four Essentials*, p. 7; and ARET, *$548,648,264.00*, pp. 28–29.

41. Simpson, *Tax Racket*, p. 8; Altman, "Chicago's Experiment," p. 152; and Comery, "A Study," p. 98.

42. Hodes, "Tax Amendment Progressive," p. 5; ARET, *1929 and 1930 Taxes Voided*, p. 9; Cook County Joint Commission, *A Study*, p. 25; and *Chicago Tribune*, 24 November 1930, p. 6.

43. Cook County Joint Commission, *A Study*, p. 31; and Altman, "Chicago's Experiment," p. 56.

44. Simpson, *Tax Racket*, pp. 226, 227; and Altman, "Chicago's Experiment," p. 152.

45. Hodes, "Obey or Revise," p. 5.

46. *People* v. *Association, Abstract*, p. 37; *Chicago Evening Post*, 16 August 1930, p. 7; and Hodes, "Tax Amendment Progressive," p. 9 (emphasis Hodes's).

47. Bistor, "Pendulum May Swing Back," p. 32.

48. Bistor, "Plans of Taxpayers' Association," p. 10; and Teninga, "Taxpayers Can Determine Taxes," p. 5.

49. ARET, *Taxes, Unemployment*; Teninga, "Taxpayers Can Determine Taxes," p. 6; and "Pratt to Direct Taxpayers," p. 13.

50. Comery, "A Study," p. 3.

51. Stark, "The Political Economy," pp. 232–33; and Holly, "The Proposed Income Tax Amendment," p. 7.

52. ARET, *$548,648,264.00*, p. 25; and ARET, *Taxes, Unemployment*.

53. ARET, *Taxes, Unemployment*.

54. *Economist and Magazine of La Salle Street* 84, 22 November 1930, p. 1; and *Chicago Tribune*, 22 November 1930, p. 12.

55. ARET, *$548,648,264.00*, p. 4.

56. *Chicago Tribune*, 17 December 1930, p. 2; and ARET, *$548,648,264.00*, p. 13.

57. *Chicago Tribune*, 14 December 1930, p. 10.

58. ARET, *$548,648,264.00*, p. 18; *Chicago Tribune*, 30 December 1930, p. 3; and *Chicago Evening American*, 18 October 1933.

59. Civic Federation of Chicago, *Bulletin* 108 (February 1930); and *Who's Who in Chicago* (1931), pp. 47, 985.

60. Civic Federation of Chicago, *Bulletin* 114 (January 1931): 1–3.

61. Ibid., p. 4.

62. King, *Public Finance*, pp. 331–32.

63. *Chicago Tribune*, 24 December 1930, p. 3.

64. Comery, "A Study," p. 10.

65. *People* v. *Association, Abstract*, pp. 38, 21, 58.

66. Ibid., p. 7.

67. *Chicago Herald and Examiner*, 4 February 1931, p. 4.

68. Ibid., 14 February 1931, p. 21.

Chapter 3

1. *Chicago Tribune*, 29 November 1930.

2. *Chicago Daily News*, 14 August 1931, p. 9.

3. White, *The Prestige Value*, pp. 139, 147.

4. Buchanan, *Public Finance*, p. 131; and Shepherd, "The Winded City," p. 17. I am indebted to Ralph Kloske for suggesting the applicability of "fiscal illusion" to "tax fixing."

5. *Chicago Tribune*, 4 February 1931, p. 11; and Coughlin, "The Municipal Follies," p. 12.

6. Murphy, "Taxation and Social Conflict," pp. 251–52; and Leet and Paige, *Property Tax Limitation Laws*, p. 23.

7. *Chicago Tribune*, 29 November 1930.

8. Comery, "A Study," p. 13.

9. Civic Federation of Chicago, *Bulletin* 116 (February 1931).

10. *Illinois Reports* 354 (December 1933): 105; *People* v. *Association, Abstract*, p. 55; and John M. Pratt to "Mr. Real Estate Taxpayer," 17 August 1931, Papers of Edmund K. Jarecki.

11. *Chicago Tribune*, 28 April 1931, p. 8.

12. By no means, however, did Hodes completely reject his past association with the taxpayers' revolt. His campaign literature featured a picture of himself and James Bistor. "Elect Barnet Hodes, Alderman 7th Ward," 1931, Papers of Barnet Hodes. Also, while in the city council, Hodes opposed draconian measures to break the strike. He characterized Cermak's campaign to shame strikers as an "attempt to bludgeon and coerce people into doing something they do not have to do." *Chicago Evening Post*, 19 February 1932, p. 1.

13. Gottfried, *Boss Cermak of Chicago*, p. 246; and *Chicago Tribune*, 28 April 1931, p. 2.

14. *Chicago Tribune*, 27 March 1931; 31 March 1931, p. 5; and *Chicago Daily News*, 13 April 1931, p. 6.

15. *People* v. *Association, Abstract*, 5; and ARET to ———, 13 April 1931, Box 2, Folder: 2–8, Papers of Charles H. Ewig.

16. According to one ARET broadside, a *"payment of any part of the 1930 tax still leaves your property subject to sale or forfeiture for the unpaid balance"*

[emphasis in the original]. ARET, *Your 1930 Tax Bill!* As usual, the CREB took the safe middle ground between violating the law and going along with the tax collector. The *Chicago Real Estate Magazine* urged real estate taxpayers to hold off paying until just before the 19 May penalty date. *Chicago Real Estate Magazine*, 18 April 1931, p. 7. It based this recommendation on the hope that the courts would void the assessment in the meantime.

17. George F. Koester was a member of ARET's board of directors. *Chicago Tribune*, 27 May 1931, pp. 1, 4; Comery, "A Study," pp. 27–29; *People of the State of Illinois* v. *Association of Real Estate Taxpayers*, No. 21697, In the Supreme Court of the State of Illinois, *Brief and Argument in Behalf of the Relator*, Illinois State Archives, Springfield, p. 93.

18. *Chicago Tribune*, 7 June 1931, p. 2.

19. *Chicago Evening Post*, 8 December 1931, p. 8; and *Chicago Tribune*, 23 October 1931.

20. *Chicago Tribune*, 20 July 1932, p. 5. McCormick's membership on the board of the First National Bank of Chicago may have also influenced his opposition to expanded personal property tax assessments. See *Who's Who in Chicago* (1931), p. 647. ARET's literature called for increased assessments on the First National Bank's intangible personal property assets. It also published a pamphlet that listed the low personal property assessments of McCormick, Traylor, Strawn, and other leading antagonists of the strike in the business community. ARET, *The Tax Strikers*.

21. *Chicago Evening Post*, 18 May 1931, p. 1. Buyers purchased only $826,579 worth of tax titles for 1929 taxes. The rest of the tax titles up for sale, worth $15,738,533, were forfeited to the county. *Chicago Daily News*, 19 April 1933, p. 3; and *Chicago Daily News*, 11 September 1931, p. 5.

22. A tax conference called by Governor Louis Emmerson endorsed an appointed assessor in its report in October 1931. See Illinois Governor's Tax Conference, *Report*. ARET achieved a public relations coup when Emmerson invited Pratt and Bistor to attend. The other members of the conference voted them down at every point, however, and no representative of ARET received a place on the executive committee. ARET activist Peter Foote hit the mark when he contended, "Exactly the same interests control the Governor's Commission which operate in the Strawn Commission. Both had the same objects, and both appear to have the same motives." Foote, "Revenue Body's Report," p. 3.

The conference also endorsed an income tax and rejected ARET's call for radically increased personal property tax assessments. ARET criticized these proposals in *A Protest Against the Acceptance of the Report*.

23. Chicago, *Journal of the Proceedings*, 29 December 1931, p. 1574. In addition to Traylor, leading bankers who testified before the legislature in favor of the Kelly bill included George M. Reynolds of the Continental Illinois Bank and Trust Company, Soloman A. Smith of the Northern Trust Company, and Joseph E. Otis of the Central Republic Bank and Trust Company, *Chicago Tribune*, 14 December 1931, p. 1.

24. Stuart, *Twenty Incredible Years*, p. 478; and *Chicago Evening Post*, 14 December 1931, p. 2.

25. *Chicago Daily News*, 30 December 1931, p. 26; *Chicago Tribune*, 17 October 1931, pp. 1, 14; and Margaret Haley to Principals and Teachers, 12 December 1931, Papers of the CTF, Box 61, Folder: November–December, 1931, Chicago Historical Society.

26. Illinois State Federation of Labor, *Proceedings*, 12–16 September 1932, p. 9.

27. *The Taxpayer of Chicago and Cook County*, 5 November 1931. ARET called the appointive system "un-American and not in keeping with ideals and standards of representative government." ARET, *The Four Essentials of Revenue Relief*, p. 7.

28. MacChesney, "The Immediate Tax Program," p. 13.

29. *Chicago Daily News*, 7 January 1932, p. 1; and *The Taxpayer*, 16 February 1932, p. 4.

30. *Chicago Tribune*, 3 December 1931, p. 2; *Chicago Union Teacher* (January 1932): 9; and *Chicago Daily News*, 5 January 1931, p. 1.

31. *Chicago Daily News*, 22 December 1931, p. 6; and *Chicago Tribune*, 14 December 1931, p. 1. Despite his strong words about the antidemocratic implications of the Kelly plan, Michael Igoe's opposition was qualified at best. He stated his willingness to support the bill if Traylor made a definite promise to buy more warrants if it passed. *Chicago Daily News*, 2 January 1932, p. 28.

32. Kerner, "Effect of Recent Illinois Decisions," p. 273.

33. Kerner, "Effect of Recent Illinois Decisions," p. 273; and *Chicago Daily News*, 17 December 1931, p. 1.

34. *Chicago Evening Post*, 31 December 1931, p. 2. For more on Hodes's association with Schaeffer and Keehn see *Chicago Tribune*, 12 April 1933, Barnet Hodes Scrapbook. *Literary Digest* 112, 16 January 1932, p. 10.

35. *Chicago Evening Post*, 25 January 1932, p. 5. On the heels of the Jarecki ruling, ARET celebrated another victory in the Koester case. A superior court judge ordered the Board of Review to bring $15 million in personal property onto the assessment rolls. The judge also delayed implementation of the ruling by giving the board a chance to appeal. *Chicago Daily News*, 11 January 1932, p. 1.

36. *Chicago Daily News*, 2 January 1932, p. 1; and *Chicago Evening Post*, 5 January 1932, p. 1.

37. Stuart, *Twenty Incredible Years*, p. 479.

38. "Chicago Teetering on the Precipice," p. 10; and Hoyt, *One Hundred Years*, p. 269.

39. *Chicago Tribune*, 1 January 1932, p. 1.

40. *People* v. *Association, Abstract*, pp. 65, 110–11; ARET, *A Protest*, p. 11; and *Chicago Daily News*, 10 June 1932, p. 5.

41. Sargent, "The Taxpayers Take Charge," p. 74.

42. Pratt to "Mr. Real Estate Taxpayer," 17 August 1931, Papers of Edmund K. Jarecki.

43. *People* v. *Association, Brief and Argument in Behalf of the Relator*, p. 114.

44. *Chicago Tribune*, 13 February 1932, p. 10.

45. *Chicago Daily News*, 19 March 1932, p. 3; Gottfried, *Boss Cermak of Chicago*, p. 254; *Chicago Evening Post*, 11 February 1932, p. 1; 24 March 1932, p. 2; and *Chicago Tribune*, 20 March 1932, p. 19.

Jarecki tried a less confrontational approach. He invited representatives from Cermak's administration, the teachers, the ARET, and the CREB to his chambers on 25 February for an informal conference. Although all parties attended, it broke up in acrimony. Pratt refused to heed Jarecki's plea to make partial payments, and Hayden N. Bell, the county attorney, attacked the tax strike, arguing that "we cannot have government with obligatory duties and permissive support." Jarecki observed that "tax crises have been at the bottom of every revolution. A tax crisis is synonymous with oppression and if our situation goes too far, I'm afraid this will happen." *Chicago Evening Post*, 25 February 1932, p. 2; and *Chicago Tribune*, 26 February 1932, p. 4.

46. *Chicago Tribune*, 20 February 1932, p. 4; 8 February 1932, p. 4; and *People v. Association, Abstract*, pp. 67–68.

47. *Chicago Daily News*, 22 January 1932, p. 2; and Chicago, *Journal of the Proceedings*, 4 May 1932, p. 2140.

48. *Chicago Evening Post*, 28 May 1932, p. 8.

49. *Chicago Tribune*, 22 February 1932, p. 1; and *Chicago Herald and Examiner*, 22 February 1932, p. 8.

50. Hallgren, "Help Wanted" p. 536.

51. *Chicago Daily News*, 13 May 1932, p. 20; *Chicago Tribune*, 14 March 1932, p. 18; and Wilson, "Bargain Hunting," pp. 4, 5.

52. *The Taxpayer*, 5 November 1931, p. 7.

53. Kuester, Interview; and Dobyns, *The Underworld*, pp. 148–55.

54. *Chicago Daily News*, 17 March 1932, p. 5; and Wrigley, *Class*, p. 214.

55. Wrigley, *Class*, pp. 214–15; Sargent, "The Taxpayers Take Charge," pp. 21, 78; Herrick, *The Chicago Schools*, p. 202; U.S. Bureau of the Census, *Financial Statistics, 1930*, p. 6; *1933*, p. 7; and Stillman, "Will Chicago Support Its Schools?" p. 7.

56. U.S. Bureau of the Census, *Financial Statistics, 1930*, pp. 400, 450; and *1933*, pp. 109, 132. Thirty-nine percent of 1932 taxes in Cook County went to debt service. Cook County, *Assessments of Real Estate*, p. 7. By contrast, debt service ate up 28.5 percent of tax collections for all local governments throughout the country in 1933. National Industrial Conference Board, *Cost of Government*, p. 79.

57. Bistor, "Majority Must Become Taxpayers," p. 9; and Mangan, Letter, p. 21.

58. *Report of the Survey*, 1:221–22.

59. *Chicago Evening Post*, 10 May 1932, p. 3; and Burbank, "Chicago Public Schools," p. 367.

60. Stenographic Report of *Proceedings at Mass Meeting called by All-City Publicity Committee*, 29 September 1932, pp. 74–75, (Papers of the CTF).

61. *Chicago Tribune*, 21 November 1931, p. 3.

62. Simpson, "Fundamentals of the Tax Situation," p. 7.

63. *Chicago Tribune*, 22 June 1932, p. 2; Mayer, "Chicago," p. 46; and *Chicago Evening Post*, 23 June 1932, p. 1.

64. *People v. Cesar*, 349, *Illinois Reports* (October 1932): 388.

65. *Chicago Daily News*, 26 July 1932, p. 3.

66. See Keller, *In Defense of Yesterday*, pp. 225–71.

67. Diller, Interview. According to Kuester, Beck suggested that ARET would have much more long-term success if it pursued a political rather than a purely litigation-oriented strategy. Kuester, Interview.

68. Biles, "Mayor Edward J. Kelly of Chicago," p. 35.

69. *Chicago Evening Post*, 3 August 1932, p. 1.

70. Cook County, *Assessments of Real Estate*, p. 7.

Chapter 4

1. Stenographic Report of *Proceedings Before Judge Jarecki In the County Court*, 21 October 1932, p. 10, Box 63, Folder: 1–21 October 1932, Papers of the Chicago Teachers' Federation; and Bogan, "Needs of the Chicago Public Schools."

2. U.S. Bureau of the Census, *Current Tax Delinquency*, p. 3.

3. The chi-square test comparing the occupational distribution between ARET's members and Chicago's population yielded the following result: $(5) = 67.17$, $p < .01$.

4. Double or multiple memberships were not common. They represented only 16.6 percent of all members. In all likelihood, the legal requirements of the suit restricted litigants to legal owners of taxable real estate.

5. *Chicago Tribune*, 22 October 1932, p. 5. See the Appendix for a description of sources and methods.

6. Abbott, *The Tenements of Chicago*, p. 366.

7. Bingham, *Insurgent America*; and Symes and Clement, *Rebel America*, p. 370.

8. Sternsher, *Consensus*, p. 221

9. *Chicago Herald Examiner*, 8 July 1932, p. 1; Copy of article submitted to the *Teacher Voter*, Box 63, Folder: July–September, 1932, Papers of the Chicago Teachers' Federation; and "The Publicity Plan," 25 May 1932, Box 63, Folder: April–May, 1932.

10. Mary L. Leitch to Joseph B. McDonough, 23 August 1932, Box 63, Folder: July–September, 1932, Papers of the Chicago Teachers' Federation; and *Chicago Evening Post*, 29 August 1932, p. 4.

11. Hayden N. Bell to Margaret A. Haley, 28 September 1932, Box 63, Folder: July–September, 1932, Papers of the Chicago Teachers' Federation.

12. *Chicago Evening Post*, 29 August 1932, p. 4; and *Chicago Tribune*, 30 August 1932, p. 5.

13. Haley to ———, 28 September 1932, Box 63, Folder: June–September, 1932, Papers of the Chicago Teachers' Federation; and Bogan, *Chicago Schools Journal* 15 (January–June 1933).

14. *Chicago Herald Examiner*, 13 July 1932, pp. 1, 4; and Bell to Robert C. Keenan, 8 July 1932, Box 63, Folder: July–September, 1932, Papers of the Chicago Teachers' Federation.

15. *Chicago Herald Examiner*, 22 July 1932, p. 5; *Chicago Evening Post*, 22 August 1932, pp. 1, 2; and *Chicago Herald Examiner*, 14 July 1932, p. 1.

16. *Chicago Tribune*, 24 July 1932, p. 12; Stenographic Report of *Proceedings of A Mass Meeting of Principals and Teachers*, 26 October 1932, 62, Box 63, Folder: October 22–November 20, 1932, Papers of the Chicago Teachers' Federation; and *Chicago Tribune*, 23 August 1932, p. 5.

17. *Chicago Evening Post*, 17 October 1932, p. 1.

18. Pratt, Interview; and *Chicago Evening American*, 18 October 1933, Barnet Hodes Scrapbook.

19. *Chicago Tribune*, 22 October 1932; Stenographic Report of *Meeting of All City Delegates*, 21 October 1932, 107, Box 63, Folder: October 1–21, 1932, Papers of the Chicago Teachers' Federation; and *Chicago Daily News*, 28 October 1932.

20. *Chicago Daily News*, 21 October 1932, p. 14.

21. For a complete text of the ordinance, see Chicago, *Journal of the Pro-*

ceedings, 26 October 1932, pp. 2994–96; and *Chicago Herald Examiner*, 27 October 1932, p. 1.

22. J. Soule Warterfield to ———, 10 November 1932, Box 62, Papers of Henry Horner.

23. *Chicago Daily News*, 28 October 1932, p. 4. From early on, ARET had anticipated that the city government might try to cut off the water supply of strikers. It took the precaution of urging members always to pay the city's separate water tax levy. *Chicago Evening Post*, 24 October 1932, p. 2; and *Chicago Tribune*, 11 November 1932, p. 12.

24. *Chicago Herald Examiner*, 4 December 1932, p. 7; and Kuester, Interview.

25. *Chicago Daily News*, 9 December 1932, p. 4.

26. *Chicago Evening Post*, 29 October 1932, p. 1.

27. *Chicago Tribune*, 11 February 1932, p. 4.

28. Ibid., 22 October 1932, p. 5.

29. Ibid., 15 November 1932; 26 October 1932; and 28 November 1932, p. 12.

30. *Chicago Evening American*, 18 October 1933, Barnet Hodes Scrapbook.

31. Kuester, Interview; *Who's Who in Chicago* (1931), pp. 90, 534; and Meites, *History of the Jews*, p. 651.

32. *Chicago Evening American*, 18 October 1933, Barnet Hodes Scrapbook.

33. Ibid.

34. *Chicago Tribune*, 4 February 1933, p. 1.

35. Kuester, Interview; Horner to Kesner, 2 March 1933, Papers of Henry Horner; Charles L. Schwerin to Henry Horner, 26 April 1933, Papers of Henry Horner; and Waller, Telephone conversation.

36. Kuester, Interview.

37. *Chicago Tribune*, 7 February 1933; and 11 February 1933, p. 4.

38. Ibid., 15 February 1933, p. 6.

39. Ibid.; and Kuester, Interview.

40. Bernhard, "Five Years' Experience," p. 38; and *Chicago Daily News*, 14 February 1933, p. 1

41. *Chicago Tribune*, 15 February 1933, p. 6; Altman, "Chicago's Experiment," p. 45; and *Chicago Evening American*, 18 October 1933, Barnet Hodes Scrapbook.

42. Bernhard, "Five Years' Experience," pp. 18–19; *Chicago Tribune*, 27 April 1933, p. 6; 25 April 1933, p. 8; 9 May 1933, p. 1; and 10 May 1933, p. 1.

43. "Tax Association Defies Kelly," p. 11; *Chicago Tribune*, 29 April 1933, pp. 1, 4; Honest Money Founders, *The Money Menace*; and Pratt, Interview.

44. U.S. Bureau of the Census, *Financial Statistics, 1930*, p. 248; and *1933*, p. 44.

45. Ibid., *1928*, p. 150; *1929*, p. 152; *1930*, p. 248; *1931*, p. 90; *1932*, p. 52; *1933*, p. 44; and *1940*, p. 15.

46. *Chicago Evening Post*, 6 July 1932, p. 5; *Chicago Tribune*, 15 November 1932; and *Proceedings of the American Municipal Association, 1931–1935*, p. 102.

47. Bernhard, "Five Years' Experience," p. 39; and Illinois Legislative Council, *Tax Delinquency*, p. 9. Instilling fear in delinquent taxpayers was the hallmark of the Skarda Act. According to Leland, a supporter of the law, "The threat that a receiver may be appointed is more effective in bringing taxes in, than the payments received under the operation of the receiverships, after appointment. It has become the game of driving the tax payer,

through fear, to pay his taxes." *Proceedings of the National Tax Association* (1935), p. 275.

48. Kuester, Interview.

49. "Tax Dodgers," p. 2.

50. Leet and Paige, *Property Tax Limitation Laws*, p. 21.

51. *Chicago Evening Post*, 27 October 1932, p. 1.

Chapter 5

1. Lutz, *Public Finance*, p. 516; and Chatters and Harris, "Tax Collection," p. 16.

2. Buttenheim, "Shall Our City Plans Gather Dust," p. 35; and Merriam, "Reducing Government Costs," p. 147.

3. Traxler, "Why Pay Taxes?" p. 81.

4. *New Republic* 76, 13 September 1933, pp. 113–14; Mayer, "When Teachers Strike," pp. 121–25; Hallgren, "Help Wanted," p. 534; and *Atlanta Constitution*, 12 February 1932, p. 9.

5. *New York Herald Tribune*, 22 March 1932, p. 2.

6. *New York Times*, 2 January 1932, p. 23.

7. *Bond Buyer*, 29 April 1933, p. 5.

8. Ibid.

9. *New York Times*, 12 June 1949.

10. *Bond Buyer*, 29 April 1933, p. 5.

11. *New York Times*, 11 October 1933, p. 37.

12. *Bond Buyer*, 17 November 1934, p. 71.

13. Ibid.; and *New York Times*, 10 March 1960, p. 31.

14. *Who Was Who*, p. 596; and *New York Times*, 9 December 1971, p. 50.

15. *Who Was Who*, p. 596.

16. *Proceedings of the Michigan Municipal League*, p. 92 (emphasis Reed's).

17. Stewart, *A Half Century of Municipal Reform*, pp. 112–13; and Committee on Citizens' Councils for Constructive Economy, *Citizens' Councils for Constructive Economy*, pp. 1–2. A few other members of CCCE were Florence Curtis Hanson, secretary-treasurer of the American Federation of Teachers, Frank Bane, director of the American Public Welfare Association, and Flavel Shurtleff, secretary of the National Conference on City Planning. Newspaper release from the Citizens' Councils for Constructive Economy, 29 March 1933, Box 246, Papers of the League of Women Voters.

18. Committee on Citizens' Councils for Constructive Economy, *Citizens' Councils for Constructive Economy*, pp. 1–2; and *Bond Buyer*, 26 August 1933, p. 7.

19. " 'Pay Your Taxes,' " p. 4.

20. National Municipal League, "What are the Prospects?" 19 June 1934, p. 3, "You and Your Government" series, Papers of the National Broadcasting Company.

21. National Municipal League, "What are the Prospects," p. 3.

22. Ibid., p. 4; and Jones, "Mr. Citizen Contemplates."

23. *Bond Buyer*, 26 August 1933, p. 7.

24. *City Manager Yearbook*, 1933, p. 105 (emphasis Leland's).

25. *Proceedings of the Investment Bankers' Association of America* (1931), p. 247; and Buttenheim, "Are Local Expenditures Excessive?" p. 2; and Anderson, "The Other Side," p. 49.

To CCCE's founders, constructive economy meant reduction in the unit cost of services through increased operating efficiency. It did not entail elimination or even reduction in the total budget of the service. Carl H. Milam to Belle Sherwin, 5 January 1933, Box 246, Papers of the League of Women Voters.

26. Buttenheim, "Are Local Expenditures Excessive?" p. 1.

27. National Municipal League, "Harmonizing the Tax System," 24 September 1935, "You and Your Government" series, Papers of the National Broadcasting Company.

28. Pay Your Taxes Campaign, *Campaign Manual*, p. 3

29. Ibid., p. 7

30. Ibid., p. 8

31. Pay Your Taxes Campaign, *Publicity Handbook*, p. 1

32. Ibid., pp. 3, 4.

33. Ibid., pp. 7, 5; and Pay Your Taxes Campaign, *Campaign Manual*, p. 16. In another violation of the pledge to avoid controversial statements, the *Campaign Manual* (p. 10) urged pay-your-taxers to show that "the city cannot reduce its expenditures to meet lowered income as can a business house, since the number of citizens remains the same and their demands in hard times are for more, not fewer services."

34. Kloske, "Fiscal Conservatism," p. 20; and Bird, *The Trend*, p. 21.

35. Bird, *The Trend*, p. 21; and Kloske, "Fiscal Conservatism," p. 21.

36. Kloske, "Fiscal Conservatism," p. 26; "Selling the City," *Public Management* 15 (January 1933): 29; and "City Advertises," p. 24.

37. Bird, *The Trend*, p. 21; Kloske, "Fiscal Conservatism," p. 27; and *Newark Evening News*, 15 September 1933, p. 4.

38. *Newark Evening News*, 15 September 1933, p. 4.

39. Ibid., 15 September 1933, p. 4, 19 September 1933, p. 8, 30 September 1933; and Hillhouse, *Municipal Bonds*, p. 432.

40. *Newark Evening News*, 30 September 1933; and Parnell, "Tax-paying Drive," p. 58.

41. *Newark Evening News*, 5 October 1933, p. 2, 28 September 1933, 16 September 1933, p. 4.

42. Ibid., 19 September 1933, p. 8, 6 October 1933, p. 1; and *Newark Star Eagle*, 11 October 1933, p. 12.

43. *Newark Evening News*, 13 October, p. 7, 30 September 1933.

44. Ibid., 3 October 1933, p. 6; and *Newark Star Eagle*, 12 October 1933, p. 13.

45. *Newark Evening News*, 10 October 1933, p. 1.

46. Ibid., 5 October 1933, p. 2, 9 October 1933, p. 14.

47. Ibid., 9 October 1933, p. 14, and 13 October 1933, p. 9.

48. Parnell, "Tax-paying Drive," p. 58; *Newark Evening News*, 25 October 1933, p. 5, 3 October 1933, p. 6; and Bird, *The Trend*, p. 21.

49. Fuller, "Tax Delinquency," p. 373; and *National Municipal Review* 23 (May 1934): 285, 286.

50. Taylor, *An Inquiry*, p. 250.

51. Anderson, "The Other Side," p. 49.

52. "Wake Up, Democracy!" pp. 64–65; and Harrison, "Taxes," p. 57.

53. National Municipal League, "Secrets of Municipal Credit," 10 October 1933, p. 2, "You and Your Government" series, Papers of the National Broadcasting System.

54. "Lotteries—A Mediaeval Throwback," *Tax Policy* 2 (October 1934): 1; and Mencken, *A Mencken Chrestomathy*, p. 147.

55. Walker, "The ABC's," p. 49.

56. Wolfe, *The Limits of Legitimacy*, p. 282 (emphasis Wolfe's); and *Proceedings of the Michigan Municipal League*, p. 91.

57. Pay Your Taxes Campaign, *Campaign Manual*, p. 16; and Pay Your Taxes Campaign, *Publicity Handbook*, p. 11.

58. Hoan, *City Government*, pp. 22–23.

59. National Municipal League, "Secrets," p. 2; *American City* 48 (June 1933): 61; and *Bond Buyer*, 14 October 1933, p. 6.

60. *Proceedings of the Investment Bankers' Association of America* (1934), p. 119; and Chatters, "Methods That Have Proved Successful," p. 37.

61. Pay Your Taxes Campaign, *Campaign Manual*, p. 14; and "Milwaukee Collects," p. 3.

62. Shultz, *American Public Finance*, p. 352.

63. Pay Your Taxes Campaign, *Campaign Manual*, p. 9; and Smith, "Recent Legislative Indulgences," p. 371.

64. Smith, "Recent Legislative Indulgences," p. 377; *American City* (August 1933): 37; and Bush, "State Centralization," p. 11.

65. Swierenga, *Acres For Cents*.

66. National Municipal League, "Secrets," p. 11; and "Memphis Has Tax Club," p. 1.

67. *Investment Banking*, 18 November 1933, p. 62; *National Municipal Review* 23 (April 1934): 234; and National Municipal League, "Why Taxpayers Strike," 12 December 1933, p. 6, "You and Your Government" series, Papers of the National Broadcasting Company.

68. Woodworth, "Delinquent Taxes," p. 423.

69. Chatters, "Michigan City Overburdened," p. 273; and Simpson, "Tax Delinquency," p. 149.

70. *National Municipal Review* 22 (July 1933): 307. On the "You and Your Government" radio series, Murray Seasongood, president of the National Municipal League, maintained, "In many places besides Chicago taxpayers are failing to pay their just public debts, some because they cannot, but many more stupidly and selfishly trying to take advantage of the situation." *Bond Buyer*, 7 October 1933, p. 6.

71. *Proceedings of the American Municipal Association*, p. 206; Pay Your Taxes Campaign, *Campaign Manual*, p. 7; Chatters, "Methods That Have Proved Successful," p. 36; William E. Leuchtenburg, "The New Deal and the Analogue of War," pp. 93–94; Springer, "The Fighting Spirit," p. 260; and Buttenheim, "Shall Our City Plans Gather Dust," p. 33.

72. *Tax Policy* 1 (May 1934): 2; and "Using Common Sense," p. 52.

73. American Municipal Association, "Anarchism Through Economania," *Illinois Municipal Review* 12 (March 1933): 58. Rush is quoted in Szasz, *The Manufacture of Madness*, p. 140.

74. Traxler, "Why Pay Taxes?" p. 104.

75. DeArmond, *Merle Thorpe*; American Municipal Association, "Anarchism Through Economania," p. 59; and Frank, "Constructive Versus Destructive Economy," p. 315.

76. Buttenheim, "A Pragmatic Experiment," p. 639.

77. Harris, "Taxpayers Strike," p. 27; American Municipal Association, *Addresses and Papers*, 1934, Annual Meeting, Report No. 100, Chicago; and

"Constructive Economy in State and Local Government," in Reed, *Government in a Depression*, p. 1

Chapter 6

1. National Advisory Council, *Four Years*, pp. 1–4.
2. Ibid.
3. "Listen and Learn About Your Government," Box 19, Folder 66, 1933, Papers of the National Broadcasting Company; National Advisory Council, *Four Years*, p. 4; and *Illinois Municipal Review* 12 (November 1932): 214.
4. National Advisory Council, *Four Years*, p. 31.
5. Tyson, *Radio and Education*, pp. 208–9.
6. NAREB, National Committee, *Bulletin*, 4 (18 August 1934): 3.
7. National Advisory Council, *Four Years*, p. 31.
8. ——— to John W. Elwood, 20 June 1933, Box 19, Folder 66, Papers of the National Broadcasting Company; and National Municipal League, "Secrets of Municipal Credit," 10 October 1933, "You and Your Government Series," Papers of the National Broadcasting Company.
9. NACRE, Education Series, 1932, Box 12, Folder 17, Papers of the National Broadcasting Company; and Reed, "The Role of Government," p. 210.
10. Tyson, *Radio and Education*, 1932, pp. 50–51. In a letter to Howard P. Jones, the secretary of CCCE, Reed termed "You and Your Government" the "first step in the National Pay Your Taxes Campaign." Reed to Jones, 26 September 1933, July–December Folder, Papers of Thomas H. Reed.
11. Tyson, *Radio and Education*, 1932, p. 50 (emphasis added).
12. National Advisory Council, *Four Years*, pp. 50, 56.
13. "Report of the National Municipal League's Committee on Citizens' Councils for Constructive Economy," 1 March 1934, Papers of the League of Women Voters, Box 276; and National Advisory Council, *Four Years*, pp. 66–68. In 1935, all NBC networks, including the blue and red, reached a total of ninety-nine stations. Ibid., p. 52.
14. Newspaper clipping, Box 19, Folder 65, Papers of the National Broadcasting Company.
15. Levering Tyson to Richard C. Patterson, 29 November 1932, Box 12, Folder 15, Papers of the National Broadcasting Company.
16. Reed observed, "The principal demand for the ["You and Your Government"] published addresses is from libraries, from certain individuals and organizations who wish to circulate them for propaganda purposes, and by teachers for classroom use in high school and colleges." Tyson, *Radio and Education*, 1932, pp. 126, 208–9. National Advisory Council, *Four Years*, p. 45; and Tyson to Patterson, 29 November 1932.
17. National Advisory Council, *Four Years*, p. 38.
18. Ibid., p. 20.
19. National Municipal League, "A Voice in the Dark," by Edward M. Barrows, 29 December 1933, "You and Your Government" series, pp. 5, 8, 9, Papers of the National Broadcasting Company.
20. National Advisory Council, *Four Years*, p. 20; and *Citizens' Councils News* 1, 1 January 1934, p. 2.
21. Tyson, *Radio and Education*, 1933, p. 125.
22. Ibid., p. 75.

23. "More Money for Public Works," *National Municipal Review* 22 (October 1933): 500–507.

24. Ibid., pp. 500–503, 507 (emphasis in the original).

25. "Report of the National Municipal League's Committee on Citizens' Councils for Constructive Economy," Papers of the League of Women Voters.

Chapter 7

1. Jones, "Mr. Citizen Contemplates," p. 165.

2. According to Reed, "The slackers have been smoked out, and the sacredness of the obligation to support government as an indispensable necessity of civilized existence brought home to the people." National Municipal League, "Civitas Redivivus—1934," p. 2, "You and Your Government" series; and White, "Turning Knowledge into Votes," p. 85.

3. *National Municipal Review* 22 (June 1933): 261; and Gray, "How Business Men Assist," pp. 24–25.

4. Thorpe, "Leave the People Something to Do!" p. 11.

5. *Tax Policy* 1 (August 1934): 2–3; and Jensen, "Property Tax Limitations," pp. 2–7; *Tax Policy* 2 (April 1935): 6; and Jensen, "Legislative Proposals," p. 631.

6. NAREB, National Committee, *Bulletin* 1 (1934); and *Tax Policy* 2 (April 1935): 1–6.

7. NAREB, *Bulletin* 4 (18 August 1934), p. 1; Jensen, "Property Tax Limitations," p. 3; and *Tax Policy* 2 (April 1935): 6.

8. Jensen, "Legislative Proposals," p. 634. After these defeats of tax limitations, George C. S. Benson suggested, "Apparently the real estate boards must revise their tactics—or subscribe to a broader outlook." Benson, "American State and Local Government," p. 285.

9. Williams, *Grants-In-Aid*, p. 125.

10. Ibid., pp. 254, 239, 234–35; and Illinois Tax Commission, *Constitutional Tax Rate Limitation*, pp. 36–37. Harold Ickes maintained that the PWA "has probably been the most important single factor responsible for the recent trend toward the use of revenue bonds as a method of financing municipal public service enterprises." Ibid., p. 234.

11. Hall, "A Cloud," p. 628; Ickes, *Back to Work*, pp. 218–19; and *Proceedings of the American Municipal Association*, pp. 370, 448.

12. Bird, *The Trend*, p. 5. Of 106 cities surveyed, delinquency declined in 77.3 percent and increased, or stayed the same, in 22.7 percent. *New York Times*, 3 March 1935.

13. "Towards Understanding," *National Municipal Review* 22 (October 1933): 490.

14. National Municipal League, "Enforcing Tax Collections," 11 December 1934, "You and Your Government" series, Papers of the National Broadcasting Company; *Municipal Finance News Letter* 3, 1 May 1933, p. 2; *Municipal Finance News Letter* 3, 15 June 1933; and *Proceedings of the Investment Bankers' Association of America* (1934), p. 121.

15. The National Municipal League, a consistent booster of the Skarda method, incorporated tax receiverships into its model real estate tax collection law. Other provisions included appointment rather than election of assessors, shortening of redemption periods, and installment payment of

taxes. *National Municipal Review* 24, Supplement (May 1935): 294–97, 301. National Municipal League, "Tax Paying Made Easier," 19 December 1934, "You and Your Government" series, Papers of the National Broadcasting Company.

16. U.S. Congress, *Home Owners' Loan Act*, p. 12; U.S. Congress, *Congressional Record*, p. 5586; Harriss, *History and Policies*, p. 130; and *Federal Home Loan Bank Review* 3 (April 1936): 306.

17. *New York Times*, 3 March 1935, p. 13; Hoan, *City Government*, p. 173; and Pay Your Taxes Campaign, *Campaign Manual*, p. 12. Another federal program, the Civil Works Administration, also subsidized the drive against delinquency. In Yonkers and other cities, it paid the wages of unemployed workers who participated in pay-your-taxes drives. Pay Your Taxes Campaign, *Publicity Handbook*, p. 17.

18. Jackson, *The Crabgrass Frontier*, pp. 196, 230; and Harriss, *History and Policies*, p. 114.

19. Ely, "Taxation in Hard Times," p. 67.

20. Mencken, "What is Going on," pp. 259–60.

21. *Tax Yields*, pp. 21, 25.

22. Ibid.

23. Leland, "Should Public Expenditures Be Reduced?" p. 393; *Weekly Legislative Newsletter* 10 (14 April 1934): 1, 3; and *Washington Taxpayer* 1 (June 1936): 2.

24. *North Dakota Taxpayer* 1 (August 1935): 1–2, 8; and (February 1935): 2.

25. *Washington Taxpayer* 1 (July 1936): 1–2.

26. Holmes, "What Makes a Tax Limitation Campaign Successful?" p. 285.

27. Karl, *Executive Reorganization*, p. 114; and Fox, *Better City Government*, p. 176.

28. Thorpe, *In Behalf of the Delinquent Taxpayer*, p. 38.

29. Merriam, "Reducing Government Costs," p. 146.

30. *Oklahoma Municipal Review* 7 (May 1933): 70; and *Comptroller* 6 (August 1932) (emphasis in the original).

31. See Hays, "The Politics of Reform," pp. 157–69; and Link and McCormick, *Progressivism*, pp. 95–96.

32. Merriam, "Reducing Government Costs," p. 150; and *Oklahoma Municipal Review* 7 (May 1933): 71.

33. *Tax Policy* 2 (November 1934): 2.

34. *Proceedings of the National Tax Association* (1934), p. 44; and Illinois Tax Commission, *Constitutional Tax Rate Limitation*, p. 23.

35. When advocates of public-choice theory Geoffrey Brennan and James M. Buchanan asserted that constitutionalism is alien to thought patterns of tax economists and reformers, they wrote from the perspective of the tax-limitation campaigns of the 1970s. This characterization has even greater applicability to the 1930s. Brennan and Buchanan, *The Power To Tax*, p. 189.

36. *Tax Policy* 1 (August 1934): 8; Lutz, *Public Finance*, p. 528; and "Cluttering up the State Constitutions," p. 1. Tax experts had long objected to uniformity clauses, which commonly dated to the nineteenth century. Uniformity came in for particular denunciation because the courts often used it to rule out any sort of graduated income tax or classified personal property tax.

37. Jensen, "Property Tax Limitations," p. 2. Brennan and Buchanan ob-

served, "that nonelectoral rules are conceivable, that they do in fact play a significant part in most recognizably democratic constitutions currently operative, and that it is not obvious on prima facie grounds that they are less significant in controlling government than are purely electoral constraints." Brennan and Buchanan, *The Power to Tax*, pp. 5, 10.

38. *Proceedings of the Michigan Municipal League*, 1932, p. 91; and "Tax Limits Prove Unwise," p. 2.

39. Karl, *Executive Reorganization*, p. 56.

40. Brennan and Buchanan, *The Power to Tax*, p. 25; and NAREB, *Bulletin* 3 (16 July 1934).

41. Brennan and Buchanan, *The Power to Tax*, p. 197; and *Weekly Legislative Letter*, 7 April 1934, p. 2.

42. Harold D. Smith, "Tax Limitation," p. 52 (emphasis mine); and NAREB, *Bulletin* 3.

43. Garet Garrett, "Insatiable Government," p. 30.

44. Ibid.

45. Ibid.

46. Ibid., p. 34.

47. Tax Policy League, *Report*; and National Municipal League, "Pruning the City Budget," 5 December 1933, p. 5, "You and Your Government" series, Papers of the National Broadcasting Company.

48. American Municipal Association et al., "Reducing the Cost," p. 54 (emphasis in the original); and "Minutes of Meeting of Executive Committee on Citizens' Councils," 18 May 1933, File: Citizens' Councils for Constructive Economy, Box 76, Papers of the League of Women Voters. "I believe," concluded Murray Seasongood, the president of the National Municipal League, "it would be best to enter them [taxpayers' organizations] from within through an individual rather than to attack them or for instance engage in a series of debates—most often fruitless." Seasongood to Howard P. Jones, 17 May 1933.

49. Of the 1,159 taxpayers' groups in the 1938 study, 17 had a national basis, 110 state, and 1,032 local. "Taxpayers' Organizations"; "Taxpayers' Organizations: Supplement," p. 1; and Elting, "You CAN Cut Taxes!" p. 10.

50. Sylvia F. Porter, "Taxpayers," p. 52; and Stewart, *A Half Century of Municipal Reform*, p. 113. For more information on taxpayers' organizations in the late 1930s and early 1940s, see Elting, "Tax Fight," pp. 12–15, 36–37; and Gaskill, "Caviar on Your Tax Bill," pp. 116–19.

51. Clifford, "The Massachusetts Taxpayers Foundation," p. 29.

52. National Municipal League, "Retrenching in State and Local Expenditures: A General View," pp. 1–2, "You and Your Government" series. Reprinted in Reed, *Government in a Depression*.

Conclusion

1. For more on the anti–New Deal activity of Bardo and Mangan, see Wolfskill and Hudson, *All But the People*, pp. 158, 347.

2. Ibid. Also see Wolfskill, *The Revolt of the Conservatives*.

3. Patterson, *The New Deal and the States*; and Graham, *The New Deal*, p, 176.

4. Braeman, Bremner, and Brody, *The New Deal*, p. xiv; and Rosen, *Hoover, Roosevelt, and the Brains' Trust*, p. 331.

5. McElvaine, *The Great Depression*, pp. 206, 146.

6. Friedel, *Franklin D. Roosevelt*, p. 363; and Roosevelt, *The Public Papers and Addresses*, pp. 671, 680. Quoted in Flynn, *Country Squire*, pp. 58–59.

7. McElvaine, *The Great Depression*, p. 200.

8. Graham, *The New Deal*, pp. x, 165–67. Also see Graham, *An Encore for Reform*, p. 25. For an example of this historical debate, see Bernstein, "The Conservative Achievements," pp. 147–62.

9. Ironically, Louis Hartz, one of the founders of the misnamed "consensus school," rejected all attempts to picture political issues in terms of "greater" or "lesser." "You do not," wrote Hartz, "get closer to the significance of an earthquake by ignoring the terrain on which it takes place." Quoted in Sternsher, *Consensus*, p. 353.

Appendix

1. *Reinecke* v. *McDonough*, #4803, In the County Court of Cook County, July Term, 1932, Illinois State Archives, Springfield.

2. Edwards, "A Social Economic Grouping," pp. 377–87. The source for the occupational profile of Chicago was from the U.S. Department of Commerce, *Fifteenth Census*.

3. Cook County, *Real Estate Assessment*.

4. Cook County, *Assessments of Real Estate*, pp. 103, 106; and Burgess and Newcomb, *Census Data*, p. xv.

BIBLIOGRAPHY

Manuscript Collections

Chicago Teachers' Federation. Papers. Chicago Historical Society.

Dodd, Walter F. Papers. Chicago Historical Society.

Ewig, Charles H. Papers. Chicago Historical Society.

Hodes, Barnet. Papers. Chicago Historical Society.

Hodes, Barnet. Scrapbook. In possession of Kay Hodes Kamin, Chicago.

Horner, Henry. Papers. Illinois State Historical Library, Springfield.

Institute for Research in Land Economics and Public Utilities. Papers. Northwestern University.

Jarecki, Edmund K. Papers. University of Illinois, Chicago.

League of Women Voters. Papers. Library of Congress, Washington, D.C.

Merriam, Charles E. Papers. University of Chicago.

National Broadcasting Company. Papers. Wisconsin State Historical Society, Madison.

Olander, Victor. Papers. University of Illinois, Chicago.

Reed, Thomas H. Papers. Bentley Historical Library, Ann Arbor, Michigan.

Public Documents

Advisory Commission on Intergovernmental Relations. *City Financial Emergencies: The Intergovernmental Dimension*. Washington, D.C., 1973.

Chicago, Illinois. *Journal of the Proceedings of the City Council*. Chicago, 1931–32.

Cook County, Illinois. Joint Commission on Real Estate Valuation. *A Study of the Assessment and Taxation of Personal Property in Cook County*. Report 4. Chicago, 1930.

———. Office of Assessor. *Assessments of Real Estate and Personal Property in Cook County, Illinois for the Tax Years of 1931–1932–1933*. Chicago, 1934.

_____. *Real Estate Assessment for 1931.* Chicago, [ca. 1933].

Illinois. Governor's Tax Conference. *Report of the Executive Committee to the Governor's Tax Conference.* Springfield, 1931.

_____. Illinois Legislative Council. *Tax Delinquency in Illinois with Particular Reference to Cook County.* Springfield, 1939.

_____. Illinois Tax Commission. *Constitutional Tax Rate Limitation for Illinois.* Chicago, 1934.

President's Conference on Home Building and Home Ownership. *Home Finance and Taxation.* Vol. 2. Washington, D.C., 1932.

U.S. Congress. Senate. *Congressional Record.* 73d Cong., 1st sess., 1933.

_____. Committee on Banking and Currency. *Home Owners' Loan Act: Hearings on S. 1317.* 73d Cong., 1st sess., 1933.

U.S. Bureau of the Census. *Current Tax Delinquency by States and Counties, Levies of 1933–34,* Vol. 2. Washington, D.C., 1934.

_____. *Fifteenth Census of the United States: 1930, Occupation Statistics, Illinois.* Washington, D.C., 1932.

_____. *Financial Statistics of Cities Having a Population of Over 30,000.* Washington, D.C., 1928–32 (published annually).

_____. *Financial Statistics of Cities Having a Population of Over 100,000.* Washington, D.C., 1933–40 (published annually).

Legal Documents

George W. Reinecke et al. v. *Joseph B. McDonough et al.,* No. 4803, In the County Court of Cook County, *List of Complaints.* July Term, 1932. Illinois State Archives, Springfield.

People of the State of Illinois, ex rel. Thomas J. Courtney v. *Association of Real Estate Taxpayers of Ilinois,* No. 21697, In the Supreme Court of Illinois, *Abstract.* June Term, 1932. Illinois State Archives, Springfield.

People of the State of Illinois, ex rel. Thomas J. Courtney v. *Association of Real Estate Taxpayers of Illinois,* No. 21697, In the Supreme Court of Illinois, *Brief and Argument in Behalf of the Relator.* June Term, 1932. Illinois State Archives, Springfield.

People, ex rel. Joseph B. McDonough v. *Lillian Cesar,* 349 *Illinois Reports,* 732–389. October 1932.

Publications of the Association of Real Estate Taxpayers (ARET)

$548,648,264.00: Our Tax Bills in 1931. Chicago, [1931]. ARET literature packet. Joseph Regenstein Library. University of Chicago.

The Four Essentials of Revenue Relief. Chicago, [ca. 1931].

1929 and 1930 Taxes Voided. Chicago, [1931].

A Protest Against the Acceptance of the Report of the Executive Committee of the Governor's Tax Conference. Chicago, 1931.

Taxes, Unemployment and Business Recovery: An Outline of Cause and Effect Relationships. Chicago, 1930. New York Public Library.

The Tax Strikers. Chicago, [1931]. ARET literature packet.
Today You Must Choose. Chicago, [ca. 1931]. ARET literature packet.
Your 1930 Tax Bill! Chicago, 1932. ARET literature packet.

Interviews

Bistor, William C. Telephone interview with author. 20 October 1985.
Chinnock, Ronald. Interview with author. Evanston, Illinois. 23 April
1985.
Diller, Ted. Interview with author. Chicago, Illinois. 21 May 1985.
Kuester, Edwin J. Interview with author. Kankakee, Illinois. 14 Novem-
ber 1985.
Pratt, John T. Telephone interview with author. 27 September 1985.
Waller, Thatcher. Telephone conversation with author. 10 November
1985.

Newspapers

Atlanta Constitution
Chicago Daily News
Chicago Evening American
Chicago Evening Post
Chicago Herald and Examiner
Chicago Tribune
Detroit Free Press
Detroit News
Milwaukee Journal
Milwaukee Leader
Newark Evening News
Newark Star Eagle
New York Herald Tribune
New York Times

Periodicals

American City
American Economic Review
American Magazine
American Mercury
American Political Science Review
Bond Buyer
Bulletin (American Library Association)
Bulletin (Civic Federation of Chicago)
Bulletin (National Association of Real Estate Boards [NAREB])
Bulletin (National Committee on Real Estate Taxation of NAREB)
Chicagoan

Chicago Real Estate Magazine
Chicago Principals' Club Reporter
Chicago Schools Journal
Chicago Union Teacher
Citizens' Councils News
Colliers
Commerce
Comptroller
Current History
Economist and Magazine of LaSalle Street
Federal Home Loan Bank Review
Federation News
Forbes
Forum
Freehold
Grain Growers' Guide
Illinois Journal of Commerce
Illinois Law Review
Illinois Municipal Review
Illinois Teacher
Independent Woman
Investment Banking
Iowa Taxpayer
Journal of American History
Journal of Libertarian Studies
Journal of the American Statistical Association
Journal of the History of Ideas
Journal of the Illinois State Historical Society
Law and Contemporary Problems
Lightnin'
Literary Digest
Michigan History
Minnesota Municipalities
Municipal Finance
Municipal Finance News Letter
Municipality
Nation
National Municipal Review
Nation's Business
Nation's Schools
New Republic
North Dakota Taxpayer
Oklahoma Municipal Review
Pacific Northwest Quarterly
Printers' Ink
Public Administrators' News Letter

Public Management
Review of Reviews
Saturday Evening Post
Survey
Tax Digest
Tax Magazine
Taxpayer of Chicago and Cook County
Tax Policy
Washington Taxpayer
Weekly Legislative Letter (New York Economic Council, Inc.)
Wisconsin Taxpayer

Books and Pamphlets

Abbott, Edith. *The Tenements of Chicago, 1908–1935*. Chicago: University of Chicago Press, 1936.

Adams, James Ring. *Secrets of the Tax Revolt*. New York: Harcourt Brace Jovanovich Publishers, 1984.

Allan and District History Book Committee. *Times Past to Present*. Allan, Sask.: Allan and District History Book Committee, 1981.

American Taxpayers' League. *Handbook on Taxation*. Washington, D.C., 1932.

Barnouw, Erik. *The Golden Web: A History of Radio Broadcasting in the United States, 1933 to 1953*. New York: Oxford University Press, 1968.

_____. *A Tower in Babel: A History of Broadcasting in the United States, to 1933*. New York: Oxford University Press, 1966.

Benson, Lee. *The Concept of Jacksonian Democracy: New York as a Test Case*. Princeton: Princeton University Press, 1961.

Bingham, Alfred M. *Insurgent America: Revolt of the Middle-Classes*. New York: Harper and Brothers Publishers, 1935.

Biographical and Genealogical History of Cass, Miami, Howard, and Tipton Counties. Vol. 2. Chicago: Lewis Publishing Company, 1898.

Bird, Frederick L. *The Trend of Tax Delinquency, 1930–1937: Cities over 50,000 Population*. New York: Dun and Bradstreet, 1938.

Braeman, John, et al. *Change and Continuity in Twentieth-Century America*. New York: Harper and Row, 1966.

Braeman, John, Robert H. Bremner, and David Brody. *The New Deal: The State and Local Levels*. Columbus: Ohio State University Press, 1975.

Brennan, Geoffrey, and James M. Buchanan. *The Power to Tax: Analytical Foundations of a Fiscal Constitution*. Cambridge: Cambridge University Press, 1980.

Brinkley, Alan. *Voices of Protest: Huey Long, Father Coughlin, and the Great Depression*. New York: Vintage Books, 1982.

Brownlow, Louis, and Charles S. Archer. *Less Government Or More?* Chicago: American Library Association, 1933.

Bryce, James. *The American Commonwealth*. New York: Macmillan Company, 1909.

Buchanan, James M. *Fiscal Theory and Political Economy: Selected Essays*. Chapel Hill: University of North Carolina Press, 1960.

———. *Public Finance in Democratic Process: Fiscal Institutions and Individual Choice*. Chapel Hill: University of North Carolina Press, 1967.

Burgess, Ernest W., and Charles Newcomb. *Census Data of the City of Chicago, 1930*. Chicago: University of Chicago Press, 1933.

Calhoun, John C. *A Disquisition on Government and Selections from the Discourse*. Indianapolis: Bobbs-Merrill Company, 1953.

Carr, William G. *School Finance*. Palo Alto, Calif.: Stanford University Press, 1933.

City Problems of 1933: The Annual Proceedings of the United States Conference of Mayors. Chicago, 1933.

Committee on Citizens' Councils for Constructive Economy. *A Citizens' Council, Why and How?* New York, [1933].

———. *Citizens' Councils for Constructive Economy*. New York, [1933].

Connolly, William, ed. *Legitimacy and the State*. New York: New York University Press, 1984.

Corey, Lewis. *The Crisis of the Middle Class*. New York: Covici, Friede, 1935.

Croly, Herbert. *The Promise of American Life*. New York: Macmillan Company, 1909.

Dahl, Robert A. *Pluralist Democracy in the United States: Conflict and Consent*. Chicago: Rand McNally and Company, 1967.

———. *Polyarchy: Participation and Opposition*. New Haven: Yale University Press, 1971.

DeArmond, Fred. *Merle Thorpe: Champion of the Forgotten Man*. Springfield, Ill.: Mycroft Press, 1959.

Denitch, Bogan, ed. *Legitimation of Regimes: An International Framework for Analysis*. New York: Sage Studies in International Sociology, 1979.

Dobyns, Fletcher. *The Underworld of American Politics*. New York: Fletcher Dobyns, 1932.

Ekirch, Arthur A., Jr. *The Decline of American Liberalism*. New York: Longmans, Green and Company, 1955.

Evans, Peter B., Dietrich Rueschemeyer, and Theda Skocpol, eds. *Bringing the State Back In*. Cambridge: Cambridge University Press, 1985.

Eyre, Virginia L. *A Study of Tax Delinquency in the Second Ward of Detroit with Special Reference to Apartment House Properties*. Detroit: Detroit Bureau of Governmental Research, 1932.

Fine, Sidney. *Frank Murphy: The Detroit Years*. Ann Arbor: University of Michigan Press, 1975.

Flynn, John T. *Country Squire in the White House*. New York: Doubleday, Doran, and Company, 1940.

Forsythe, Dall W. *Taxation and Political Change in the Young Nation, 1781–1833*. New York: Columbia University Press, 1977.

Fox, Kenneth. *Better City Government: Innovation in American Urban Politics, 1850–1937*. Philadelphia: Temple University Press, 1977.

Friedel, Frank. *Franklin D. Roosevelt: The Triumph*. Boston: Little, Brown and Company, 1956.

Gottfried, Alex. *Boss Cermak of Chicago: A Study of Political Leadership*. Seattle: University of Washington Press, 1962.

Graham, Otis L., Jr. *An Encore for Reform: The Old Progressives and the New Deal*. New York: Oxford University Press, 1967.

_____, ed. *The New Deal: The Critical Issues*. Boston: Little, Brown and Company, 1971.

Griffith, Ernest S. *A History of American City Government: The Conspicuous Failure, 1870–1900*. New York: Praeger Publishers, 1974.

Habermas, Jürgen. *Legitimation Crisis*. Translated by Thomas McCarthy. Boston: Beacon Press, 1973.

Hallgren, Mauritz A. *Seeds of Revolt: A Study of American Life and the Temper of the American People during the Depression*. New York: Alfred A. Knopf, 1933.

Harriss, C. Lowell. *History and Policies of the Home Owners' Loan Corporation*. New York: National Bureau of Economic Research, 1951.

Herrick, Mary J. *The Chicago Schools: A Social and Political History*. Beverly Hills: Sage Publications, 1971.

Higgs, Robert. *Crisis and Leviathan: Critical Episodes in the Growth of American Government*. New York: Oxford University Press, 1987.

Hillhouse, A. M. *Municipal Bonds: A Century of Experience*. New York: Prentice-Hall, 1936.

Hoan, Daniel W. *City Government: The Record of the Milwaukee Experiment*. New York: Harcourt, Brace and Company, 1936.

_____. *Taxes and Tax Dodgers*. Chicago: Socialist Party of America, 1934.

Hofstadter, Richard. *The American Political Tradition and the Men Who Made It*. New York: Vintage Books, 1948.

Honest Money Founders, Inc., *The Money Menace: A Warning to All American Citizens*. N.p., n.d.

Hoyt, Homer. *One Hundred Years of Land Values in Chicago: The Relationship of the Growth of Chicago to the Rise of its Land Values, 1830–1933*. Chicago: University of Chicago Press, 1933.

Ickes, Harold L. *Back to Work: The Story of the PWA*. New York: Macmillan Company, 1935.

Illinois Legislative Council. *Tax Delinquency in Illinois with Particular Reference to Cook County*. 1939.

Jackson, Kenneth T. *The Crabgrass Frontier: The Suburbanization of the United States*. New York: Oxford University Press, 1985.

Journal of Proceedings of the Ohio State Grange. 1932.

Karl, Barry D. *Charles E. Merriam and the Study of Politics*. Chicago: University of Chicago Press, 1974.

_____. *Executive Reorganization and Reform in the New Deal: The Genesis of Administrative Management, 1900–1939*. Cambridge: Harvard University Press, 1963.

Keller, Morton. *In Defense of Yesterday: James M. Beck and the Politics of Conservatism, 1861–1936*. New York: Coward-McCann, 1958.

Kimmel, Lewis H. *Cost of Government in the United States, 1934–1936*. New York: National Industrial Conference Board, 1937.

King, Clyde L. *Public Finance*. New York: Macmillan Company, 1935.

Leet, Glen, and Robert M. Paige, eds. *Property Tax Limitation Laws: The Evidence and the Arguments for and against Them by Twenty-four Authorities*. Chicago: Public Administration Service, 1934.

Leff, Mark H. *The Limits of Symbolic Reform: The New Deal and Taxation, 1933–1939*. Cambridge: Cambridge University Press, 1984.

Leggett, William. *Democratick Editorials: Essays in Jacksonian Political Economy by William Leggett*. Edited by Lawrence H. White. Indianapolis: Liberty Press, 1984.

Link, Arthur S., and Richard L. McCormick. *Progressivism*. Arlington Heights: Harlan Davidson, 1983.

Lutz, Harley L. *Public Finance*. New York: D. Appleton-Century Company, 1936.

McCormick, Anne O'Hare. *The World at Home: Selections from the Writings of Anne O'Hare McCormick*. Edited by Marion Turner Sheehan. New York: Alfred A. Knopf, 1956.

McCormick, Robert R. *Tax Eaters, Tax Eating, and Tax Eaten*. Chicago: The Tribune Company, 1933.

McDonald, Terrence J., and Sally K. Ward, eds. *The Politics of Urban Fiscal Policy*. Beverly Hills: Sage Publications, 1984.

McElvaine, Robert S. *The Great Depression in America, 1929–1941*. New York: Times Books, 1984.

Meites, Hyman. *History of the Jews of Chicago*. Chicago: Jewish Historical Society of Illinois, 1924.

Mencken, Henry Louis. *A Mencken Chrestomathy: Edited and Annotated by the Author*. New York: Alfred A. Knopf, 1974.

Merriam, Charles E., et al. *The Government of the Metropolitan Region of Chicago*. Chicago: University of Chicago Press, 1933.

Morton, William Lewis. *The Progressive Party in Canada*. Toronto: University of Toronto Press, 1950.

Musgrave, Richard A., and Alan T. Peacock. *Classics in the Theory of Public Finance*. London: Macmillan, 1962.

National Advisory Council on Radio and Education et al. *Four Years of Network Broadcasting*. Chicago: University of Chicago Press, 1936.

National Association of Real Estate Boards. *Over-all Limitation of Real Estate Taxation*. Chicago, 1935.

National Industrial Conference Board. *Cost of Government in the United States, 1933–1935*. New York: National Industrial Conference Board, 1935.

National Municipal League. *The Crisis in Municipal Finance*. New York, 1934.

O'Connor, James. *The Fiscal Crisis of the State*. New York: Martin's Press, 1973.

Olcott's Land Values Blue Book of Chicago. Chicago: George C. Olcott and Company, 1932.

Patterson, James T. *The New Deal and the States: Federalism in Transition*. Princeton: Princeton University Press, 1969.

Pay Your Taxes Campaign. National Committee. *Campaign Manual*. New York: National Municipal League, 1935.

Pay Your Taxes Campaign. National Committee. *Publicity Handbook*. New York: National Municipal League, 1935.

Proceedings of the American Municipal Association, 1931–1935. Chicago: Public Administration Service, 1936.

Proceedings of the Investment Bankers' Association of America. Published annually. 1930–35.

Proceedings of the Michigan Municipal League. Ann Arbor: Michigan Municipal League, 1932.

Proceedings of the National Tax Association. Published annually. 1930–35.

Reed, Thomas H., ed. *Government in a Depression: Constructive Economy in State and Local Government*. Chicago: University of Chicago Press, 1933.

Report of the Survey of the Schools of Chicago, Illinois. Vol. 1. New York: Bureau of Publications, Teachers' College, Columbia University, 1932.

Ribuffo, Leo P. *The Old Christian Right: The Protestant Far Right from the Great Depression to the Cold War*. Philadelphia: Temple University Press, 1983.

Roosevelt, Franklin D., *The Public Papers and Addresses of Franklin D. Roosevelt*. Edited by Samuel I. Rosenman. New York: Random House, 1938–50.

Rosen, Elliot A. *Hoover, Roosevelt, and the Brains Trust: From Depression to New Deal*. New York: Columbia University Press, 1977.

Rothbard, Murray N. *America's Great Depression*. Kansas City: Sheed and Ward, 1972

Shultz, William L. *American Public Finance and Taxation*. New York: Prentice-Hall, 1931.

Simpson, Herbert D. *Tax Racket and Tax Reform in Chicago*. Chicago Institute for Economic Research, 1930.

Sitkoff, Harvard, ed. *Fifty Years Later: The New Deal Evaluated*. Philadelphia: Temple University Press, 1985.

Slaughter, Thomas P. *The Whiskey Rebellion: Frontier Epilogue to the American Revolution*. New York: Oxford University Press, 1986.

Social Register. Chicago: Social Register Association, 1930–33.

Steed, Hal. *Georgia: Unfinished State*. New York: Alfred A. Knopf, 1942.

Sternsher, Bernard. *Consensus, Conflict, and American Historians*. Bloomington: Indiana University Press, 1975.

Stewart, Frank Mann. *A Half Century of Municipal Reform: The History of the National Municipal League*. Berkeley: University of California Press, 1950.

Strayer, George D., director. *Report of the Survey of the Schools of Chicago, Illinois*. New York: Bureau of Public Teachers' Colleges, 1932.

Stuart, William H. *Twenty Incredible Years*. Chicago: M. A. Donohue and Company, 1935.

Sutherland, Douglas. *Fifty Years on the Civic Front*. Chicago: The Civic Federation, 1943.

Swierenga, Robert P. *Acres for Cents: Delinquent Tax Auctions in Frontier Iowa*. Westport, Conn.: Greenwood Press, 1976.

Symes, Lillian, and Travers Clement. *Rebel America: The Story of Social Revolt in the United States*. New York: Harper and Brothers Publishers, 1934.

Szasz, Thomas S. *The Manufacture of Madness: A Comparative Study of the Inquisition and the Mental Health Movement*. New York: Harper and Row, 1970.

Szatmary, David P. *Shays' Rebellion: The Making of an Agrarian Insurrection*. Amherst, Mass., 1980.

Tax Policy League. *Report of Special Committee on Tax Policy to Aid Economic Recovery and Permanent Property*. New York, 1935.

Tax Yields: 1940: Tax Collection Statistics for the Various Units of Government with Explanatory Text and Analysis. Philadelphia: Tax Institute, 1941.

Taylor, John. *An Inquiry into the Principles and Policy of the Government of the United States*. New York: Bobbs-Merrill Company, 1969.

Teaford, Jon C. *City and Suburb: The Political Fragmentation of Metropolitan America, 1850–1970*. Baltimore: Johns Hopkins Press, 1979.

Thorpe, Merle. *In Behalf of the Delinquent Taxpayer—Present and Prospective*. N.p., 1932.

Tickton, Sidney G. *An Analysis of Tax Delinquency*. Detroit: Detroit Bureau of Economic Research, 1932.

Traylor, Melvin A. *What Can Be Done About Taxes: An Address by Melvin A. Traylor*. Traylor for President Club, 1932.

Tyson, Levering, ed. *Radio and Education*. Chicago: University of Chicago Press, 1932, 1933.

Walsh, George. *Gentleman Jimmy Walker: Mayor of the Jazz Age*. New York: Praeger Publishers, 1974.

West Virginia Taxpayers' Association. *The Tax Burden in West Virginia*. Charleston, 1932.

White, Leonard D. *The Prestige Value of Public Employment in Chicago*. Chicago: University of Chicago Press, 1929.

Who's Who in Chicago and Vicinity. Chicago: A. N. Marquis Company, 1931–45.

Who Was Who in America. Vol. 5. St. Louis: Von Hoffman Press, 1973.

Wickens, David L. *Residential Real Estate: Its Economic Position as Shown by Values, Rents, Family Incomes, Financing and Construction, Together with Estimates for All Real Estate*. New York: National Bureau of Economic Research, 1941.

Williams, Elmer Lynn. *They Got Their Man: A Story of Income Tax Persecution*. Milwaukee: Wisconsin Cuneo Press, 1941.

Williams, J. Kerwin. *Grants-In-Aid under the Public Works Administration:*

A Study in Federal-State-Local Relations. New York: Columbia University Press, 1939.

Wolfe, Alan. *The Limits of Legitimacy: Political Contradictions of Contemporary Capitalism.* New York: Free Press, 1977.

Wolfskill, George. *The Revolt of the Conservatives.* Boston: Houghton-Mifflin Company, 1962.

Wolfskill, George, and John A. Hudson. *All but the People: Franklin D. Roosevelt and His Critics, 1933–39.* London: Collier-Macmillan, 1969.

Wrigley, Julia. *Class, Politics, and the Public Schools: Chicago, 1900–1950.* New Brunswick, N.J.: Rutgers University Press, 1982.

Yearley, Clifton K. *The Money Machines: the Breakdown and Reform of Governmental and Party Finance in the North, 1860–1920.* Albany: State University of New York Press, 1970.

Articles

Allen, H. K. "Collection of Delinquent Taxes by Recourse to the Taxed Property." *Law and Contemporary Problems* 3 (June 1936): 397–404.

American Municipal Association et al. "Anarchism through Economania." *Illinois Municipal Review* 12 (April 1933): 58–60.

_____. "Reducing the Cost of Local Government." *Illinois Municipal Review* 12 (April 1933): 54–57.

Anderson, William. "The Other Side of the Tax Problem." *Illinois Municipal Review* 11 (March 1932).

Babcock, James. "Farm Revolt in Iowa." *Social Forces* 12 (March 1934): 369–73.

Barrows, Edward M. "A Challenge to Reform." *National Municipal Review* 22 (May 1933).

Benson, George C. S. "American State and Local Government." *American Political Science Review* 31 (February 1937): 284–85.

Bernstein, Barton J. "The Conservative Achievements of Liberal Reform." In *The New Deal: The Critical Issues,* edited by Otis L. Graham, Jr. Boston: Little, Brown and Company, 1971.

Bilharz, Millard J. "Solon's Slur Brings Hot Retort." *Taxpayer of Chicago and Cook County,* 5 November 1931, p. 7.

Bistor, James E. "Majority Must Become Taxpayers." *Chicago Real Estate Magazine* 9, 3 September 1932.

_____. "Pendulum May Swing Back." *Chicago Real Estate Magazine* 5, 20 September 1930.

_____. "Plans of Taxpayers' Association." *Chicago Real Estate Magazine* 4, 31 May 1930, pp. 10–11.

Bogan, William J. "Needs of the Chicago Public Schools." *Chicago Schools Journal* 15 (January–June 1933).

Burbank, Lyman B. "Chicago Public Schools and the Depression Years of 1928–1937." *Journal of the Illinois State Historical Society* 64 (Winter 1971): 365–81.

Buttenheim, Harold S. "Are Local Expenditures Excessive?" *Municipality* 28 (January 1933).
_____. "A Pragmatic Experiment With Taxes," *Survey* 68, 1 December 1932, p. 639.
_____. "Shall Our City Plans Gather Dust—Or Make the Dirt Fly?" *Illinois Municipal Review* 14 (February 1935): 33–35.
Chatters, Carl H. "Methods That Have Proved Successful in Collecting Delinquent Taxes." *American City* 48 (August 1933): 36–37.
_____. "Michigan City Overburdened by Assessments." *Tax Digest* 8 (August 1930).
Chatters, Carl H., and Walter Harris. "Tax Collection Legislation, 1933." *Municipal Finance* 6 (November 1933): 16–17.
"Chicago Teetering on the Precipice." *Literary Digest* 112, 16 January 1932, p. 10.
"City Advertises to Collect Taxes." *Printers' Ink* 29 (September 1932): 24.
Cline, Denzel C. "Economic Recovery and the Public Employee." *National Municipal Review* 23 (September 1934): 471–76.
"Cluttering Up the State Constitutions." *Tax Policy* 2 (December 1934): 1–10.
Coughlin, Francis. "The Municipal Follies." *Chicagoan* 26 (October 1929).
"Dayton Citizens' Council in Action." *National Municipal Review* 22 (June 1933): 259–60.
Dunstan, E. Fleetwood. "Report of Municipal Securities Committee." *Investment Banking* 3, 18 November 1933, pp. 61–69.
Edwards, Alba M. "A Social Economic Grouping of the Gainful Workers of the United States." *Journal of the American Statistical Association* 27 (1933): 377–87.
Elting, John. "Tax Fight." *Forbes* 43, 15 February 1939.
_____. "You CAN Cut Taxes!" *Forbes* 43, 1 March 1939.
Ely, Richard T. "Taxation in Hard Times." *Review of Reviews* 67 (August 1931): 67–68.
Fairchild, Fred Rogers. "The Problem of Tax Delinquency." *American Economic Review*, Supplement. (March 1934): 140–50.
Farr, Newton C. "Board to Organize Owners." *Chicago Real Estate Magazine* 5, 16 August 1930, pp. 5–6.
Foote, Peter. "Revenue Body's Report Is Called Unfair, Unjust, Iniquitous." *Taxpayer of Chicago and Cook County*, 5 November 1931.
Frank, Glenn. "Constructive Versus Destructive Economy." *National Municipal Review* 22 (July 1933): 313–76.
Franklin, Jay. "Taxes, Taxes, Taxes!" *Forum* 87 (April 1932): 200–203.
Fuller, Denton A., Jr. "Tax Delinquency." *Tax Magazine* 13 (June 1935).
Garrett, Garet. "Insatiable Government." *Saturday Evening Post* 204, 25 June 1932.
Gaskill, Gordon. "Caviar on Your Tax Bill." *American Magazine* 131 (April 1941): 116–19.
Gray, Welles A. "How Business Men Assist Officials to Lower Municipal Expenditures." *Comptroller* 5 (August 1932): 22–27.

Greenman, Edward D. "Bringing in Taxes Through Penalties or Discounts." *National Municipal Review* 23 (June 1934): 305–98.

Hall, Albert H. "A Cloud on the New York State Tax Horizon." *National Municipal Review* 24 (November 1935): 626–30.

Hallgren, Mauritz A. "Help Wanted—for Chicago." *Nation* 134, 11 May 1932, pp. 534–36.

Harp, Gillis J. "Taylor, Calhoun, and the Decline of a Theory of Political Disharmony." *Journal of the History of Ideas* 46 (January–March 1985): 107–20.

Harris, Joseph P. "Taxpayers Strike in Washington." *National Municipal Review* 22 (January 1933).

Harrison, J. L. "Taxes and 'The Little Home Town.' " *American City* 48 (June 1933): 56–58.

Hays, Samuel P. "The Politics of Reform in Municipal Government in the Progressive Era." *Pacific Northwest Quarterly* 55 (1964): 157–69.

"Help Forced on the Farmer." *Nation's Business* 19 (December 1931): 1.

Hodes, Barnet. "Law of Uniformity Confiscates." *Chicago Real Estate Magazine* 5, 28 June 1930, pp. 5–7.

_____. "Obey or Revise!" *Chicago Real Estate Magazine* 5, 30 August 1930, pp. 5–7.

_____. "Tax Amendment Progressive." *Chicago Real Estate Magazine* 5, 26 July 1930, p. 5.

Holly, William H. "The Proposed Income Tax Amendment to the Constitution of the State of Illinois Analyzed and Its Iniquities Bared." *Federation News* 24, 18 October 1930, p. 7.

Holmes, Lawrence G. "What Makes a Tax Limitation Campaign Successful?" *Freehold* 4, 15 April 1940.

Jensen, Jens P. "Legislative Proposals Last Year and This." *National Municipal Review* 24 (November 1935): 631–34.

_____. "Property Tax Limitations." *Tax Policy* 2 (February 1935): 2–9.

Jones, Howard P. "Mr. Citizen Contemplates the City Hall." *Public Management* 16 (June 1934): 163–67.

_____. "Unrest in County Government." *National Municipal Review* 21 (August 1932): 470.

Kerner, Otto, Jr. "Effect of Recent Illinois Decisions on Taxpayers' Remedies." *Illinois Law Review* 28 (June 1933): 272–76.

Leland, Simeon E. "Should Public Expenditures Be Reduced?" *Public Management* 13 (December 1931): 393–98.

Leuchtenburg, William E. "The New Deal and the Analogue of War." In *Change and Continuity in Twentieth-Century America*, by John Braeman et al. New York: Harper and Row, 1966.

Lindheimer, Benjamin F. "Both Groups to Fight for One Goal." *Chicago Real Estate Magazine* 5, 16 August 1930, p. 6.

MacChesney, Nathan William. "The Immediate Tax Program." *Chicago Real Estate Magazine* 6, 9 May 1931, pp. 11–15.

Mangan, John J. Letter. *Chicago Real Estate Magazine* 8, 12 March 1932, p. 21.

Mayer, Milton S. "Chicago—City of Unrest." *Forum* 89 (January 1933): 46–51.

———. "When Teachers Strike." *Forum* 90 (August 1933): 121–25.

"Memphis Has Tax Club." *Municipal Finance News Letter* 2, 1 September 1933, p. 1.

Mencken, H. L. "What Is Going on in the World." *American Mercury* 30 (November 1933): 257–62.

Merriam, Charles E. "Reducing Government Costs." *Illinois Municipal Review* 11 (July 1932): 145–48, 150.

Merrill, Julia Wright. "The Taxpayer Looks at Government." *American Library Association Bulletin* 26 (December 1932): 801.

"Milwaukee Collects Delinquent Taxes." *Municipal Finance News Letter* 3, 1 March 1935, p. 3.

"More Money for Public Works." *National Municipal Review* 22 (October 1933): 499–507.

Munro, William B. "Taxation Nears a Crisis." *Current History* 37 (March 1933): 656–62.

Murphy, Marjorie. "Taxation and Social Conflict: Teacher Unionism and Public School Finance in Chicago, 1898–1934." *Journal of the Illinois State Historical Society* 74 (Winter 1981): 242–60.

Ortquist, Richard T. "Tax Crisis and Politics in Early Depression Michigan." *Michigan History* 59 (Spring–Summer 1975): 91–119.

Parnell, Reginald. "Tax-Paying Drive Successfully Organized." *American City* 48 (December 1933): 58.

" 'Pay Your Taxes.' " *Public Administrators' News Letter* 3 (July 1933): 4.

Porter, Sylvia F. "Taxpayers on the War Path." *American Magazine* 130 (October 1940).

Pratt, John M. "Rural Municipal Affairs." *Grain Growers' Guide* 10, 28 November 1917.

"Pratt to Direct Taxpayers." *Chicago Real Estate Magazine* 5, 23 August 1930, p. 13.

Raico, Ralph. "Classical Liberal Exploitation Theory: A Comment on Professor Liggio's Paper." *Journal of Libertarian Studies* 1 (Summer 1977): 179–83.

Reed, Thomas H. "Organizing to Save Communities." *National Municipal Review* 22 (July 1933).

———. "The Role of Government in Business Recovery." *Illinois Municipal Review* 11 (November 1932).

"Revolt of the Chicago Taxpayers." *Literary Digest* 110, 18 July 1931, p. 6.

Sargent, Fred W. "The Taxpayers Take Charge." *Saturday Evening Post* 205, 14 January 1933.

"Selling the City." *Public Management* 15 (January 1933): 29.

Shepherd, William G. "The Winded City." *Colliers*, 12 April 1930.

Simpson, Herbert D. "Fundamentals of the Tax Situation." *Illinois Journal of Commerce* 13 (December 1931).

———. "Tax Delinquency—Economic Aspects," *Illinois Law Review* 28, (June 1933).

Smith, Harold D. "Tax Limitation." *Municipal Finance* 6 (August 1933): 47–52.

Smith, Wade S. "Recent Legislative Indulgences to Delinquent Taxpayers." *Law and Contemporary Problems* 3 (June 1936): 371–75.

Springer, Gertrude. "The Fighting Spirit in Hard Times." *Survey* 68, 15 June 1932.

Steed, Hal. "Adventures of a Tax Leaguer." *Saturday Evening Post* 208, 4 November 1933.

Stillman, Charles B. "Will Chicago Support its Schools?" *Chicago Union Teacher* (April 1932).

"Tax Association Defies Kelly." *Lightnin'* (May 1933): 11.

"Tax Dodgers and How They Get Away With It." *Federation News* 27, 13 February 1932, p. 2.

"Tax Limits Prove Unwise." *Tax Policy* 1 (December 1933): 1–5.

"Tax Strikes a la 1934." *National Municipal Review* 23 (September 1934): 485.

"Taxation and Tyranny." *New Republic* 73, 16 November 1932, pp. 4–6.

"Taxpayers' Organizations in the United States." *Tax Policy* 5 (September 1938).

"Taxpayers' Organizations: Supplement." *Tax Policy* 6 (March 1939): 1–26.

"Taxpayers' Revolt." *Minnesota Municipalities* 17 (January 1932): 5.

Teninga, Cornelius. "Taxpayers Can Determine Taxes." *Chicago Real Estate Magazine* 5, 14 June 1930, pp. 6–7.

Thelen, David P. "Social Tensions and the Origins of American Progressivism." *Journal of American History* 56 (September 1969): 323–41.

Thorpe, Merle. "Leave the People Something to Do!" *Nation's Business* 20 (August 1932): 11.

"Towards Understanding." *National Municipal Review* 22 (October 1933): 490.

Traxler, Henry. "Why Pay Taxes?" *Municipality* 28 (July–August 1933).

"Using Common Sense in the Tax Saving Crusade." *American City* 47 (July 1932): 52.

"Wake Up, Democracy!" *Nation's Schools* 11 (March 1933): 64–65.

Walker, Mabel L. "The ABC's of Taxation." *Independent Woman* 13 (February 1934).

"When to Pay 1929 Tax Bills." *Chicago Real Estate Magazine* 6, 18 April 1931, p. 7.

White, William Allen. "Turning Knowledge into Votes." *National Municipal Review* 23 (February 1934): 85–86.

Wilson, Irvin A. "Bargain Hunting in Education." *Chicago Principals' Club Reporter* (May 1932): 3–7.

Woodworth, Leo Day. "Delinquent Taxes." *Tax Digest* 12 (December 1934).

Dissertations, Theses, and Papers

Altman, Oscar Lewis. "Chicago's Experiment in Personal Property Taxation, 1931–1936." Ph.D. diss., University of Chicago, 1936.

Bernhard, Russell Sherman. "Five Years' Experience under the Illinois Tax Receivership Act." Master's thesis, Northwestern University, 1938.

Biles, William R. "Mayor Edward J. Kelly of Chicago: Big City Boss in Depression and War." Ph.D. diss., University of Illinois, 1981.

Bush, Chilton Rowlette. "State Centralization: General Property Tax Rate Limitation and Its Relation to Municipal Finance." Ph.D. diss., University of Wisconsin, 1935.

Carey, Richard J. "Taxpayer Protests in the Great American Depression, 1931–1935." Ph.D diss., University of Hawaii, 1979.

Clifford, Guy C. "The Massachusetts Taxpayers' Foundation: Its Influence in Massachusetts Politics, 1932–1966." Master's thesis, University of Massachusetts, 1967.

Comery, George Richard. "A Study of the Enforcement of the Personal Property Tax in Cook County, 1929–1934." Master's thesis, Northwestern University, 1935.

Hardy, Bruce Allen. "American Privatism and the Urban Fiscal Crisis of the Interwar Years: A Financial Study of the Cities of New York, Chicago, Philadelphia, Detroit, and Boston, 1915–1945." Ph.D. diss., Wayne State University, 1977.

Kloske, Ralph. "Fiscal Conservatism in New Jersey." University of Wisconsin, 1985. Chapter in forthcoming Ph.D. dissertation.

Palmer, Tom G. "Toward a Liberal Theory of Class." Unpublished paper, St. Johns University, 1982.

Stachcowski, Floyd J. "The Political Career of Daniel Webster Hoan." Ph.D. diss., Northwestern University, 1966.

Stark, Bennett S. "The Political Economy of State Public Finance: A Model of the Determinants of Revenue Policy: The Illinois Case, 1850–1970." Ph.D. diss., University of Wisconsin, 1982.

INDEX